The Book of Acts
Chapters 15–28

BOOKS BY JAMES D. QUIGGLE

DOCTRINAL SERIES

Biblical History
Adam and Eve, a Biography and Theology
Angelology, a True History of Angels

Essays
Biblical Essays
Biblical Essays II
Biblical Essays III
Biblical Essays IV

Marriage and Family
Marriage and Family: A Biblical Perspective
Biblical Homosexuality
A Biblical Response to Same-gender Marriage

Doctrinal and Practical Christianity
First Steps, Becoming a Follower of Jesus Christ
A Christian Catechism (with Christopher McCuin)
Why and How to do Bible Study
Thirty-Six Essentials of the Christian Faith
The Literal Hermeneutic, Explained and Illustrated
The Old Ten In the New Covenant
Christian Living and Doctrine
Spiritual Gifts
Why Christians Should Not Tithe

Dispensational Theology
A Primer On Dispensationalism
Understanding Dispensational Theology
Covenants and Dispensations in the Scripture
Dispensational Soteriology
Dispensational Eschatology, An Explanation and Defense of the Doctrine
Rapture: A Bible Study on the Rapture of the New Testament Church
Antichrist, His Genealogy, Kingdom, and Religion

God and Man

God's Choices, Doctrines of Foreordination, Election, Predestination
God Became Incarnate
Life, Death, Eternity
Did Jesus Go To Hell?

Small Group Bible Studies

Elementary Bible Principles (with Linda M. Quiggle)
Counted Worthy (with Linda M. Quiggle)

COMMENTARY SERIES

The Old Testament

A Private Commentary on the Bible: Judges
A Private Commentary on the Book of Ruth
A Private Commentary on the Bible: Esther
A Private Commentary on the Bible: Song of Solomon
A Private Commentary on the Bible: Daniel
A Private Commentary on the Bible: Jonah
A Private Commentary on the Bible: Habakkuk
A Private Commentary on the Bible: Haggai

The New Testament

James Quiggle Translation New Testament

The Gospels and Acts

A Private Commentary on the Bible: Matthew's Gospel
A Private Commentary on the Bible: Mark's Gospel
A Private Commentary on the Bible: Luke 1–12
A Private Commentary on the Bible: Luke 13–24
A Private Commentary on the Bible: John 1–12
A Private Commentary on the Bible: John 13–21
A Private Commentary on the Bible: Acts 1–14
A Private Commentary on the Bible: Acts 15–28

Other Works On the Gospels
Four Voices, One Testimony (a Gospel Harmony)
Jesus Said "I Am"
The Parables and Miracles of Jesus Christ
The Passion and Resurrection of Jesus the Christ

The Christmas Story, As Told By God

Pauline Letters
A Private Commentary on the Bible: Galatians
A Private Commentary on the Bible: Ephesians
A Private Commentary on the Bible: Philippians
A Private Commentary on the Bible: Colossians
A Private Commentary on the Bible: Thessalonians
A Private Commentary on the Bible: Pastoral Letters
A Private Commentary on the Bible: Philemon

General Letters
A Private Commentary on the Book of Hebrews
A Private Commentary on the Bible: James
A Private Commentary on the Bible: 1 Peter
A Private Commentary on the Bible: 2 Peter
A Private Commentary on the Bible: John's Epistles
A Private Commentary on the Bible: Jude

Revelation
A Private Commentary on the Bible: Revelation 1–7
A Private Commentary on the Bible: Revelation 8–16
A Private Commentary on the Bible: Revelation 17–22

REFERENCE SERIES
James Quiggle Translation New Testament
Dictionary of Doctrinal Words
Old and New Testament Chronology (With David Hollingsworth)
(Also in individual volumes: Old Testament Chronology; New Testament Chronology)

TRACTS
A Human Person: Is the Unborn Life a Person?
Biblical Marriage
How Can I Know I am A Christian?
Now That I am A Christian
Thirty-Six Essentials of the Christian Faith
What is a Pastor? / Why is My Pastor Eating the Sheep?
Principles and Precepts of the Literal Hermeneutic

(All tracts are in digital format and cost $0.99)

Formats
Print, Digital, Epub, PDF. Search "James D. Quiggle" or book title.

A Private Commentary on the Bible

Acts 15–28

James D. Quiggle

Copyright Page

A Private Commentary on the Bible: Acts 15–28

Copyright © 2023 James D. Quiggle. All rights reserved.

ISBN: 979-8-9871044-5-3

All New Testament translations are from the *James Quiggle Translation New Testament*, copyright © 2023.

Old Testament translations.

Brenton translation of the Septuagint (Public Domain, see Sources).

The Holy Bible, English Standard Version (ESV). Copyright © 2000, 2001 by Crossway Bibles, A Division of Good News Publishers, 1300 Crescent Street, Wheaton, Illinois 60187, USA. All rights reserved.

This print edition of *A Private Commentary on the Bible: Acts 15–28* contains the same material as the digital editions.

Table of Contents

Preface 13
Introduction 15
Acts Fifteen 23
Acts Sixteen 57
Acts Seventeen 83
Acts Eighteen 109
Acts Nineteen 133
Acts Twenty 151
Acts Twenty-one 177
Acts Twenty-two 193
Acts Twenty-three 203
Acts Twenty-Four 215
Acts Twenty-five 223
Acts Twenty-six 229
Acts Twenty-seven 243
Acts Twenty-eight 255
Appendix: Election 265
Appendix: Free Will 279
Appendix: Paul's Roman Imprisonments 283
Sources 287

Preface

The *Private Commentary* series on the Old and New Testaments is my interpretation of the Bible, neither more nor less. I am responsible for the use made of all quoted and cited material.

In this book I use the word "believers" to identify those who have placed saving faith in Jesus Christ and submit to the Scripture as the rule of faith and practice. Not all who call themselves Christians are believers. The use of "believer" versus "Christian" in no way states or implies those who disagree with me are not believers or Christians.

The genuine Christian, or believer, is the person who has placed saving faith in Jesus Christ, submits to the Scripture as the rule of faith and practice, and holds to the essential doctrines of the Christian faith.

In this commentary I mention one or more of my books. The purpose is not advertisement, but to refer the reader to in depth explanations in those books. I never worry about sales. The Holy Spirit decides who will read my works, and I trust in his decisions.

Introduction

The Book of Acts is Luke's continuation his account of the good news, showing the ministry of the Christ through the Holy Spirit, as the Holy Spirit acted through the Twelve, Paul, and other disciples, to take the good news throughout the known world. The Book of Acts was written ca. AD 62–63, during the time Paul was awaiting trial before the Caesar, and reveals selected events between the AD 33 Pentecost and AD 63, when Paul was released from his Roman imprisonment.

The Book of Acts is often subtitled in our Bibles as "of the Apostles." No, Luke wrote about the acts of the Holy Spirit through many individuals.

Why did Luke write Acts? One purpose of Acts might have been to show the Holy Spirit active in the New Testament church. The history of Spirit's works present a pattern by which each generation might recognize and understand how the Holy Spirit continues his work in every generation of the New Testament church.

Others have suggested Luke wrote a history of the early New Testament church to tell the New Testament church of its origin. This view has biblical precedence, as the Pentateuch was written by Moses as a history of the origin of the nation Israel.

Another view was suggested by John W. Mauck, in his book, *Paul on Trial*. The book's subtitle is *The Book of Acts as a Defense of Christianity*. Mauck's thesis is the book was written as a legal brief for Theophilus, "the Roman official responsible for the judicial investigation of trials to be conducted before Emperor Nero" [Mauck, ix]. Luke's legal brief would show Christianity was not a threat to the Roman Empire, and Paul was innocent of the accusations brought against him by the Jews. If you believe, as I do, Paul was released as "not guilty" from his first imprisonment, then Luke's history may have been instrumental in achieving that outcome, whether or not written for that specific purpose.

Luke's two volume history of the Christ and the New Testament church certainly instructed believers about their faith. Acts informs the believer what the earliest Christians believed and how they lived out those beliefs, thereby showing a pattern of faith and the Christian life for the New Testament church. Certainly theology as both faith and

Introduction

Christian living is part of the acts of the Holy Spirit in the Book of Acts.

None of the above purposes are mutually exclusive. Whatever Luke's personal motivations, the Holy Spirit worked through his servant to present to the New Testament church the early history of the church, and how those believers lived out their faith in their particular historical-cultural circumstances: through their relationship with God in Christ, by the power of the indwelling Holy Spirit, and a regenerated human nature.

So also the Holy Spirit works in every generation of believers, as he did in the first, and every generation of believers is to live out their faith through their relationship with God in Christ, by the power of the indwelling Holy Spirit, and a regenerated human nature.

The structure of the Acts has been extensively analyzed by commentators over the many centuries from then to now. So also matters of authorship, date, and historicity. It is not my purpose to duplicate introductory information that may be found in other resources.

I consider the Book of Acts to be the genuine composition of a man named Luke, who was a sometime companion of the apostle Paul, written as superintended by the Holy Spirit (inspiration). The act of writing the book probably began during Paul's detention under Festus, Acts 25:12, and the act of writing the book ended sometime after Paul's meeting with the Jews in Rome, Acts 28:29. Acts 28:30–31 seems like an epilogue, probably added ca. AD 63 after Paul was judged innocent of all charges brought against him by the Jews.

Outline Of Acts

The Book of Acts naturally divides into four sections.

Prologue

   Luke's Introduction, 1:1–3.

   Jesus' final commands and ascension, 1:4–8.

   Disciples waiting for the promise of the Father, 1:9–26.

The ministry of Peter

   Using the "keys of the kingdom" (Matthew 16:19) to open the door of the kingdom to the Jews, Acts 2–7.

   Using the "keys of the kingdom" to open the door of the

Introduction

kingdom to those of mixed Jew and gentile heritage, i.e., the Samaritans, Acts 8 (with a subsection, Philip opening the door to gentile proselytes).

Using the "keys of the kingdom" to open the door of the kingdom to the gentiles (Acts 10:1–11:18; 15:7–11).

The ministry of Paul

His conversion and early life as a believer, Acts 9; 11:19–30.

His life as apostle to the gentiles, Acts 12:25—20:38.

His arrest, trials, and journey to Rome, Acts 21:1–28:16.

Epilogue

Paul's gospel defense to the Jews in Rome, 28:17–29.

Succinct summary of Paul's life in Rome, Acts 28:30–31.

Purpose Of The Commentary

The purpose of this commentary is to present a detailed explanation of the Book of Acts for use by Bible students, teachers, and pastors, for learning, teaching, and preaching. My method of interpretation is the Historical-Grammatical Hermeneutic (HGH), also known as the Literal hermeneutic. For an explanation of how I understand and use the Literal hermeneutic, see my book, *The Literal Hermeneutic, Explained and Illustrated*. The following is an extract from that book.

Hermeneutical Method

The purpose of biblical hermeneutics is to discover the intent of the biblical authors in order to understand the interpretation of the text. The literal hermeneutic is really the application of seven methods of analysis to the biblical text: historical-cultural, contextual, lexical-syntactical, theological, literary (genre), and doctrinal aspects of Scripture, and comparison with other interpreters using the same methods (the first five are from Virkler, 76). The interpreter synthesizes the facts discovered through judicious application of these analyses to arrive at an understanding of the biblical text. These analyses are described as follows:

Historical-Cultural analysis: considers the historical-cultural milieu in which the author wrote. The facts of the historical-cultural background involve the task of reconstructing or comprehending the historical and cultural features of the specific passage. This requires an understanding of:

> The situation of the writer, especially anything that helps explain why he or she wrote the passage.
>
> The situation of the people involved in the text and/or the recipients of the book that can help explain why the writer penned this material to them.
>
> The relationship between the writer and audience or the people involved in the text.
>
> The cultural or historical features mentioned in the text.

Contextual analysis: considers the relationship of a given passage to the whole body of an author's writing.

Lexical-Syntactical analysis: develops an understanding of the definitions of words (lexicology) and their relationships to one another (syntax).

Theological analysis: studies the level of theological understanding at the time the revelation was given in order to ascertain the meaning of the text for its original readers. It takes into account related Scriptures, whether given before or after the passage being studied.

Literary (Genre) analysis: identifies the literary form or method used in a given passage: historical narrative, letters, doctrinal exposition, poetry, wisdom, prophetic.

Doctrinal analysis: the harmonization of doctrine in a specific passage with the full teaching of Scripture on that doctrine.

After the analyses are performed, one should compare his or her tentative interpretation with the work of other interpreters who also use the literal hermeneutic. This step will substantiate a valid interpretation or alert the interpreter to a novel or aberrant interpretation, perhaps one already considered and discarded in the past history of interpretation. Certainly a novel or new interpretation should be re-examined and validated by careful exegesis if it is to be retained.

Introduction

The "literal" hermeneutic is in reality the "grammatical-historical-contextual-lexical-syntactical-theological-genre-doctrinal" hermeneutic, judiciously applied to the various literary genres in Scripture, the results of which are compared with other competent interpreters of past and present, and used to understand just what it is the Bible is teaching, whether in a particular verse or passage, or in relation to doctrine.

What Does "Literal" Mean

The meaning of "literal interpretation" has been and still is subject to misinterpretation and caricature. Here is what "literal interpretation" means:

> The literal hermeneutic understands the words and language used by the human authors of the Bible in the normal and plain sense of words and language as used in everyday conversation and writing.
>
> Understanding words in their plain and normal sense means all words in all languages have a semantic content and range that reflects the historical-cultural background of the original writer and reader.
>
> Understanding words in their plain and normal sense means that languages also communicate meaning through well-defined rules of vocabulary, grammar, and syntax.
>
> Understanding words in their plain and normal sense means recognizing all language includes idioms, slang, figures of speech, and symbols specific to that language and the historical-cultural circumstances of original writer and reader, and that these must be interpreted for the modern reader in terms of his or her language.
>
> Understanding idioms, slang, figures of speech, and symbols in the plain and normal sense of language means an idiom, slang, figure of speech, or symbol is based on something literal and is intended by the writer or speaker to communicate something literal. And the corollary: A symbol is not intended to communicate the literal thing on which it is based.

Introduction

Understanding the biblical use of words, figures of speech, idioms, slang, and symbols means recognizing the biblical authors sometimes used and invested these parts of language with specific theological or spiritual meanings, and that the Holy Spirit maintained the consistency of those meanings among the several human authors.

If an interpretation invests an author's words, figures of speech, idioms, slang, or symbols with a meaning other than the plain and normal meaning of their use in the language in which he is communicating, then it is not a literal interpretation, but is an allegorical or spiritual interpretation: an abstract distortion of the meaning of the text dependent on the interpreter's imagination, not the biblical writer's truth-intention.

Considering the above propositions, a "literal" hermeneutic determines the biblical author's intended meaning (his truth-intention) through the normal and plain sense of the words and language he used. To discover the author's truth-intention the "literal" method applies historical, cultural, contextual, grammatical, lexical, syntactical, theological, genre, and doctrinal analysis to the author's text.

The Translation

The translation of the Greek text of Acts (and Translation Notes) is from my book, *James Quiggle Translation New Testament*. See that book for an explanation of translation conventions and resources.

Identifying Believers And Non-Believers

In the commentary I have used several terms to identify the people. Those who are saved I have variously identified as believers, Jewish Christians, and Christians. The unsaved are identified as Jews, God-fearers, gentile proselytes (to Judaism), and pagan gentiles. Luke the author of Acts identifies believers as a sect of the Nazarenes, as members of the Way, and as Christians, Acts 24:5; 9:2; 22:4; 11:26.

A Suggested Chronology Of Acts 15–28

Acts 15, Jerusalem Council, ca. AD 50

Acts 16–18:22, Paul's second missionary journey, ca. AD 51–54

Acts 18:23–19:3, Paul's Third missionary ca. AD 54–58

Introduction

Acts 20–21:16, Paul's journey to Jerusalem, ca. AD 58
Acts 21:17–23:22, Paul arrested in Jerusalem, ca. AD 58
Acts 22:33–26:32, Paul prisoner in Caesarea, ca, AD 58–60
Acts 27–28:16, Paul taken to Rome, ca. AD 60–61
Acts 28:17–31, Paul prisoner in Rome, ca. AD 60–63

How those events work out is the subject of this commentary.

Acts Fifteen

Translation Acts 15:1

1 And certain ones who came down from Judea were teaching the brethren, "If you are not circumcised according to the custom of Moses you are not able to be saved."

EXPOSITION

For the first thirteen to fourteen years of the existence of the New Testament church (AD 33 – ca. AD 46-47), the New Testament church was composed of saved Hebrews, a few saved gentiles who had first proselytized to Judaism, and a few saved gentile God-fearers. The first pagan gentiles to be saved (as documented in Acts) were in Antioch of Pisidia, Acts 13:13–52. How saved pagan gentiles were to be integrated into what was essentially a Hebrew New Testament church was the question of the moment.

Acts 14 (see volume 1, *Acts 1–14*) ends about AD 49. Acts 15 begins about a year later, ca. AD 50. Certain believers came from Jerusalem to Antioch of Syria. Their message was gentiles had to proselytize to Judaism to be saved.

Just as the phrase "John's immersion" incorporated his entire teaching of repentance and immersion as preparation for the Messiah, and "the cross" means the entire message of the good news, even so in 15:1, the word "circumcision" represents all the Law of Moses. That statement may seem too broad a conclusion from, "If you are not circumcised according to the custom of Moses you are not able to be saved." But circumcision was the next to last step for males in converting to Judaism. After the circumcision had healed, then a water immersion was performed to complete their conversion. To be "circumcised according to the custom of Moses" was to convert to Judaism.

These teachers from Jerusalem of Christianized Judaism were not evil men. The Old Testament Law and prophets taught gentiles were to be part of Messiah's Kingdom. Longnecker [439] lists some of those Scriptures: Genesis 22:18; 26:4; 28:14; Isaiah 49:6; 55:5–7; Zephaniah 3:9–10; Zechariah 8:22. The leader of the council, Jacob (half-brother of Jesus Christ) agrees, quoting the prophet Amos, that gentiles were part of the kingdom.

(Why am I calling James, half-brother of Jesus Christ, by the name "Jacob?" Because in the Greek text his name is *Iakōbos* [Zodhiates, s. v. 2384], which transliterates to "Jacob." Every other biblical character's name in English translations of the New Testament is transliterated, but "James" is not a transliteration of *Iakōbos*, it is not even a translation of *Iakōbos*. The name "James" is from "the Old French 'Gemmes,' a variation of the later Latin 'Jacomus,' itself a variation of the early Latin 'Jacobus'" [Vlachos, *James*, 9]. The James son of Zebedee in the gospels is really Jacob. The half-brother of Jesus, who is the "James" of Acts 15:13 and the "James" of the Book of James, is actually Jacob the half-brother of Jesus, Jacob of Acts 15:13, and Jacob who wrote the New Testament Book of "James.")

The history of Israel indicated the way gentiles would share in the blessing of Messiah, was to be administered by Israel proselytizing gentiles into the kingdom. That the YHWHism of their fathers had devolved into Judaism did not materially change their evangelistic mission, although it had changed the faith into which gentiles were proselytized, cf. Matthew 23:15. The Christian Hebrews wanted to bring the gentile Christians under the Law, because that's the way it had always been done, according to the Old Testament Scripture. Therefore, in this new age of Messiah's kingdom, those who were zealous for the Law believed for a gentile to be saved he or she must conform to the Law.

These "Judaizers" in Acts 15:1 believed circumcision was the price of entry into the covenant of the Law, that those believing in the Messiah were under the Law covenant, and therefore gentile believers in the Messiah must be circumcised according to the Law or they were not part of the covenant—and if not part of the Law covenant then you were not saved, because the Law covenant required every member of the covenant to be circumcised.

The Judaizers logic was flawless, but the conclusion was false, because the premise was wrong. Every saved person is removed from the Law covenant and placed in a New covenant made in the death and resurrection of the Christ, where the only "price" for entry was the "coin" of faith." More simply, the New Testament church is not Israel.

Others more discerning knew circumcision was actually a symbol of the Abrahamic covenant given to identify Abraham's physical descendants through Isaac as members of that covenant. But the Judaizers conflated the Abrahamic covenant with the Law covenant, because both required circumcision. Gentiles are not the subjects of the Abrahamic covenant, although gentiles are beneficiaries of one aspect of that covenant, the blessing through Abraham to all peoples, see Galatians 3:7–9. But again, without circumcision, which an aspect of the covenant given later to mark the physical descendants of Abraham through Isaac as members of the covenant.

Let me briefly mention that in addition to the principle of continuity (for example, "Jesus Christ the same yesterday and today and to the ages," Hebrews 13:8), the Scripture also teaches the principle of discontinuity: God does not always do the same things in the same way. For example, Abraham's content of saving faith may be summarized by Genesis 15:6. Today's content of faith may be summarized by Acts 16:31. Today no believer brings a lamb to make a sacrifice for the forgiveness of an act of sinning, as was done under the Law, but follows 1 John 1:9 because of 1 John 2:2. From time to time God changes the ways in which he interacts with humankind, and there is always some kind of demarcation to let his people know some things have changed. Even so, the demarcation between the Law and Christ is revealed at Acts 10:44–48; 13:46–48; 15:6–29.

Let me also insert here that the genius of Christianity in the ancient world was the elimination of social and religious distinctions among the saved. The saved are one body, in one Christ, under one Father, sealed by one Spirit. The social statuses of slave, free, male, female, Jew, Greek, or barbarian do not apply within the New Testament church. In the New Testament church there is no Judaism or paganism, there is no distinction of Jewish Christian and gentile Christian. Some Christians are Hebrew, just as some are African, or American, or Arabic, Chinese, European, etc. But all are citizens of one father, having one fatherland in one heaven, all saved by the limitless merit of one person, Christ, and all gathered together by the Holy Spirit into one body, the New Testament church, where religious and social and ethnic distinctions do not apply to those who are saved.

The prevailing view of the young and Jewish New Testament church, was that that Messiah had come, and it was supposed the

Davidic-Messianic kingdom was to be built by the church—by the Jews of the New Testament church. Therefore it had become necessary to bring these believing gentiles under the Law. The saved Jews were the faithful remnant [Longnecker, 440], who would incorporate the gentiles into the Kingdom.

The history in Acts 1–9 tells us Jews were being saved. In comments on Acts 1–14 (see that volume) I have assumed gentile proselytes were also being saved. Then a gentile God-fearer was saved, Acts 10. Cornelius and his relatives and friends were not proselytes, they were not circumcised, but they did have a relationship with YHWH through the Law, which in the view of the Jewish believers, meant they could easily be proselytized and circumcised, and therefore God-fearers believing on Christ could be accepted into the Kingdom. Conversion to Judaism and circumcision, if proposed, would have seemed natural to the saved God-fearer Cornelius, as the reasonable next step in his conversion to faith in the Messiah.

In every practical way, conversion to Christianity had not, to date, changed the Jewishness of the Jewish believers, nor their Judaism. They assumed as the natural course of things that gentile conversion to Christianity would make those gentiles Jewish, to be proselytized and circumcised.

But there was a bump in the road. Paul had proclaimed the good news to pagan gentiles, and they had been saved, and he had not required them to become Jewish. His scriptural basis, Acts 13:47, was naturally suspect, because it did not include conversion to Judaism ("For so the Lord has commanded us: 'I have set you [Christ] for a light of the gentiles, for you to be salvation to the uttermost part of the earth'").

Of course the seeds of change had already been planted. Forgiveness of sins by faith in Christ automatically excluded temple sacrifices for sin. Anyone paying attention to Peter's sermon and Stephen's defense could see the Law was growing old and passing away. Paul's good news had made both things clear.

> Acts 13:38–39, Therefore be it known to you, men, brethren, that through this one, to you forgiveness of sins is proclaimed. And from all things from which you were not able in the Law of Moses to be justified, in him everyone believing is justified.

The first great theological conflict of the New Testament church had arrived. Did the salvation of pagan gentiles require conversion to the Law, or was salvation of pagan gentiles without the Law?

The other issue at stake was more far reaching. Did the coming of the Christ mean the faithful remnant of national ethnic Israel was to build the prophesied Davidic-Messianic Kingdom? I will answer that question when I discuss 15:16–17.

Translation Acts 15:2–3

2 Then, no small dispute and debate by Paul and Barnabas with them having occurred, they appointed Paul and Barnabas to go up, and certain others out of them, to the apostles and elders, to Jerusalem, about this question. 3 Therefore, they indeed having been sent forth by the church, passed through both Phoenicia and Samaria, telling in full the conversion of the gentiles, and they were bringing great joy to all the brethren.

EXPOSITION

No Small Dispute

Paul and Barnabas, having experienced the salvation of pagan gentiles apart from the Law, entered into a spirited debate with the teachers from Judea. Three great questions of salvation were at the heart of this dispute: what is salvation; when is a person saved; is Christianity a religion of works or a relationship with God in Christ? Those debating the issues might not have framed the discussion in this way, but lacking a documented record of their debate, this is the way I will discuss the issues.

Question one: What is salvation? It is tempting to define salvation by what one must believe in order to be saved. But the journey, how to be saved, is not the destination. What is salvation?

> Salvation. The remission of sin's penalty by the application of the merit of Christ's propitiation of God on the cross to the sinner's spiritual need. In salvation, God rescues a sinner out of the state of spiritual death and delivers him/her into a permanent state of spiritual life.

Here is the one way of salvation, the one essential doctrine: "Saved by God's grace through the sinner's faith in God apart from personal merit of the sinner but by Christ's merit alone."

That scripture, Ephesians 2:8–9, defines the object of saving faith as God. What is the content of saving faith? God's testimony as to the way or means of salvation, as given by the Holy Spirit in the historic progressive revelation of truth. What the Holy Spirit told Seth, Enoch, Noah, and Abraham in the revelation he had given to them prior to and during their times, was sufficient for their salvation. That revelation did not include a coming Redeemer (the Christ), but spoke of the ever-present Redeemer, YHWH.

That is why there is no such a thing as a partial salvation. God's grace and the sinner's faith in God and God's testimony, as given in the historic progressive revelation of truth, whatever that testimony might have been at any one time during the history of redemption, was sufficient to save, by grace through faith. Therefore one either is, or is not, saved, by faith in God through God's historically current testimony. Any theology that requires something else, anything else, to effect a complete or completed salvation is a false doctrine. By requiring circumcision, those teachers of the Law were saying the uncircumcised gentiles who had believed on Christ as Savior were not saved because not circumcised.

The modern "Hebrew Roots" movement is a descendant of the Acts 15:1 doctrine. Hebrew Roots requires adherence to certain parts of the Mosaic Law to complete a person's salvation (to make the person complete in his or her salvation). The error is this: no works of the Law save and no works of the Law complete salvation. To keep only parts of the Law is to be guilty of violating the Law, because the law is one Law, though having many parts; the argument of the Book of James, 2:10.

Another example of the error is the belief among some, that the Old Testament believers were saved, but had to go to a "good side" of hades (aka: Abraham's Bosom), not heaven, upon physical death. Why? To wait for Christ's to make his propitiation on the cross, so the merit of that propitiation could be applied to their spiritual needs and complete their salvation, and then they went to heaven. I address that theology in my book, *Did Jesus Go To Hell?* I will just say here that the one and only merit required to save a sinner was decreed before the creation of the universe (Ephesians 1:4), and therefore was always in effect from the beginning of humankind to fully and completely save sinners

I will say it again: any theology that requires something else, anything else, to effect a complete or completed salvation is a false doctrine. One either is, or is not, saved. The Old Testament believers either were saved, and therefore went to heaven upon physical death, 2 Corinthians 5:8, or they were not saved and went to hades (there is no good side) upon physical death.

In the case of the Old Testament believers, God is not temporally bound. Before God created the universe, God decreed Christ's propitiation as the only merit for salvation. The act that would create the merit at a particular moment in time was certain, because decreed. God acted on the certainty of his decree from the beginning, because 1) God is not temporally bound, 2) God decreed Christ's propitiation to be only merit that saves, and 3) there is no such thing as a partial salvation. Like being pregnant, like being alive, like being dead, one either is or is not fully and completely saved. If fully and completely saved, the 2 Corinthians 5:8 applies.

The principle of 2 Corinthians 5:8, "absent from the body, present with the Lord" either applies to all who are saved or it applies to none who are saved. That is how a principle works: if it applies to one meeting the condition, then it applies to all meeting the condition, else it is not a principle affecting any meeting the condition. (That is why the false doctrines of "limbo" and "purgatory" exist: to make salvation complete and completed. The Old Testament saved going to hades to wait for Christ's propitiation is a purgatory-like doctrine.)

Question two: When is a person saved? When the sinful human nature is regenerated (born-again). As Charnock said [22], "No age, no time, no administration excludes it ... For being by nature spiritually dead, there must be a restoration to a spiritual life ... How can any, in any age, enjoy an infinite holy God, without being changed from their impurity?"

The indwelling of the Holy Spirit is not required for the sinner to be saved and his or her sinful human nature to be regenerated. Christ and the New Testament writers present the indwelling of the Holy Spirit as a new spiritual reality—new because of the New covenant created in Christ's death (either as an application of the Jeremiah 31:31–33 New Covenant to the New Testament church, or as a separate but similar New covenant, Hebrews 10:11–18, between Christ and his New Testament church; opinions differ).

What does it mean to be born-again?

The first part of "born-again" is the believer's faculty of spiritual perception is brought to life, thus enabling the spiritual understanding required to be convicted of sin, the Savior, and salvation. This is accomplished through God's gift of grace-faith-salvation (Ephesians 2:8) by the work of the Holy Spirit to accomplish the salvation decreed by God (Ephesians 1:4; 2 Thessalonians 2:13; 1 Peter 1:2).

Upon the exercise of saving faith by the sinner, God imparts to him/her eternal life, John 10:27–29; 17:2–3; Romans 6:23b; 1 John 2:25, which is God sharing (in a participatory way) the communicable aspects of his eternal life, creating communion with God and spiritual understanding. To be born-again, or regeneration, is the result of God sharing the communicable aspects of his eternal life. The attributes of human nature, which were jumbled and wrongly prioritized by the sin attribute, are normalized, which is to say, godliness is restored to human nature through the godly attributes of holiness, righteousness, love, mercy, etc. The believer is given new wants and new desires. His/her human nature is re-prioritized toward God.

Upon the exercise of saving faith, God imputes the righteousness of Christ to the now-believing sinner, freeing him or her from the judicial guilt and penalty of sin (justification) because Christ has satisfied God's law on behalf of the sinner, Romans 6:23. The now-saved sinner has been reconciled to God, 2 Corinthians 5:18–19. This brings peace with God, Romans 5:1, because with sin forgiven (Ephesians 1:7), and the judicial penalty satisfied through Christ's propitiation (1 John 2:2), there is no more enmity between God and the believer.

Upon the exercise of saving faith, the Holy Spirit accomplishes the sanctification of the believer, which is to set the believer apart from the defilement caused by sin and dedicate him to God, Ephesians 1:4; 1 Corinthians 1:30; 1 Peter 1:2. In the act of sanctification sin loses its dominating power, Romans 6:14–23, and a new principle of life, holiness, is added to the believer,

Ephesians 4:24, becoming the dominating principle in his human nature, 1 Thessalonians 4:7; 1 Corinthians 3:17b; Colossians 3:12; 1 Peter 1:15.

The believer now stands before God in Christ as forgiven, justified, sanctified, regenerated, filled with eternal life, and indwelt by the Holy Spirit. He is freed from the penalty, power, and pleasure of sin, with absolute assurance of the future transformation and glorification of his/her human nature and body, so that he/she will be freed eternally from the presence of sin. The believer is empowered to resist sin's temptations, live a holy life, understand the Scripture, worship, obey, fellowship with, and serve God. God hears and answers his prayers, and he (or she) perseveres in the faith to lead a holy life, looking toward resurrection and an eternal life in God's presence.

The norm for those saved in this age of the New Testament church, is the Holy Spirit takes up permanent residence in the believer's sanctified soul, John 14:17; Acts 10:44–48; 1 Corinthians 6:19, because a New covenant has begun.

Question three: Is Christianity a religion of works or a relationship with God in Christ? The answer is "both." But one must arrange the order of events in the scriptural order. Because of the prior salvific relationship the believer has gained with God in Christ by grace through faith, Ephesians 2:8–9, Christianity becomes a religion of good works that God has "previously prepared in order that we should conduct our manner of life in them," Ephesians 2:10, because the believer has been "created in Christ Jesus for good works" (same reference).

The dispute and debate between Judaism and Christianity in the first century AD turned on that proper order of "salvation, then works." The teachers of a Christianized Judaism were saying the works of the Law, specifically circumcision (but not excluding the rest of the Law), were necessary to complete the salvation of the gentiles. Paul and Barnabas said otherwise. The future of Christianity as faith based or works based turned on the outcome of this debate, which would be decided by the council in Jerusalem.

They Appointed Paul And Barnabas To Go Up

Because the teachers had come from Judea, it was necessary to discover if their teaching was the teaching of the apostles in Judea. Christianity had originated from the Twelve, and Christianity had been defined by the Twelve; both were aspects of their apostolic office. Were Paul and Barnabas teaching a different version of the good news than the Twelve?

Paul stated his source for the good news he proclaimed was the risen Jesus Christ.

> Galatians 1:11–12, ... the good news proclaimed by me, that it is not according to man. For I did I did not receive it from man, nor was I taught but by means of revelation from Jesus Christ.

The dating of the letter to the Galatians is debated, but that issue is not relevant to Paul's meeting with the Jerusalem Council, because Paul was taught by Christ during his three years in Arabia, Galatians 1:17, which occurred soon after his salvation.

The teachers of Christianized Judaism were claiming the Old Testament Scripture as the source of their soteriology (doctrine of salvation), and may have claimed the authority of the Twelve. Paul was claiming Old Testament Scripture (see comments Acts 13:47) and divine inspiration (taught by revelation from Christ) as source for his soteriology.

Paul's chronological marker in Galatians 2:1, "after fourteen years," is the AD 50 Jerusalem Council. Either as part of that council, or in a separate meeting during that time, Paul was recognized by the Twelve as Christ's apostle to the gentiles.

> Galatians 2:6–9, Now of those esteemed to be someone—of what sort at one time or another to me it does not make a difference, for God does not accept the person of any man—to me the esteemed added nothing. 7 But on the contrary, they having seen I had been entrusted with the good news of the uncircumcision, just as Peter of the circumcision—8 for the one having worked in Peter to apostleship of the circumcision did also in me to the gentiles—9 and having known the grace given to me, Jacob and Cephas and John, those esteemed to be pillars, gave right hands to me and Barnabas, of fellowship, that we to the gentiles, but they to the circumcision.

The Jerusalem Council not only decided salvation was faith based not works based, but the key members of the council recognized Paul as an apostle equal to the Twelve. (Did Paul deny he was an apostle at 1 Corinthians 15:9? No, that would contradict his appointment by Christ. He said he was not worthy of the honor. And so he is not the thirteenth apostle, because not counted as part of the Twelve.) Paul's office is Apostle to the Gentiles, and we see him exercising that office at the Jerusalem Council.

The local church at Antioch of Syria decided to send Paul and Barnabas, and others as witnesses, to seek the counsel of "the apostles and elders" in Jerusalem. The traveled "through both Phoenicia and Samaria." They might have walked inland through Hamath and Damascus to Jerusalem, but they chose a different route. They may have walked the trade route down the coast to Caesarea and then inland through Samaria to Jerusalem. Or they may have taken a ship to Sidon, Tyre, walked to Caesarea, then inland to Jerusalem.

Their purpose was to visit local churches on their way to Jerusalem, in order to tell "in full the conversion of the gentiles." In so doing "they were bringing great joy to all the brethren." Perhaps they were also building a consensus that agreed with their proclamation of the good news to the gentiles.

The Christians at Antioch wanted to know who was right according to the Lord. The Holy Spirit undoubtedly prompted them to send a deputation to Jerusalem. In the Lord's timing the time had come to resolve the issue of the Law's relationship to Christianity. Put another way, should the new wine of Christianity be put into the old wine bottle of the Law.

Translation Acts 15:4–6

4 Then arriving at Jerusalem, they were welcomed by the church and the apostles and the elders. Then they declared all that God had done with them. 5 Now certain of those of the party of the Pharisees who believed, rose up, saying, "It is necessary to circumcise them, then to command to keep the Law of Moses." 6 Then the apostles and the elders gathered together to take care of this matter.

EXPOSITION

The Jerusalem Christian community welcomed Paul and Barnabas. In AD 50, Jacob of Nazareth, brother of Jude and half-brother of Jesus of Nazareth, was pastor of the Jerusalem church. It would be interesting to know with whom they first met upon arrival in Jerusalem. Were the Twelve still meeting in John's Jerusalem house (as they were in Acts 1, 2)? Both Paul and Barnabas knew that house. Did they meet Jacob and the church elders in Jacob's house? Galatians 2:9 mentions (pastor) Jacob and the apostles Peter and John. At Acts 11:22, ca. AD 44, the Jerusalem church had sent Barnabas to Antioch of Syria. Jacob was almost certainly pastor of the Jerusalem church when they sent Barnabas to Syria.

At an appointed time, the Jerusalem church gathered together to hear Paul and Barnabas. As noted in volume 1, local churches met in the house of certain members, probably the homes of the elders. Small churches met in one home, Colossians 4:15; Philemon 2. Larger churches, such as at Jerusalem, met in several homes, but would have had a place where most could meet as one congregation from time to time, probably outdoors, though a large, rented place cannot be excluded.

In a suitable place, where all or most of the Jerusalem church could gather and listen, Paul and Barnabas declared all that God had done with them on their first missionary journey. They disclaimed the works as originating in them, but rather God worked through them. This was a speech they had developed and practiced as they "passed through both Phoenicia and Samaria, telling in full the conversion of the gentiles." The essential content was this: God has saved gentiles out of their paganism; God has given those saved gentiles the Holy Spirit; God did not require those saved gentiles to become Jews.

That report of God's activities provoked a response from "certain of those of the party of the Pharisees who believed." Here we see one of the doctrinal problems in the early church: those saved out of Judaism continued to practice Judaism. That belief in the Law was so strong, it was so certain, that there were some saved Jews who continued to be Pharisees, a religious group whose sole purpose for existing was to keep the Law. Their belief the Law caused them to apply the Law to those believing on Messiah for forgiveness of sin.

The Pharisees came from all walks of life, but in general they were successful businessmen, Levites, scribes, and priests. They were notable (and notorious) for their strict adherence to Judaism—to the traditional interpretations of the Mosaic Law. They did not understand—

apparently few Christians had come to the inevitable conclusion—that the outcome of the good news of salvation by faith in Christ was to be the destruction of the temple system and the passing away of the Mosaic law.

In the early church, the believers in Christ continued to practice the Law; some continued to be Pharisees; all continued bound to the Law and the temple. But God was about to make a change, and he did it through the church leadership, having previously given the new revelation that announced the change, and demonstrated that change through "all that God had done with" Paul and Barnabas.

The new revelation of salvation apart from the Law had begun at the beginning. Peter had proclaimed salvation through faith, not sacrifices or good works, Acts 2:38. Stephen had proclaimed the same, and those hearing but disbelieving truly understood the good news would destroy the temple and change the customs of Moses, Acts 6:14. Paul had proclaimed "from all things from which you were not able in the Law of Moses to be justified, in him everyone believing is justified." Paul's good news to the gentiles put the new revelation into practice: salvation did not include the works of the Law.

Wrong doctrine leads to wrong practices. Certain believers who held to the doctrine of the Pharisees stood up and said, "It is necessary to circumcise them [saved gentiles], then to command to keep the Law of Moses." That was their faith and practice, and they insisted every saved person must do as they did, whether Jewish, saved gentile proselytes, saved God-fearers, or saved formerly pagan gentiles.

Let us try to place ourselves in the sandals of those in the Jerusalem church who were not "of the party of the Pharisees who believed." They also would have conformed their beliefs and practices to the Mosaic Law, but they may not have expected gentiles to do likewise.

Most reading these comments know, from personal experience, the divisions that can occur in a local church. They understand that some of the congregation sided with the Pharisees and some with Paul and Barnabas. All were common in their belief the Law continued to apply, but not all believed the Law must apply to gentiles who were neither proselytes, nor God-fearers, but saved out of paganism. This division in the church led the apostles and elders to "gather together to take care of this matter." A time and place was appointed to discuss the issue, and thus the first general council of the New Testament church was convened. Although the place was probably not large enough to hold all the church members, many would have attended as spectators.

Translation Acts 15:7–11

7 Now much discussion having occurred, Peter standing up said to them, "Men, brethren. You know that from early times, God chose among you through my mouth the gentiles to hear the word of the good news, and to believe. 8 And God, knowing the heart, bore witness in them, giving them the Holy Spirit, as also to us, 9 and he made not one distinction between us and them, by faith having cleansed their hearts. 10 Now therefore, why are you putting God to the test, to put a yoke upon the neck of the disciples, that neither our fathers, nor we, have been able to bear? 11 But through the grace of Lord Jesus Christ, to be saved, we believe in the same manner as they also."

EXPOSITION

From 15:12 we discover the discussions did not begin with a report of God's work through Paul and Barnabas. All present had heard the previous report in 15:4, "the conversion of the gentiles." On the basis of that report, the council had been convened to decide one question: is it necessary to circumcise saved gentiles and command them to keep the Law of Moses?

The phrase "much discussion having occurred" means exactly what anyone having attended such a meeting has experienced: everyone with an opinion on the matter said something. Some helpful, some not; some scriptural, some not. The apostles and elders let everyone who wanted to speak contribute. Then, "Peter standing up said to them."

Peter rehearses the history all knew, but not all had applied. God had sent Peter to the gentiles, "to hear the word of the good news, and to believe." That in itself was significant, because at the time no one had thought to proclaim the good news to gentiles. Some proselytes had heard and believed, but their faith, as was the faith of the Jewish believers, was in Judaism and Christ. No God-fearer had heard the good news, until Peter told Cornelius, because a God-fearer was still a gentile.

What Peter says next directly addresses the issue at hand. Based on his experience with Cornelius the gentile, Peter concluded these things.

> God knows the heart: God knows when faith is genuine.
>
> God bore witness their faith was genuine: God gave them the indwelling Holy Spirit.
>
> God gave the indwelling Holy Spirit to them the same as to us: their salvation is as genuine as our salvation.
>
> God did not make a distinction between them and us: salvation is the same whether Jew or gentile.
>
> God by their faith cleansed their heart: salvation is the same whether Jew or gentile.

The sum of his words is this: saved apart from the Law.

We may make a relevant application: salvation is the same for all skin tones, languages, ethnicities, nationalities, tribes, and any other kind of superficial differences. From the first person saved, Abel, to the last person saved before the Great White Throne judgment, the one and only way of salvation is God's grace through the sinner's faith apart from personal merit by the sinner but Christ's merit alone. The means of salvation is for the sinner to believe on God and God's testimony of the means of salvation that has been given to you in God's historic progressive revelation of truth. In this current age of the New Testament church that means is Jesus Christ.

Acts 15:10 amounts to this. God saved gentiles apart from the Law. Why would you require those God saved apart from the Law to be under the Law? Why would you test God in that manner (to tell God he must do something he chose not to do)? Why would God put a yoke on the saved that no one—not our fathers, not you and me—has been able to bear?

A "yoke ... that neither our fathers, nor we, have been able to bear," is the seed of a doctrine that comes to full fruition in Paul's writings. The Law served three purposes.

> The Law was given to inform us what God requires of us: a righteous life pleasing to God lived according to God's moral values and principles.
>
> The Law was given to protect us from all those things that

violate God's moral values and principles.

The Law was given to show us no one can live a righteous life pleasing to God apart from God's grace.

These three purpose of the Law are parts of the whole: a yoke that no one is able to bear. The Law is perfect, but human beings are not. Because of the sin attribute resident in human nature, no one can achieve the perfect righteousness required by the Law, and therefore no one can be saved by the Law, nor can anyone live perfectly according to the Law (during this mortal life), after salvation. You yourselves, says Peter, the kind of lives you live, are witness to the truth. Why then require the gentiles to do something "neither our fathers, nor we, have been able to" do throughout our entire lives, unsaved or saved?

Peter's final statement is a brilliant summation. He said, "through the grace of Lord Jesus Christ," we Jews will be saved *in the same manner* those pagan gentiles were saved (emphasis mine). He means Jews are also saved apart from the Law, just like gentiles are saved apart from the Law. There is no difference, all who are saved have been saved apart from the Law.

We may make an application. During the 1,500 or so years of the Mosaic Law, *no one* was saved by the Law. Salvation is always "saved by God's grace through the sinner's faith." When a person under the Law brought the sacrifice for sin required by God in the Law, he or she was not saved by obedience to the Law, but by faith in God's testimony in the Law as to the means by which faith accessed God's grace and Christ's merit to save. (Not that they saw Chris in the sacrifices, but they saw a propitiation of God [atonement] in the sacrifices.)

Bringing the sacrifice was the demonstration of personal faith in God and God's testimony that the proper sacrifice, presented by faith and repentance, would result in forgiveness of sin. That was the truth God had given them, that was the truth that could save them, and faith in that truth did save them. Faith in God and God's testimony, not obedience to the Law, was always (and is always) the path to salvation and righteousness.

The Law told the sinner the content of saving faith, it did not save nor did it create saving faith. By God's grace you were saved, through your faith, not by the works of any law, and by God's grace, not by the works of any law, you continue in your salvation by faith. For neither God's grace, nor your faith, nor your salvation, are from you as the source, because they are God's gift to you, he alone is the source of his grace, your faith, and your salvation, just as he alone is the origin and source of the limitless merit that saves the sinner.

Translation Acts 15:12

12 Now all the many kept silent, and were listening to Barnabas and Paul telling what God had done, signs and wonders among the gentiles through them.

EXPOSITION

Peter's statement made them listen. I suspect those who believed gentiles must be under the Law to be saved had doubted Paul and Barnabas' perception that gentiles had truly been saved apart from the Law. Now, willing to listen, they paid close attention to Barnabas and Paul's report, which was probably more detailed than their previous account, 15:4. Here the account includes "what God had done, signs and wonders among the gentiles through them [Paul and Barnabas]." Let us remember the Jews were accustomed to validating God's work by God's signs and wonders.

Translation Acts 15:13–18

13 Now after, they were silent. Jacob responded, saying, "Men, brethren, hear me. 14 Simon has said how first God looked with mercy, to take out of the gentiles a people for his name. 15 And with this the words of the prophets agree. As it is written: 16 'After these things I will return and will build again the tabernacle of David which has fallen in ruins, and the ruins of it I will build again, and will set it upright, 17 so that the remnant of men may seek out the Lord, and all the gentiles, upon whom my name has been called in them, says the Lord, doing these things' 18 known from eternity."

TRANSLATION NOTE

In Acts 15:16–17, Jacob is quoting Amos 9:11–12, which ends with the words "doing these things." The words in 15:18, "known from eternity," are Jacob's comment on the prophecy. The reading of 15:18 in the KJV, "known unto God are all his works from the beginning of the world" (so also the NKJV), are by later scribes attempting to explain what they thought an incomplete sentence [Metzger, *Textual*, 379].

EXPOSITION

In quoting Amos, Jacob used the LXX, not the Hebrew text.

Amos 9:12 (Hebrew text), That they [Israel, 9:9] may possess the remnant of Edom, and all the gentiles who are called by my name, says YHWH who does these things.

Amos 9:12 (LXX), that the remnant of men, and all the Gentiles upon whom my name is called, may earnestly seek me, saith the Lord who does all these things.

Acts 15:17, so that the remnant of men may seek out the Lord, and all the gentiles, upon whom my name has been called in them, says the Lord, doing these things.

The Hebrew text says Israel will possess the remnant of Edom and all the gentiles called by the name of YHWH, i.e., those gentiles whom YHWH has saved or will save. The LXX text does not mention Edom and says all the gentiles upon whom God's name is called will seek the Lord. One might view that particular phrase as pointing to God's election of sinners to salvation.

Amos. That the remnant of men, and all the Gentiles upon whom my name is called, may earnestly seek me

Acts. So that the remnant of men may seek out the Lord, and all the gentiles, upon whom my name has been called in them

When will the remnant of men and all gentiles seek the Lord? Jacob says the timing agrees with Peter's encounter with Cornelius the gentile.

Acts 15:14–15, Simon has said how first God looked with mercy, to take out of the gentiles a people for his name. 15 And with this the words of the prophets agree.

Jacob has applied Amos's prophecy to the salvation of the gentiles that was happening in his, Jacob's, times.

Our task is to understand how Amos 9:11–12 agrees with Peter's encounter with Cornelius the gentile. Here is the timing in Amos, and Jacob's application of Amos.

Amos 9:11 (LXX), In that day [see 9:9] I will raise up the

tabernacle of David that is fallen, and will rebuild the ruins of it, and will set up the parts thereof that have been broken down, and will build it up as in the ancient days:

Acts 15:16 (JQTNT), 'After these things I will return and will build again the tabernacle of David which has fallen in ruins, and the ruins of it I will build again, and will set it upright,

The question is, what did Jacob mean when he said "after these things I [the Lord] will return" instead of quoting Amos' words "in that day?"

In Amos 9:11, "in that day" refers to Amos 9:9 (LXX), "For I will give commandment, and sift the house of Israel among all the Gentiles, as corn is sifted in a sieve, and yet a fragment shall not in any wise fall upon the earth."

In Amos 9:11, "in that day," are the days in which YHWH will sift the house of Israel among all nations, Amos 9:9, and the day in which the tabernacle of David will be rebuilt, 9:11. Amos 9:9, 11 is a reference to the Day of the Lord-Tribulation.

Jacob does not say "in that day," but says, "after these things I [the Lord] will return." Jacob also says Peter's encounter with Cornelius the gentile agrees with Amos' prophecy. Obviously Peter's encounter with Cornelius was not part of the Day of the Lord-Tribulation. Therefore, in Jacob's interpretation of Amos, the rebuilding of the tabernacle of David, and the remnant and gentiles seeking the Lord, comes "after these things," which things are the salvation of gentiles currently taking place, as initiated by Peter's encounter with Cornelius.

Could Jacob be saying the salvation of the gentiles that was happening in his times is the rebuilding of the house and kingdom of David ("the tabernacle of David")? No, for three reasons.

> One, we know Jacob is not referring to the restoration of David's kingdom that will take place after the Tribulation-second advent, because he uses a translation (the LXX) that does not mention the "remnant of Edom." Edom was an enemy of Israel. Edom plays a role in the Tribulation, e.g., Isaiah 34; 63; Daniel 11. Some think the believing remnant of national ethnic Israel during the Tribulation flee to Petra (Revelation 12:14, a place in the wilderness). Petra is now part of Jordan, but in Old Testament times it was in the nation Edom.

Two, the Lord did not "return and will build again the tabernacle of David." That had not happened. Israel remained under the control of the gentiles, the "times of the gentiles," Luke 21:24.

Three, the "tabernacle of David" is the Davidic-Messianic kingdom promised to national ethnic Israel, 2 Samuel 7:13–16; Psalm 2. The New Testament church is not Israel, did not replace Israel, is not a continuation of Israel. The Scripture always maintains a distinction between national ethnic Israel and the New Testament church. See the lengthy discussion in my book, *Dispensational Eschatology*, pp. 47–84. Scripture cannot contradict, so Jacob cannot be saying the New Testament church is to build the kingdom God promised to national ethnic Israel through King David's heir.

There are three possible interpretations of Jacob's application of Amos.

Possibility One. The New Testament church is the Tabernacle of David rebuilt. Therefore those gentiles "upon whom my name has been called" are seeking out the Lord. There are at least three problems with that interpretation.

(1) Where is the "remnant of men" mentioned by Amos (LXX) and Jacob? During the New Testament church age there is no remnant of men. After the Tribulation, yes, because at least two-thirds of the earth's population will die during the tribulation, leaving a remnant. The times of the Tribulation are so deadly to human life, that "if those times had not been shortened, there would not have been anybody saved," Matthew 24:22.

(2) Gentiles in this New Testament church age are not earnestly seeking the Lord, as Amos 9:12 says, but the Lord is seeking out the gentiles, as Jacob said, 15:14.

(3) An allegorical interpretation is required, that spiritualizes the New Testament church age as the Davidic Kingdom, and spiritualizes each salvation as a return of Christ to build the kingdom.

Possibility Two. The New Testament church is to rebuild the tabernacle of David. This is the same as saying the New Testament church has become Israel or is the continuation of

Israel, which I briefly discussed above. Those with this interpretation will say one of two things: the kingdom is here and now in the New Testament church (Amillennialism); the kingdom is being built by the church and the Holy Spirit for Christ to receive when he returns (Postmillennialism).

Possibility Three. Jacob is saying Amos' prophecy will come to pass after the salvation of the gentiles. Jacob says, "after these things I [the Lord] will return." What things? This thing: "Simon has said how first God looked with mercy, to take out of the gentiles a people for his name." Therefore the salvation of the gentiles now during this New Testament church age is necessary prior to the Lord's return and the Davidic Kingdom.

Looking at the history of the New Testament church age, interpretation three seems the most agreeable to the Scripture. By consistently applying the historical-grammatical hermeneutic (the Literal hermeneutic) to all the applicable scriptures, only interpretation three agrees with the Scripture.

There is a fourth reason the New Testament church is not the promised Davidic-Messianic kingdom: gentiles are not under the Law, Acts 15:24. If the New Testament church was the promised Davidic-Messianic Kingdom, or the New Testament church is building the promised Davidic-Messianic Kingdom, then the gentiles must be placed under the Law. Again Amos: after the Day of the Lord-Tribulation, 9:9, on that day, 9:11, the kingdom will be rebuilt and, 9:12, Israel will possess the remnant of Edom and all the gentiles who are called by YHWH's name. But in the New Testament church there is no distinction between Israel and gentiles, the New Testament church is one body.

Jacob says the gentiles are not to be placed under the Law, Acts 15:24. Gentiles will not be under the Law, because the proclamation of the good news is not the renewal of national ethnic Israel, contra Peterson [428ff.], or the restoration of the kingdom of David, contra Alexander [544], but the beginning of a new people group, the New Testament church. Paul clearly says (see Ephesians 3:1–7) the New Testament church is a new people group composed of Hebrews and gentiles—not Jews and gentiles, not gentiles converted to Judaism, but Hebrew Christians and gentile Christians who are one body in Christ.

Using the prophecy of Amos, Jacob has said the recent appearance of the heir of David, Jesus the Christ, is why gentiles are being saved, and "after these things" Jesus will return and rebuild the house and kingdom of David. In other words, Jacob is speaking of the New Testament church age that lies between the two advents.

Excursus: The Kingdom

In volume 1 (Acts 1–14) I briefly discussed the several kingdoms in Scripture. I won't repeat that discussion here, but a reminder of the different kingdoms in Scripture will be helpful.

A kingdom consists of ruler(s), ruled, and realm. Scripture teaches several aspects of the kingdom.

> The Universal Kingdom: God's universal rule over his creation. This kingdom is present for all time and eternity.
>
> Kingdom of God/Kingdom of Heaven. The reign of God through Jesus Christ (1 Corinthians 15:24–28).
>
> The Spiritual Kingdom: the kingdom during the New Testament church age between the two advents, composed only of believers saved during the New Testament church age, entered by the new birth. This is the New Testament church that is the body of Christ.
>
> The Mystery Kingdom: the kingdom during the New Testament church age between the two advents, composed of believers saved during the New Testament church age, and of people professing (not possessing) faith, rejecters of faith, and opponents of faith, who are visibly in the New Testament church, but are not spiritually part of the New Testament church through the new birth. This is the church the world sees.
>
> The Davidic-Messianic Kingdom: based on the Davidic covenant (2 Samuel 7:11b-17; 1 Chronicles 17:10b-15) promised to national ethnic Israel through King David's heir, who is Christ. The ruler is Christ through national ethnic Israel. The ruled will be all the inhabitants of the earth. The resurrected church will reign with Christ in this kingdom (2 Timothy 2:12; Revelation 5:10; 20:6).

Returning to the exposition.

The Kingdom of Amos 9:11 is the Davidic-Messianic Kingdom. The Kingdom, rather kingdoms, of this New Testament church age are the Spiritual Kingdom and the Mystery Kingdom.

Translation Acts 15:19–21

19 "Therefore I judge to trouble not those who from the gentiles

are turning to God, 20 but to send word to them by letter to abstain from the pollutions of idols, and sexual immorality, and that which is strangled, and from blood. 21 For Moses, from generations of old, has in every city those preaching him in the synagogues, being read on every Sabbath."

EXPOSITION

Trouble Not

By "trouble not" Jacob means that according to Amos' prophecy, the time has not yet come for gentiles to be under the Law. Will gentiles be under the Law in the Davidic-Messianic Kingdom? Yes, although the exact form of that Law cannot now be determined. We know there will be a literal temple in that kingdom with literal offerings, as described in Ezekiel 40–48 and Zechariah 14. In the Davidic-Messianic Kingdom, there will be living saved and living unsaved. There is a need, therefore, for a temple.

A temple is a place where man meets God through a mediator. How awesome the New Testament believer is the temple of the Holy Spirit, 1 Corinthians 6:19. Sinners meet God through his saved people, to whom God has given the message of reconciliation, 2 Corinthians 5:18–19. How awesomely fearful we should be not to defile the temple of God with our sins, and daily cleanse God's temple with confession and repentance.

The mediator in the Davidic-Messianic Kingdom is the Messiah. The saved during the Davidic-Messianic Kingdom enter a literal, physical temple to worship. The unsaved enter that literal, physical temple to hear the word of salvation and receive the opportunity to believe and be saved. Compare Revelation 21:22, the new heavens and earth, where all are saved and no temple is needed. [See discussion, *Dispensational Eschatology*, 236–239.]

Abstain From

Jacob understood, from the report given by Barnabas and Paul, that in some places a local church would be saved Hebrews and saved gentiles, but in other places saved gentiles only. The gentiles were not to be under the Law, but were there values in the Law that would guide their behavior? Moreover, there was the principle to not give offense to a brother in Christ through one's behavior and practices. Those things seem to be the origin of the letter to the saved gentiles from the Jerusalem Council.

Let us pause briefly to consider the authority of the Council. All those present assumed they had the authority to decide the issue of the Law, and the power to exhort, if not command, the behavior of the saved gentiles. All present at the council assumed that as the "mother church," those Christians in Jerusalem had the authority and power to command other local churches. Obviously believers at Antioch of Syria believed that was true: "they [the local church at Antioch] appointed Paul and Barnabas to go up, and certain others out of them, to the apostles and elders, to Jerusalem, about this question," Acts 15:2.

There have been seven other general church councils in New Testament church history, before the New Testament church divided into denominations. Each had the authority and power, and the consent of the whole church, to decide important issues for the whole church. The last general church council was AD 787.

This example of properly exercised authority and power later led to ecclesiastical hierarchies and the improper use of authority and power. Yet unlike the ecclesiastical hierarchies that later developed—Roman Catholic Church, Church of England, and other organizations—the Council restricted itself to the matter of the Law: (1) were gentiles required to conform to the Mosaic Law to be saved; and (2) did the Mosaic Law have certain values that could be applied to the gentiles?

Unlike the ecclesiastical hierarchies that later developed, Jacob was not declared head of the New Testament church, the ecclesiastical organization of the local church was not decided, and a from-the-top-down organization of local churches was not initiated—no archbishop-bishop-pastor-laymen, or any other kind of ruling hierarchy. Just recognized and trusted leaders led by the Holy Spirit deciding an issue of importance to the whole New Testament church, and bringing an unruly faction into submission.

Returning to 15:20, "abstain from the pollutions of idols, and sexual immorality, and that which is strangled, and from blood." Why these four things? Did this list of proscribed behaviors place the gentiles under the Law? To answer that question, one must remember the three functions of the Mosaic Law I mentioned earlier.

    One to make known God's moral values—God's rules for living—

that he requires of all human beings.

Two, to protect his saved people from moral harm by their keeping the commandments.

Three, to reveal the sinner's inability to keep God's commandments without grace from God.

None of these functions has expired.

Through the moral values and principles within the Mosaic Law, which are repeated in the New Testament (see my book *The Old Ten in the New Covenant*), it is by God's laws that the Christian is able to know God's moral values, which are God's rules for living—the "Do this, Don't do that" commandments—and is able to keep God's commandments because his human nature has been regenerated and is now inclined to obedience, not for salvation, but to work out his or her salvation, Philippians 2:12.

The one who said, "if you love me keep my commandments," John 14:15, and "you are my friends if you do whatever I command you," John 15:14, had no other moral principles and values to give except those he had given to humankind through Moses. For example, "Love one another," Leviticus 19:18, John 13:34; Romans 13:9, and many other New Testament scriptures.

As John Calvin wrote [*Institutes*, 3.19.2], "The whole life of Christians ought to be an exercise of piety, since they are called to sanctification (Eph. 1:4; 1 Thess. 4:3, 7). It is the office of the law to remind them of their duty and thereby excite them to the pursuit of holiness and integrity."

Jacob selected four moral values from the Law for the saved gentiles.

> Abstain from the pollutions of idols. Exodus 20:3–4, "I am your God YHWH. You will not have other gods beside me. You will not make to yourself an image: any form which is in the heaven above, which is in the earth under, which is in the water under the earth."

> Abstain from sexual immorality. Exodus 20:14, You will not commit adultery. Leviticus 18:6–18; 20:11, 17, You will not commit incest. Leviticus 18:23; 20:15–16, You will not commit bestiality. Leviticus 19:28, You will not commit prostitution.

> Leviticus 20:13, You will not commit homosexuality. Exodus 20:17; 34:16; Numbers 25:1; Deuteronomy 23:17, You will not commit fornication.
>
> Abstain from that which is strangled. This is from the prohibition not to eat an animal that was not properly slaughtered and prepared, Leviticus 22:8. Not eating blood may also have been a factor.
>
> Abstain from blood. YHWH said very clearly "blood makes atonement [propitiation] for the soul," Leviticus 17:11. This prohibition encompass engaging in sacrifices to idols and eating blood, which some cultures were doing (and many still do).

The two prohibitions to abstain from blood and from things strangled appear to say the same thing. For that reason, a few early commentators thought the prohibition, "abstain from blood," might be a figurative reference to murder. But that seems unlikely.

Why did Jacob select these four prohibitions? Most commentators say so as not to offend Hebrew Christian brethren in a local church. Undoubtedly that is an application. But what about local churches composed only of gentiles? For example, at Derbe and Lystra? There are, therefore, other reasons.

> The heart of paganism was worship of idols. Idolatry violates the holiness of the Christian faith, and denies there is one God, Father-Son-Holy Spirit, who is the only God and Savior.
>
> Sexual immorality violates the sanctity of marriage. The sanctity of marriage as between one man and one woman was the second moral value God gave humanity, Genesis 2:24. (Obedience was the first, Genesis 2:17.)
>
> Sexual immorality violates the sanctity of the believer as the temple of the Holy Spirit, 1 Corinthians 6:15–20.
>
> The prohibition against eating blood, whether in the flesh or by itself, was the first moral value God gave humankind after the flood, Genesis 9:4. Blood is holy—meaning it is set apart—because it symbolizes life and the propitiation for sin that saves lives.

Jacob says the gentiles already know these moral values from the Law, because "Moses, from generations of old, has in every city those preaching him in the synagogues." Preventing divisions in the local churches between saved Hebrew and saved gentiles was Jacob's main priority. But we must also recognize that some cities, like Derbe, Lystra, and even a major city such as Philippi, did not have a synagogue. Jacob's second priority was to help saved gentles escape the ungodliness of their former paganism, by not defiling themselves before their God and Savior with practices that were common to their former way of life.

Is there an application for today? Of course. We have the completed Old Testament and New Testament revelation, which clearly teaches us God's moral values—God's "Do this, Don't do" rules for godly living taught in the Scripture. Many cultures in the world still practice these four prohibitions named by Jacob. As Christians we should be careful to live by God's moral values and principles of behavior and practice.

Translation Acts 15:22–23

22 Then it seemed good to the apostles and to the elders, with all the church, having chosen men out from them, to send to Antioch with Paul and Barnabas, Judas called Barsabbas, and Silas, leading men among the brethren, 23 having written by their hand:

"The apostles and the elders, brethren, to those in Antioch and Syria and Cilicia, brethren among the gentiles, Greeting."

EXPOSITION

There was a church-wide vote on the matter. The letter was approved by the Twelve (now eleven by Jacob's [brother of John] death), the elders of the Jerusalem church, and "all the church," which would be the membership of the Jerusalem church (those present representing all), those from Antioch of Syria representing that church, and Paul and Barnabas representing the churches they had founded.

A scribe was called; perhaps already present recording the "minutes" of the meeting. The letter was discussed, the wording chosen, and the whole was dictated to the scribe. Then several copies would be made, because the letter was to go out to "those in Antioch and Syria and Cilicia."

This is the first mention of Cilicia having a local church. Looking ahead to 15:36–41, when Paul wants to "go back and look after the brethren in every city in which we declared the word of the Lord," he means those cities which were in Galatia. Luke says, "he was passing through Syria and Cilicia," 15:41 to visit those churches. So whether or not there were local churches in Cilicia, Paul meant he would pass through the regions of Syria and Cilicia to visit the local churches they had founded in the region of Galatia. The council probably meant the same thing, intending the letter go out to all the gentile churches.

The letter begins, "The apostles and the elders, brethren, to those in Antioch and Syria and Cilicia, brethren among the gentiles, Greeting." The one difficulty is the letter is not also sent to the local churches in Galatia, where Paul had founded churches composed only of gentiles, such as Derbe and Lystra. Nor are any local churches in Cyprus mentioned. Bruce said [314],

> The letter is addressed to the Gentile Christians of Antioch and of the province of Syro-Cilicia of which Antioch was the capital. The recently founded churches of South Galatia might be looked upon as an extension of the work in Antioch, Tarsus, and the rest of Syro-Cilicia and not as a separate "province."

Bruce's opinion seems reasonable. (I remind the reader once again Tarsus of Cilicia is never mentioned as having been evangelized, nor a local church founded in Tarsus, so to include it as having a local church is an assumption by Bruce. Tarsus, all mentions, Acts 9:11, 30; 11:25; 21:39; 22:3.)

Notice no one person claims himself as the origin of the decision. This is not a "Papal Bull," or a letter from the ecclesiastical head of a monolithic church, such as the Church of England. Christians viewed as and selected to be wise leaders together reached these decisions, together wrote this letter, and together sent the letter out to "brethren among the gentiles," at the same time declaring they were also "brethren." A genuine Christian community of faith is an assembly of equals. Some fulfill the offices of a local church, others have no office but exercise their spiritual gifts, and all are spiritually equal brethren in the Lord. As Paul wrote, 1 Corinthians 4:7.

> For who makes you differ one from another? But what do you have which you did not receive? Now if also you did receive, why do you boast as not receiving?

There are different offices and different gifts and different means of serving the Lord, but all are equally brethren in the Lord.

Translation Acts 15:24–26

24 "Because now we have heard that some from us going out troubled you by words, upsetting your minds, saying to be circumcised and keep the Law, to whom we had not given command, 25 it seemed good to us, having come with one mind, having chosen men to send to you with our beloved Barnabas and Paul, 26 men having committed their lives for the name of our Lord Jesus Christ."

EXPOSITION

The reason for the letter was this, some coming from Jerusalem and claiming to speak for the apostles and elders taught you something we did not authorize: "to be circumcised and keep the Law." The letter immediately gives the decision of the assembled Council, with the "apostles and the elders" speaking for the whole. Here is the decision: gentiles are not under the law.

The proper order of salvation in Christianity had been decided: salvation by faith, nothing added. Not because the Council said so, but because the decision of the Council was according to Scripture—both the written revelation of the Old Testament, and the new revelation given to the apostles and about to be written. A split in Christianity was derailed. However, the enemy of souls never stops trying. We must always be on our guard.

The consequence of the Council was a decision to inform the gentile churches by both letter and by representatives who would say the same as the letter. These men had proved their commitment to Christ. Notice the Council approves of Barnabas and Paul, which implies approval of the good news they are proclaiming to the gentiles.

That one or more of the apostles did not accompany the letter, at least as far as Antioch of Syria, speaks to their diminishing role in the day-to-day life of the local churches. Having created the New Testament church, they did not continue to manage the New Testament church. The Hebrew churches had centuries of experience in congregational meetings, which were easily adapted to the needs of those particular bodies of Christ. The Holy Spirit gave Paul to manage the gentiles churches for a little while, to establish a proper order for gentile congregations, whose only prior experience was an inconsistent paganism divided among the many gods.

Translation Acts 15:27–29

27 "Therefore we have sent Judas and Silas, and they by speech are telling you the same things. 28 For it seemed good to the Holy Spirit and to us, to lay no more burden upon you, except these necessary things: 29 to abstain from whatever is sacrificed to an idol, and from blood, and from what is strangled, and from sexual immorality. Keeping yourselves from these, you will do well. Be well."

EXPOSITION

The Council's messengers are introduced: Judas and Silas. Judas we hear of no more. Silas becomes an important companion of the apostle Paul, and later is found with Peter, 1 Peter 5:12.

The letter then gives the exhortation. The change in the order of those things suggests three are linked as parts of pagan worship: "abstain from whatever is sacrificed to an idol, and from blood, and from what is strangled." Setting apart the fourth "abstain from sexual immorality," highlights this important prohibition. Modern views of sexuality closely mirror the ancient pagan gentile view of sexuality.

What is sexual immorality? The following is an extract from my book *Biblical Homosexuality*.

The times and cultures and peoples (Hebrews and Gentiles) within which the Bible was written possessed erotic literature, visual depictions of nudity and sexual activity, practiced sexual activity with minors, practiced homosexuality, practiced prostitution (including prostitution as religious worship), and practiced heterosexuality outside the context of marriage. All these actions are comprehended under the Old Testament term *zānâ* (sexual activity outside the context of marriage) and the New Testament term *porneía* (to commit any sexual sin).

"Sexual morality" is sexual attraction and sexual activity that puts the biblical standards into daily practice. "Sexual immorality" is sexual attraction and sexual activity that does not meet the biblical standards. The Bible defines sexual immorality using certain representative terms: incest, adultery, fornication, prostitution, homosexuality, bestiality.

God's standards of sexuality morality may be summarized:

> Moral: Heterosexual attraction, heterosexual marriage, heterosexual sexual activity, in that order of occurrence.

> Immoral: whether occurring in person or presented in any media, acts of rape, incest, adultery, unmarried sex, bestiality, homosexuality, prostitution, pornography, public sexual activity, or public display of sexual organs (butt, genitals, female breasts).

> Immoral: within the context of the marriage relationship any sexual activity that may be demeaning or degrading to either spouse. Within the context of the marriage relationship any sexual activity displayed for public view whether occurring in person or presented in any media.

The letter sent by the Council used the word *porneía* [Zodhiates, s. v. 4202], translated as "sexual immorality." The gentiles knew what this word meant. The *Theological Dictionary of the New Testament*, [6:579ff.] lists the following as meanings of *porneía* used in the gentile world: prostitution (male and female), those who used prostitutes, adultery, fornication (unmarried sex), homosexuality (male and female), to live licentiously.

By keeping themselves from these things, the apostles and elders believed they would "do well." The letter closes with "Be well."

The remarkable thing about this letter is it is informative, not threatening or commanding. The believer's manner of life must be guided by God's moral values, of that there is neither doubt nor ambiguity. Equally as certain is the believer must choose to live by God's moral values. Morality cannot be legislated, it must be chosen. Yes, punishment for immorality may be legislated, or not, as a culture decides, and the moral values of any particular culture agrees, or not, with God's moral values. But God's standards do not change, and the believer is always obligated to live by those standards. Choose wisely, so that you may do well and be well.

Translation Acts 15:30–35

30 They therefore, indeed, having been sent, went to Antioch *of Syria*. And gathering the many, they delivered the letter. 31 Now having read, they rejoiced at the encouragement. 32 Both Judas and Silas, themselves also being prophets, through speech much exhorted and strengthened the brethren. 33 Continuing for a time, they were sent

away in peace from the brethren to those having sent them. [34 see translation note] 35 But Paul and Barnabas stayed in Antioch, teaching and preaching, with many others also, the word of the Lord.

TRANSLATION NOTE

Acts 15:34, is almost certainly a scribal addition to explain 15:40. The added sentence reads, "But it seemed good to Silas to remain there."

EXPOSITION

The letter was delivered. The people rejoiced at the decision, which encouraged them in their faith. Paul and Barnabas had previously reported to the church, "all that God had done with them, and that he had opened to the gentiles a door of faith," Acts 14:27. They had undoubtedly repeated the good news they had proclaimed to the gentiles, just as they had taught how gentiles were being saved apart from the Law. We know that Paul and Barnabas "stayed a long time with the disciples" at Antioch of Syria, 14:28, so there may have been saved, formerly pagan, gentiles in the local church, saved apart from the Law.

Judas and Silas, were prophets, and we see what kind of prophets they were, "through speech much exhorted and strengthened the brethren." In common parlance they preached and taught the word. They discipled, they did not predict. There were five teachers at Antioch, who graciously stepped aside so Judas and Silas could minister.

Then, "continuing for a time, they [Judas and Silas] were sent away in peace from the brethren to those having sent them." They returned to Jerusalem. The Jerusalem Council was during the year AD 50, Acts 15:40 during the year AD 51. Luke reports Silas left Antioch with Judas, so at a later time Silas returned.

In the interim, "Paul and Barnabas stayed in Antioch *of Syria*, teaching and preaching, with many others also, the word of the Lord." The Jerusalem teachers having left, and no longer disrupted by those of the party of the Pharisees who believed, the Antioch teachers resumed their duties.

Life returned to normal. For Paul this would mean evangelizing, teaching, discipling, and working at his trade, tentmaker (18:3) to support himself and his local church.

Translation Acts 15:36–41

36 Now after some days, Paul said to Barnabas, "Truly, let us go back and look after the brethren in every city in which we declared the word of the Lord, how they are." 37 Now Barnabas decided to also take John called Mark. 38 But Paul thought suitable not to take along the one having left from them from Pamphylia and not going with them to the work. 39 But a sharp disagreement arose, so that they separated from one another. And Barnabas, taking Mark, sailed to Cyprus. 40 But Paul chose Silas, and left, being commended to the grace of the Lord by the brethren. 41 Then he was passing through Syria and Cilicia, confirming the churches.

EXPOSITION

How much time had passed is not relevant, but those interested in such matters believe this second missionary journey of Paul began ca. AD 51. Paul's second missionary endeavor is usually reckoned as beginning at 15:36, lasting ca. AD 51–54, and ending at 18:22.

Although this second missionary work extended into Achaia (Macedonia, Greece), 16:11–18:18a, the initial purpose was "let us go back and look after the brethren in every city in which we declared the word of the Lord, how they are." Those things he did, 15:41; 16:1–2, 16:6.

A disagreement arose between Barnabas and Paul. Barnabas wanted to take his cousin Mark with them. Paul dissented because Mark had returned early from the first missionary work. The disagreement was "sharp ... so that they separated from one another."

But this was not an end to their friendship. I said in volume 1 [409], "Acts 15:39 is the last mention of Barnabas in the Book of Acts." And so it is. But Barnabas and Paul worked together again, and it was during this second missionary work. First Corinthians 9:6, "or do only I and Barnabas have no authority to work or not?" Though not mentioned in Acts, Barnabas was with Paul in Corinth, sometime between Paul's arriving, Acts 18:1, and leaving, Acts 18:18a.

After the disagreement, "Barnabas, taking Mark, sailed to Cyprus" and "Paul chose Silas, and left ... he was passing through Syria and Cilicia." Because of their disagreement over Mark they divided the work. But that was not the end of Mark and Paul's relationship. Paul mentions Mark, "the cousin of Barnabas" as with Paul during his first Roman imprisonment (Mark as a visitor, not a prisoner), Colossians 4:10; Philemon 24. A few years later, Timothy is to bring Mark with him to see Paul because Mark "is useful for the ministry," 2 Timothy 4:10. Apparently that young man did some growing up.

Now, "Paul chose Silas, and left, being commended to the grace of the Lord by the brethren." Was Barnabas not also commended to the grace of the Lord by the brethren? Luke does not say, but it is hard to imagine either man allowing a schism in the church. Luke follows the usual biblical method of reporting history: to finish with one history before beginning another. He completes his report of Barnabas, and turns his focus on Paul, who will occupy the remainder of the history of the Acts of the Holy Spirit.

We see Paul and Silas went overland, "passing through Syria and Cilicia, confirming the churches." Were there local churches in Syria and Cilicia not mentioned anywhere else in the New Testament? Acts 16:1 opens with two conjunctions, "then also," indicating after confirming the churches in Syria and Cilicia, then also Paul "came to Derbe and to Lystra." There is always more happening than the Holy Spirit tells us, if we pay attention to what he does tell us. There was more missionary work going on than what Luke reports in Acts.

Acts Sixteen

Translation Acts 16:1–3

1 Then he also came to Derbe and to Lystra. And behold, a certain disciple was there named Timothy, the son of a believing Jewish woman, but his father a Greek, 2 who bore honorable testimony by the brethren in Lystra and Iconium. 3 This one Paul wanted to go out with him, and taking him he circumcised him, on account of the Jews being in those parts. For they all knew that his father was a Greek.

EXPOSITION

The Roman provinces (now parts of modern-day Turkey) in which Paul had evangelized and is now visiting were local churches in the Imperial Provinces of Syria, Cilicia, and Galatia.

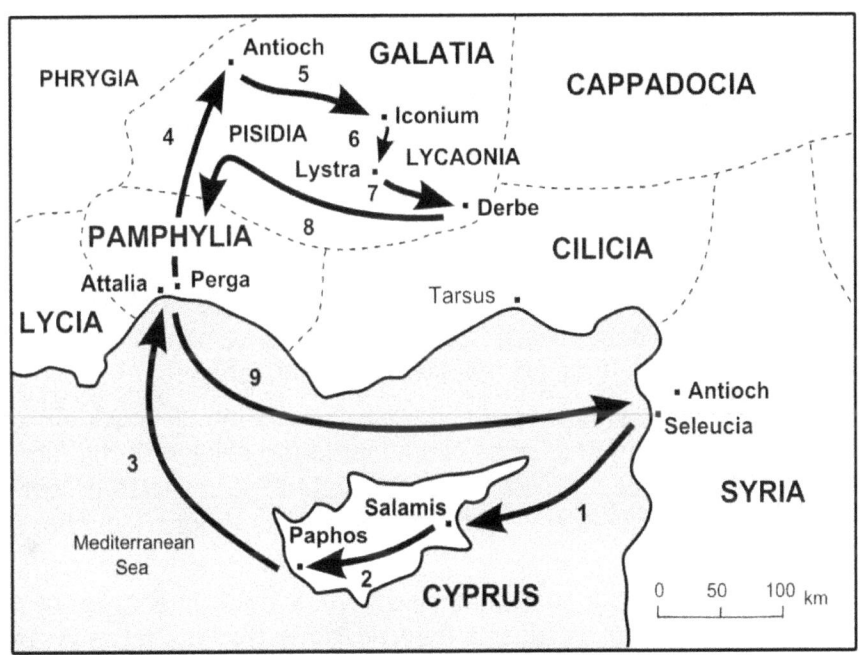

[https://www.thebiblejourney.org/]

(Ephesus was in the Senatorial Province of Asia [modern day Turkey], Philippi was in the Senatorial Province of Macedonia, and Corinth was in the Senatorial Province of Achaia [modern day Greece])

There is no mention in Acts that Paul ever evangelized in Tarsus of Cilicia. He may have, but Luke does not tell us. Derbe and Lystra were in the Imperial Province of Galatia, in a part of Galatia known as Lycaonia. Think of Galatia as a state, Lycaonia as a county, Derbe and Lystra as major cities in the county of Lycaonia.

Paul was last in Lycaonia ca. AD 48–49. The year is now ca. AD 51. In Lystra "a certain disciple was there named Timothy." The local church had been busy evangelizing during those two to three years, although Paul may have met Timothy in AD 48–49. Now, two to three years later, Timothy had grown into an adult disciple, whose personal character and understanding of Scripture caught Paul's notice. Timothy had gained "honorable testimony by the brethren in Lystra and Iconium," showing he was actively ministering in two local churches in different cities. Paul himself said of Timothy many years later, "from childhood you have known the sacred writings able to make you wise unto salvation through faith in Christ Jesus," 2 Timothy 3:15.

Paul wanted Timothy to come with him. Looking ahead, we see Paul's goals for this missionary trip, which began as "go back and look after the brethren in every city in which we declared the word of the Lord, how they are." Paul also intended to evangelize in other cities in other provinces. Timothy may (or maybe not) have been too old to be a proper apprentice, but essentially Paul took Timothy as his apprentice to learn the trade of the proclaiming the good news. There were no Christian colleges or seminaries to train men and women to understand Scripture and serve the Lord. Paul was the seminary.

Now, Timothy's mother was Jewish but his father Greek. In the ancient world, the mother and child adopted the religion of the father, at least outwardly. So Timothy was not circumcised, as was proper to the Greeks, but his mother (and grandmother) taught him the Old Testament Scripture.

Paul took Timothy and circumcised him. Why? "On account of the Jews being in those parts. For they all knew that his father was a Greek," Acts 16:3. Paul knew an uncircumcised man would not be accepted in the synagogues where Paul evangelized. That is to say, he could observe, and worship YHWH, but he could not speak. Timothy knew the Old Testament Scripture, but no Jew would accept his testimony, because if he was not circumcised he was Greek not Jewish.

Therefore Paul removed a hindrance to ministry.

Now this circumcising Timothy seems strange, does it not? Paul had the year before spent weeks of debate, culminating in the Jerusalem Council, against the requirement for circumcision. Indeed, in Galatians 2:3 he says he refused to circumcise another fellow-worker, Titus the Greek. Is Paul being inconsistent in his theology? No.

The circumcision issue was this, did non-Jews need to follow the Law in order to be saved, or in order to be completed Christians as obedient disciples of Jesus Christ? That question was answered with a resounding "No." Where that principle of salvation by works or faith was the issue, Paul would not bend: no circumcision. But if circumcision was not a matter of salvation or becoming a completed Christian, but rather a hindrance to the proclamation of the good news, Paul could adapt, because the salvation principle, saved by grace through faith, was not the issue.

Circumcising Timothy after delivering the Jerusalem Letter on not having to be circumcised, undoubtedly cause some issues in the Lystra church. There would have been some who fell away from Paul over the issue. By looking at Paul's letters, we see Paul maintained his opposition to circumcision as part of salvation. We may also see Paul's argument for circumcising Timothy.

Let us begin by looking at a simpler issue as an example. I was recently asked, "Is drinking alcohol a sin?" Answer. No. Consuming alcohol is not a sin. Intoxication is a sin. A definition of intoxication: "a noticeable change in behavior occurring as a result of consuming alcohol." That is, noticeable by others. The intoxicated person is usually clueless, especially in the early stages.

Now suppose the Christian who does occasionally consume alcohol, let's say as part of an evening meal, is called upon by the Holy Spirit to evangelize an alcoholic, and in the processes of testimony invites the alcoholic sinner into his home for an evening meal. Should not the Christian set aside his liberty to consume alcohol, because it is a hindrance to his evangelization of this man? Yes, of course. Voluntarily curtailing one's liberty when it is a hindrance to others is maturity in the Lord. Say this of myself? Or does the Scripture say it?

> Romans 15:20–21, Do not because of food destroy the work of God. Truly all *is* clean, but harmful to the person eating with

offence. 21 *It is* good to not eat meat, neither to drink wine, nor *that* in which your brother stumbles.

1 Corinthians 8:13, Therefore, if food offends my brother, never no never may I eat meat to the age, so that I may not offend my brother.

Here is a Scripture passage that speaks to the propriety of circumcising Timothy but not Titus.

1 Corinthians 9:19–23, For being free from all, to all I myself become a servant, so that I may gain the more. 20 And I became to the Jewish, as a Jew, so that I might gain Jewish. To those under Law, as under Law, not being myself under Law, so that I might gain those under Law. 21 To those outside Law, as outside Law—not being outside God's law but under law to Christ—so that I might gain those outside Law. 22 I became to the weak, weak, that the weak I might gain. To all these things I have become all, so that by all means I might save some. 23 Now I do all for the sake of the good news, that I might become a joint partaker with it.

Paul makes an important distinction between an essential of the faith, and an accommodation to the weaknesses of others. One cannot compromise an essential of the faith. Circumcision is not required for salvation, no compromise. But one may accommodate others in a non-essential practice that becomes a hindrance to evangelism. Does the person I am evangelizing believe caffeine is an addictive drug not to be consumed under any circumstances (e.g., some Mormons)? Then I will set aside my morning cup of tea to proclaim the good news.

And if the Lord should be pleased to save that person, I will teach him from the Scripture. Romans 14:14, "I know and I am persuaded in the Lord Jesus, that nothing is unclean of itself, except to him reckoning something to be unclean: to that one it is unclean," and 14:17, "For the kingdom of God is not eating and drinking, but righteousness and peace and joy in the Holy Spirit," and 14:22, "The faith that you have, keep to yourself before God. Blessed the one not judging himself in what he approves."

Paul took Timothy to himself as an apprentice, and took the first step to prepare Timothy for a life of service to Jesus Christ to both Jews and Greeks.

Translation Acts 16:4–5

4 Then, as they were passing through the cities, they charged them to keep the decisions decided by the apostles and elders who were in Jerusalem. 5 Truly, therefore, the churches were strengthened in the faith, and increased in number every day.

EXPOSITION

As they visited established local churches, Paul and Silas gave them copies of the Jerusalem Council's letter, and added their own exhortations. The immediate impact was confirmation in the faith, increased evangelization to all peoples, and salvations as the Lord was pleased to save. The phrase "the churches ... increased in number every day," probably means individuals joining established churches through salvation. However, the ambiguity may be deliberate on the part of the Holy Spirit, and might also mean the number of local churches increased.

Translation Acts 16:6–8

6 Then passing through Phrygia and the Galatian region, the Holy Spirit having forbid them to speak the word in Asia, 7 then coming down to Mysia they tried to go into Bithynia, and the Spirit of Jesus did not

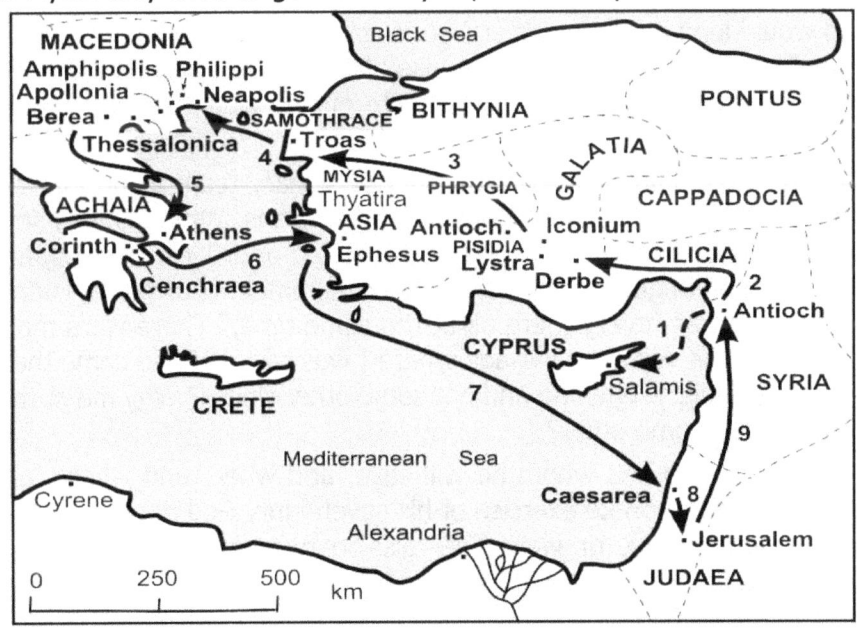

permit them. 8 Then passing by Mysia they came down to Troas.

EXPOSITION

Luke does what he sometimes does, he reverses the order of events. Paul, Silas, and Timothy passed through Galatia and into Phrygia. Looking at the map [https://www.thebiblejourney.org/], we see Phrygia was a county in the state of Asia, just as Iconium was a county in the state of Galatia. We would more accurately say Derbe of Lycaonia in Galatia, Lystra of Lycaonia in Galatia, Iconium of Lycaonia in Galatia, Antioch of Pisidia in Galatia. Then passing into Asia through the state of Phrygia, they went to Mysia of Asia and Troas of Asia. By limiting the path to Phrygia, Luke is saying the missionary team did not intend to go to the major seaport of Ephesus. They also did not stop at Mysia of Phrygia in Asia, but went on to Troas of Asia.

They went to Troas of Asia because, as Luke tells us, when the missionary team was near Mysia, they wanted to go into Bithynia, but the Holy Spirit would not allow them. A decision to go into Bithynia tells us they had no intention of crossing the Aegean Sea, but intended to evangelize in Bithynia, Pontus, and Cappadocia, then continue south back to Antioch of Syria.

Evangelizing in Bithynia, Pontus, and Cappadocia was a good plan, and would lend itself to further "let us return and see how everyone is doing" journeys out of the home base of Antioch in Syria. Paul thought of Antioch of Syria as his home church, but he would see it only one more time, 18:22.

The Holy Spirit did not allow the missionary team to go into the state of Bithynia. The Holy Spirit had other plans. Why this was so is not explained. The simple fact is God is a God of order not chaos, and God has an evangelistic plan for his New Testament church that cannot be described as "everywhere all at the same time," There were many unsaved in the very small village where I was saved (I had come there 6 months earlier). Why me and not some other sinner? Why me at that time and not some other?

Only God knows whom he will save, and when, and where, and why. In an appropriate exercise of his sovereignty God does not tell us who, when, where, or why. The missionary team chose to bypass Mysia, and were not allowed to go into Bithynia. God is sovereign over the affairs of humankind. He is always just in every decision and every action, or lack of action. Romans 9:15, "'I will show mercy to whom I may show mercy' and 'I will have compassion on whom I may have compassion.'" We either the have the faith to trust him, or not.

We never again hear of the churches in Galatia by name; they are the churches Paul wrote to in his letter to the Galatians, but that was before this second missionary trip, which confirmed what was said in the Jerusalem Letter, "they charged them to keep the decisions decided by the apostles and elders who were in Jerusalem."

Translation Acts 16:9–10

9 And a vision appeared to Paul during the night, a certain man of Macedonia was standing and imploring him and saying, "Passing over into Macedonia, help us." 10 Now when he had seen the vision, we immediately desired to go into Macedonia, concluding that God had called us to proclaim the good news to them.

EXPOSITION

The team has arrived in Troas. Luke does not mention any evangelistic activity, and perhaps there was none, but we know from later mentions there was a New Testament church at Troas, e.g., Acts 20:6–12.

The city of Troas was a small seaport on the north coast of the Roman Province of Asia (Turkey). They had stopped at Troas because they did not know where to go next. Their missionary plan, Bithynia-Pontus-Cappadocia-home, had been denied by the Holy Spirit. They were not inactive—that would be contrary to all else Luke has said, and will say, about this missionary team. They kept busy proclaiming the good news whole awaiting further instructions.

One night while they were in Troas, the Holy Spirit gave Paul a vision. "A certain man of Macedonia was standing and imploring him and saying, 'Passing over into Macedonia, help us.'" Some commentators say the man did not identify himself as a Macedonian. But the man in the vision said, "Passing over into Macedonia, help us." The "us" includes the man in the vision, who by using "us" self-identified as a Macedonian.

How Luke became attached to the missionary team is not stated.

Perhaps Luke found Paul in a synagogue (but there is no historical documentation of a synagogue in Troas). Perhaps there was already a local church in Troas and Luke met Paul there. Or perhaps Paul founded a local church in Troas before receiving the vision and that was how Luke and Paul met.

Neither Luke nor the Holy Spirit thought it important for us to know how they met. We only know this. One, the author of both gospel and Acts is assumed to be Luke, an assumption supported by early church testimony and internal evidence. Two, the author of Acts accompanied Paul to Macedonia, identifying himself by the "we" passages in the narrative. The first one is here, 16:10 and continues to 17:1. Luke remained in Philippi, because "they" left Philippi and went to Thessalonica, 17:1. The "we" passages pick up at 20:6.

Having received the vision, the missionary team knew where the Holy Spirit wanted them to go and evangelize. "We [Luke, Paul, the missionary team] immediately desired to go into Macedonia, concluding that God had called us [Luke, Paul, the missionary team] to proclaim the good news to them."

Translation Acts 16:11–13

11 Then sailing from Troas, we took a straight course to Samothrace. Then the next day to Neapolis, 12 and from there to Philippi, which is a leading city of the region of Macedonia, a colony. Now we remained in this city for some days. 13 Then on the day of the Sabbaths, we went out, outside the city gate, where we supposed there was to be prayer by a river. And sitting down, we spoke to the women having gathered.

EXPOSITION

To Philippi

Samothrace is a volcanic Island in the Aegean Sea about 70 miles by ship from Troas, and then another 86 miles by ship to Neapolis. They would have stopped at Samothrace for the night, then sailed to Neapolis. Neapolis was part of Macedonia, but Luke does not say Paul evangelized in Neapolis; the tempo of the narrative suggests he did not. As was his habit, Paul selected one of the major cities in the region to begin his work in Macedonia. From Neapolis there was a Roman road, the Via Egnatia, that going west from Neapolis went up an elevated ridge, through a narrow pass, then down into a flat and well-watered, fertile plain to the Roman colony of Philippi, a distance of about 10 miles from Neapolis to Philippi.

Emperor Augustus (63 BC – AD 14) had made Philippi a Roman colony [Conybeare, 223] to memorialize his victory over Brutus and Cassius. As a Roman colony the city was deliberately made into a "miniature resemblance of Rome" [Conybeare, 223], and its people were Roman citizens, a valuable status. Latin was the official language, the city had a Roman military garrison, and many military veterans had been rewarded with land in or near Philippi to colonize the area. Their government was their own, ruled by magistrates, not subject to local governors. Many of the residents were Italians.

The Day Of The Sabbaths

The plural "Sabbaths" occurs many times in the New Testament, but most translations change it to the singular form. The New Testament writers meant that particular day of the week, the seventh, on which a sabbath is practiced. Every week has a Sabbath, so, "Sabbaths." Sabbath means rest. The Sabbath day was a day of rest from productive employment. It was not given by God, Exodus 20:8, as a worship day; every day was a worship day. When the synagogue system was developed during the intertestamental period, the local synagogues adapted the Sabbath day of rest as a day of worship.

The missionary team had used the time before that particular Sabbath day to discover if there was a synagogue, and not finding one, were there any Jews in Philippi, and if so, where did they meet? Apparently they heard there were Jews in Philippi. On the day of the Sabbaths, the missionary team went outside the city gate to the river, where they supposed there was to be prayer by the resident Jews. Philippi lay between the Strymon and Nestos rivers.

Many sources say ten Jews were required to found a synagogue—ten of either gender, or a combination—but there were apparently only Lydia and some members of her household, all women, but not amounting to ten. Because all these Jews were women, some believe that is why there was not a synagogue. But the rule of ten males in the first century AD is not certain. Today only the Orthodox denomination requires ten males. The Reformed denomination requires ten persons.

Some [e.g., Longnecker, 460] like to point to m. *Sanhedrin* 1.6,

"And whence do we learn that a congregation is made up to ten?" in order to say it must be ten males. But two things are important here. One is the Mishnah was compiled during the 400 years between the 2nd century BC and 2nd century AD, and our story takes place in ca. AD 51. Two, *Sanhedrin* 1.6 quotes Numbers 14:27, which refers to the congregation, not to males only. But the patriarchalism of the times would have resisted women as founding members without at least one male. Christianity has no such problem. If there are only women to begin a local church, women can preach to women and teach children.

Lydia might also have been a gentile God-fearer, and the question about a synagogue irrelevant. If so she would have received instruction on Jewish ways of worship somewhere, if not in Philippi, then perhaps in Thyatira. Prayer would be natural, and if a God-fearer then the home was a suitable a place as any on a Sabbath. Seeking out a river for prayer most likely indicates she was Jewish. Why a river? Living (running) water for ritual cleansing. Without a synagogue there was no mikvah (bath for immersion) for cleansing.

The missionary team joined the prayer group, which was sitting on the banks of one of the two rivers. Had they begun the prayer time, or completed their prayer time? Standing for prayer was not required (although some today say it is required for some kinds of prayer). Regardless the people were sitting when the missionary team came upon them and, "we spoke to the women having gathered." The "we" means not only was Luke present and speaking to the women, but the team divided themselves among the women in order to speak to them individually. Proclaiming the good news is not the work of one person.

Translation Acts 16:14–15

14 And a certain woman named Lydia, a seller of purple cloth, of the city of Thyatira, worshiping God, was listening, whom the Lord opened her heart to give attention to the things spoken by Paul. 15 Then when she was immersed, and her household, she implored, saying, "If you have judged me to be faithful to the Lord, come into my house and abide." And she persuaded us.

EXPOSITION

Thyatira was a city a little north of Ephesus in the Asian province, on the great circular road that ran thorough the province (in Revelation

2, 3, all the cities mentioned were on that road). The city was formerly part of a kingdom known as "Lydia" before becoming part of the Roman Empire. Many in Paul's times continued to call the province Lydia. [Longnecker, 461]. Thus, "a certain woman named Lydia," might mean the "Lydian Lady," but most likely means she was named after the ancient kingdom. Thyatira was famous for purple dyes and dyeing cloth. Purple dye was obtained from the marine snail Bolinus brandaris, also known as the murex shellfish. Lydia had moved across the Aegean Sea to Philippi, Macedonia, to start a business selling purple cloth. Purple cloth was prized as the color of royalty, and a status symbol (because it was expensive). Thousands of snails were required to obtain purple dye in sufficient quantities for dyeing cloth.

In one sentence Luke tells us the story of Lydia's conversion.

> a certain woman named Lydia
>
> [who was] worshiping God [when Paul, "sitting down … spoke to the women having gathered" 16:13]
>
> [and] was listening [to Paul proclaim the good news]
>
> whom [Lydia] the Lord opened her heart to give attention to the things spoken by Paul

A certain woman named Lydia, a seller of purple cloth, of the city of Thyatira, who was worshiping God when Paul, sitting down, spoke to the women having gathered, and she was listening to Paul proclaim the good news, whom the Lord opened her heart to give attention to the things spoken by Paul. Having believed, she was immersed as a testimony of her faith, and as the first act of obedience every believer should render to Christ.

What did Paul speak? "Therefore be it known to you, women, brethren, that through this one, to you forgiveness of sins is proclaimed. And from all things from which you were not able in the Law of Moses to be justified, in him everyone believing is justified," Acts 13:38–39.

How do we know she believed and was saved? Because "she was immersed [in the river], and her household," an event that happens in Acts only after a credible profession of saving faith. Her Jewish heritage would have told her immersion was the next step after conversion; Paul would have told her immersion was a believer's act of obedience to the

Savior Jesus Christ. Some discipleship probably took place between salvation and immersion. Notice there was nothing dramatic about these salvations: they heard, they believed, they were instructed, they were immersed. The simplicity of the good news gospel believed and practiced. The Holy Spirit came to indwell without any outward manifestation of his abiding presence.

"Household" would include servants, some of whom might also have been employees in her business. No husband is mentioned, but in the ancient world that was not unusual, because being widowed was commonplace, and it may have been the reason she left Thyatira for Macedonia. No children are mentioned, but that also is not unusual, because children are seldom mentioned in the New Testament.

Lydia then offered the missionary team lodging in her home. The offer was culturally conditioned, it was normal to her Jewish culture to offer one's home to traveling prophets (preachers) for a brief time of lodging. Compare Luke 10:5–7. Such an offer was usually accepted. But there was also a cultural problem: men staying unchaperoned in a household of women only.

Therefore, her offer came with a condition: "If you have judged me to be faithful to the Lord, come into my house and abide." Patterson says [462], the offer of her home "reflected the possibility that the missionaries might not yet consider her 'a believer in the Lord.'" That view neglects the fact that in Acts immersion always follows, and is only administered, upon a *credible* profession of salvation. Her salvation was not the issue.

Lydia was saying, "if you judge (evaluate) me to be a righteous and chaste woman whose reputation is above reproach." Even gentiles would have looked askance at men staying unchaperoned in a household of women only. So the effect on the men's reputation was also a factor. However, let us also remember it was normal for local churches to be established in homes. Lydia might have been offering more than temporary hospitality, she may have been opening her home as a local church to others who might be saved in Philippi. As a woman known to all as chaste and respectable, she was offering to house the missionaries and host other believers.

Translation Acts 16:16–18

16 Now it happened, in our going to the place of prayer, a certain girl having a spirit of Python, met us; who much gain was bringing her masters by fortune-telling. 17 This one, following Paul and us, was calling aloud, saying, "These men are servants of the God the Most High, who proclaim to you the way of salvation." 18 Then this she continued for many days. Then Paul became wearied, and turning to the spirit he said, "I command you in the name of Jesus Christ to come out of her." And it came out the same hour.

EXPOSITION

The missionary team met the girl "having a spirit of Python" on their way to the place of prayer where they had met with Lydia and her household, an event that kept on occurring each time they went to the place of prayer. In Greek myth, Python was the son Gaia, the goddess representing the planet earth, and he was a serpent. The sun god Apollo killed Python and built a temple at Delphi over Python's grave. The site at Delphi was home to female prophets, known as the oracles. The serpent's name became both a place name and a title. The priestess of the oracle at Delphi was known as the Pythia. A "spirit of Python" means a spirit of prophecy, an oracle.

The oracle at Delphi would enter a trancelike state to utter the prophecies. Some believe the probable cause of the trancelike state of the Priestess (the Pythia) at the oracle of Delphi was produced by inhaling ethylene gas or a mixture of ethylene and ethane from a naturally occurring vent of geological origin [Hiller et al, https://pubmed.ncbi.nlm.nih.gov/].

The Scripture writers were men of their culture, and both Luke and Paul knew the story of Python, and Luke correctly uses the terminology of the day to describe someone who worked as an oracle. But Luke and Paul were also men of the Scripture, and informed by the Holy Spirit. This particular Pythia (oracle) was inhabited by a fallen messenger.

Fallen messengers don't know the future any more than you or me, which is to say not at all. But their intelligence allows them to make good guesses based on what they did know, and their numbers gave them access to a large amount of relevant information about the Pythia's clients. One should also never underestimate the human capacity for self-delusion, for even today "fortune tellers" make a good living.

Notice in 16:18 Paul addresses the fallen messenger, not the girl. A human being in whom a fallen messenger (demon) resides cannot cast out the fallen messenger. The person so inhabited cooperates, willingly or unwillingly, with the indwelling demon.

When Luke says the spirit "came out" of the girl "the same hour," he does not mean a lengthy period of time elapsed between Paul's command and the fallen messenger leaving the girl. We would say "came out that very minute." Luke is simply writing consistent with the way things were said in in his times. The fallen messenger may have resisted, as some did when Christ cast out fallen messengers.

In the days following Paul's initial meeting with the girl, she continued to follow them as they went about the city proclaiming the good news, and during the everyday activities normal to life. For many days, wherever they went, the girl followed, saying "These men are servants of the God, the Most High, who proclaim to you the way of salvation." One wonders why, as the constant attention led to the fallen messenger being cast out.

Perhaps the fallen messenger thought by proclaiming the truth he might not be cast out. Perhaps he wanted to antagonize Paul and the Holy Spirit only allowed him to proclaim the truth. (Balaam is an example, Numbers 21:35.) When Jesus confronted a fallen messenger residing in a human being, some gave a true message that he was the Messiah. For example, Mark 1:24; Luke 4:34. Jesus, "did not allow them to speak, because they knew him to be the Christ," Luke 4:41.

The fallen messenger may have thought to disrupt the proclamation of the good news by being the louder and more insistent voice. He may also have thought to be associated with the missionary team in the minds of the people, in order to lead the people to think Paul was also an oracle of Python. That kind of association would have discredited the good news. The missionaries would not be seen as speaking in the name of Jesus Christ but with a spirit of Python. Whatever people thought about the men who employed the girl, would be transferred to the missionaries, who would then be seen as proclaiming salvation for money—the girl brought her masters much gain by fortune telling. Many teachers of Greek learning went from town to town preaching philosophy for money.

Regardless of the reason or reasons, and they are not at all mutually exclusive, after many days, "Paul became wearied, and turning to the spirit he said, 'I command you in the name of Jesus Christ to come out of her.'" Again we are confronted with more questions than answers. Why did Paul wait many days? Perhaps Paul delayed hoping to avoid trouble with the girl's masters? What did Luke mean by "Paul became wearied?" Did Paul act out of frustration, or some nobler principle? These questions cannot be answered; all one may do is try to walk a little in Paul's shoes and seek reasonable answers.

Regardless of why Paul waited, after many days he cast the fallen messenger out the girl. Were those days productive, i.e., were some saved during those days? Or did the girl's interference, i.e., the fallen messenger's interference, cause others to avoid the missionaries? Luke does not say, and we may only speculate.

Translation Acts 16:19–21

19 Now her masters, seeing that the hope of their profit was gone, seizing Paul and Silas, they dragged them into the market place before the rulers. 20 And bringing them to the magistrates, they said, "These men greatly disturb our city, being Jews, 21 and proclaim customs it is not lawful for us to accept nor practice, being Romans."

EXPOSITION

Certainly sin makes you stupid in the ways of God, but not the ways of the world. The "customs it is not lawful for us to accept nor practice" would be turning from the many gods to one God, YHWH. Worshiping one God was lawful for Jews, but not for Romans. If there had been a synagogue in Philippi the charge might have carried less weight, because the Jews did legally proselytize gentiles to Judaism, and worshiping one God became lawful upon conversion and circumcision, because by those actions a gentile became a Jew.

The men bringing the accusation did not care the missionaries were Christians, and either knew not or cared not they were proclaiming Christ. The difference between a "Jew" and a "Christian" was not discernable to gentiles during these early years of Christianity. Paul and Silas certainly dressed like Jews, Timothy was half-Hebrew and probably dressed like a Jew, Lydia was a Jew, and of her household most, if not all, were Jews. Where was Luke, who was a gentile? We know Luke remained in Philippi when the missionary team left, so he was probably not with them when arrested, having business in the community that kept him busy.

Paul and his team had not broken any Roman laws. The Roman treaty with Jews allowed them to proselytize. In another city the accusation might have amounted to nothing. In Corinth the proconsul refused to become involved with "a dispute about a word, and names, and according to your [Jews'] law, Acts 18:15. But Philippi was a Roman colony, so they were zealous about Roman customs and desired to preserve their status. Less zeal and more Roman law would have prevented what came next. But the magistrates let themselves be influenced by the crowd. Such is the way of many politicians.

Why were the magistrates in the marketplace? The Greek *agora* originated as a place for political gatherings. A Roman *agora* was mostly a marketplace (an open market). Philippi, having once been a Greek city, probably incorporated both uses. Certainly the *agora* was suitable for the public administration of justice. Even if the magistrates had not been in the marketplace, those accusing the missionaries would have first brought them to the *agora* to inflame public opinion.

Translation Acts 16:22–24

22 And the crowd rose up together against them, and the magistrates, having torn their clothing, commanded they be beaten with rods. 23 Then having given them many blows, they cast them into prison, charging the jailor to keep them securely, 24 who having received such an order, threw them into the inner prison, and fastened their feet in the stocks.

EXPOSITION

The accusation had the desired result. The crowd's reaction gives us another reason Lydia and her household met outside the city gate. Jews were not popular in gentiles lands, as they were considered atheists because they worshiped only one God, and their customs kept them socially and culturally isolated from the gentiles.

Tearing clothes was a universal sign among the peoples of the times for anger, great fear, mourning, or repentance; an outward expression of a strong emotional state. There are two possible explanations to "having torn their clothing." The first, and most likely, is the pronoun "their" refers to the preceding noun "magistrates." The politicians did what politicians do, they took the pulse of the populace and responded by publicly demonstrating they understood what their constituents felt, by tearing their own clothing.

The second possible explanation is the pronoun "their" refers to the previous pronoun "them," meaning Paul and Silas. That would be an unlikely syntax. Luke would have written, "the magistrates commanded their clothing be torn and they be beaten with rods."

The magistrates illegally had Paul and Silas beaten. The beating was illegal because neither man had been arrested or convicted of a crime. A beating was sometimes administered after an arrest as a means to elicit a confession of a crime. But usually a beating was the result of being convicted of a crime. Paul and Silas were given the *fustigatio* form of punishment, but beaten as though a Freedman (a slave who had been given his freedom or had bought his freedom). Romans, which is to say citizens, could not be beaten. Beating a Roman citizen without an arrest, a legal trial, and a verdict of guilty was a serious crime.

Excursus: Beatings Under Roman Law

The Romans used different forms of corporal punishment, depending on who the person was and what he had done. A Freedman (a slave who had been given his freedom or had bought his freedom) was beaten with rods of birch or elm bound together in a bundle. Slaves and non-Romans were flogged (also known as scourging). Flogging was performed using a whip made out of leather straps or knotted cords (rope) often weighted with pieces of metal or bone.

Flogging was used in four circumstances: (1) as torture during questioning of a prisoner; (2) as punishment (the *fustigatio* and the *flagellatio*); (3) for execution (the *verberatio*); (4) as preparation for crucifixion (the *verberatio*).

The *fustigatio* was a less severe beating meted out for relatively light offences, (think misdemeanor). The *flagellatio* was a brutal flogging administered to criminals whose offences were more serious, (think felony). The *verberatio* was used as capital punishment for people sentenced to death by flogging, or as preparation for crucifixion. (Definitions see Bromiley, *Encyclopedia*, s. v. "Scourge.")

Pilate had Jesus given the *fustigatio* in an effort to satisfy the crowd—justified by having been arrested and the public disturbance—and then the *verberatio* after being condemned to execution by crucifixion. (See volume 2 of my commentary on John's gospel.)

Paul and Silas were given the *fustigation* with rods on the assumptions 1) they legally deserved a bearing, and 2) they were free or freedman.

Returning to the exposition.

Paul and Silas were cast into prison. This was not illegal. In ancient times, imprisonment was not used for punishment. A person was imprisoned to hold them until a trial was held. A person might be imprisoned during an investigation and released if there was insufficient evidence for a trial. A debtor could be held in prison until the debt was paid. Imprisonment was used after a trial to keep the convicted prisoner secured until the punishment (beating, exile, execution, a fine) could be accomplished. Bear in mind, under Roman Law (in fact the laws of most countries at the time) the accused was presumed guilty unless or until evidence or a trial declared them innocent.

Paul and Silas were presumed guilty of public disturbance and proclaiming illegal customs. They would be held in prison until a trial could determine their innocence or punishment. The only thing the magistrates did wrong was administering punishment without investigation (torture during questioning) or trial. If Paul and Silas had not been Roman citizens, then beating them would not have been a crime; premature, yes, but not a crime.

The jailor, most likely a Roman soldier, was charged "to keep them securely." Now, Roman prisoners were always kept securely. Jail breaks and prison uprisings were unlikely; Roman soldiers took no prisoners, so-to-speak, if one or more of the imprisoned dared attempt a riot or escape. The reason was the prison guard would suffer the punishment due the escaped prisoner. So the charge "to keep them securely" was no idle command or threat.

The jailor, probably knowing little to nothing about the preceding events, upon receiving such a charge, assumed Paul and Silas were dangerous persons. He "threw them into the inner prison, and fastened their feet in the stocks." Roman prisons were filthy, poorly ventilated, and were underground. The prisons would be divided into outer and inner areas. The inner parts of the prison were more secure and darker. [Robinson, 113]. Putting their feet into stocks was excessive, but ensured there was no escape.

Translation Acts 16:25–28

25 Now about midnight, Paul and Silas were praying and singing praises to God. Now the prisoners were listening to them. 26 Then suddenly there was a great earthquake, so that the foundations of the prison were shaken. Then immediately the doors of all were opened, and the chains of all were loosened. 27 Then the jailor having been awakened, and seeing the doors of the prison opened, drawing his sword, he was about to kill himself, supposing the prisoners to have escaped. 28 But Paul called out in a loud voice, saying, "Do no harm to yourself, for we are all here."

EXPOSITION

Why midnight? No one can say for sure, only God knows and he did not say, but it did give Paul and Silas time and opportunity to pray and sing praises to God—most likely singing the Psalms in Greek and Latin. The moment is reminiscent of Acts 5:41, "rejoicing that they had been counted worthy to suffer dishonor for the Name."

The prisoners in the inner jail may have been in individual prison cells, but an open area was just as likely. Whether in a cell or an open area, Paul and Silas had their feet in stocks, and the stocks were probably secured to the floor or wall.

Did some evangelism take place? Possibly. I believe it to be an accurate assumption the accusation before the magistrates took place during the daylight hours. There was a crowd, which would indicate popular shopping hours. In a world lit only by oil lamps, not streetlights, darkness was a time for honest citizens to be at home. Paul and Silas had been in the inner prison for many hours, "praying and singing praises to God." Even if there were no individual conversations, praying and singing praises to God was evangelism among that gentile crowd.

A stock for holding feet was made of two long and wide pieces of wood boards, with two semicircles cut out of one board, which formed the bottom of the stocks. The ankles would be laid in the semicircles, and the upper board laid atop the ankles, the two boards securely holding the ankles. The two boards would be tightly secured together on both ends with a latch and lock.

The position required the legs be straight, and depending on the height of the semicircle in relation to the body, the position could be quite uncomfortable. The only relief for stretched leg muscles and tendons would be lying down on one's back for a while. Depending on the size of the semicircle holding the ankles, it might not have been possible to bend the knees, even a small amount. The two men were definitely not sitting comfortably.

Most likely the earthquake was localized to the prison. The earthquake itself was not what opened the doors, or loosen the chains, including the locks and chains holding the stocks. God did that as well as cause the earthquake. The earthquake was to wake the guard. He was allowed to sleep because the doors were secured and the prisoners chained. But now, being awakened, he saw the doors were open.

The jailor knew what happened to guards who let prisoners escape. He did not look beyond the open doors—open prison doors meant prisoners escaping. He decided to kill himself rather than be executed, possibly tortured first. The inner prison would be for the worst criminals, whose punishment might include death by flogging (the *verberatio*), crucifixion, or beheading. Guards who allowed a prisoner to escape suffered the punishment due the prisoner.

Paul knew these things, just as you and I know the laws of our country. Paul called out in a loud voice, saying, "Do no harm to yourself, for we are all here." That "we are all here" is the work of God keeping the prisoners in the inner prison, even though the doors are open. Luke's account has up to now made us used to seeing certain kinds of miracles. The earthquake, the opening of doors and loosing of chains, and keeping the prisoners from escaping, are all miracles. The sleeping jailor of the inner prison was not the only soldier on duty that night. Others would soon come and once again secure the prisoners. The miracle was to free Silas and Paul, not those deserving of their punishment, and give the opportunity to present the good news to the jailor.

Translation Acts 16:29–34

29 Then having called for lights, he sprang in, and being terrified, he fell down before Paul and Silas. 30 And bringing them out he said, "Sirs, what is necessary to do that I may be saved?" 31 And they said, "Believe on the Lord Jesus, and you will be saved, you and your household." 32 And they spoke to him the word of the Lord, and with all those in his house. 33 And taking them in that hour of the night, he

washed the wounds from them; and he was immersed, he and his household immediately. 34 Then bringing them into the house he laid a table for them, and rejoiced with all his household having believed in God.

TRANSLATION NOTE

In 16:31, the texts used by the KJV read "the Lord Jesus Christ." The majority of other texts read "the Lord Jesus."

EXPOSITION

What Is Necessary To Do?

Was the jailor's question prompted by earlier hearing Paul and Silas praying and singing praises to God? Possibly. We are conditioned by our entertainments to think of prison doors as iron bars. But the door to the inner prison really was a door, probably made of iron. There was probably a small opening cut into the door so the interior might be viewed. Through this opening the jailor may have heard Paul and Silas as they sat with their feet bound in stocks, praying and singing praises to God. But his question was prompted by more immediate concerns.

Th jailor called for a light, indicating there was more than one soldier present. The others secured the prisoners while the one in charge brought Paul and Silas out of the inner prison room; probably to the small room he used as an office, just outside the door to the inner prison.

The jailor asks his question, "Sirs, what is necessary to do that I may be saved?" He did not mean to save his soul from the penalty of sin. He meant to be saved from certain death should even one prisoner escape. Because Paul had spoken, he assumed Paul was in charge. The jailor was placing his life in the hands of Paul. What he had heard through the opening in the door, and the miracles he had witnessed, led him to believe Paul was an honorable man with some connection to the gods.

Paul's answer was "believe on the *kúrios* Jesus." The word *kúrios* means "lord, master, sir" [Zodhiates, s. v. 2962]. In the cultural context of this gentile Roman soldier, Paul's statement to believe on "*kúrios* Jesus," was probably understood by the jailor as "believe on this Jesus who has been anointed to be lord," in the same sense Caesar was Lord, or the man's military superior was his lord, and the magistrates were his lords. The jailor may have believed this Jesus, like Paul himself, had some kind of connection to the gods.

This one sentence Paul spoke is isolated from a context you and I assume because we have the completed New Testament revelation. That context, which might be summarized as "sin, the Savior, and salvation," was what the jailor *did not have* in the moment. Paul and Silas had not spent the night proclaiming the good news. They had spent the night "praying and singing praises to God."

The jailor understood this one sentence as this: "In order to be rescued from death, transfer your loyalty from all the other *kúrios* in your life to this one *kúrios*, Jesus." To read an understanding of the statement within the context of the Old and New Testament Scripture, which this gentile *did not have* in the moment, is eisegesis: reading into the text what we want to see in the text.

In that one moment, Paul needed to say one thing that would both satisfy the man's immediate distress and later lead to satisfying his eternal spiritual needs. The sentence had an immediate effect. This Roman soldier acted against everything he had been taught to do and obey. He removed Paul and Silas from the prison. How he justified this action to the other soldiers guarding the prison is unimportant. Myself having served in the military, I would attribute it to rank having its privileges. The jailor of the most important part of the prison, the inner prison, may have outranked other soldiers on duty that night.

They Spoke To Him The Word Of The Lord

As I said above, Paul said one sentence that would later lead to satisfying the jailor's eternal spiritual needs. We know Paul later said more to the man and to all who were in his house. We do not know what he said, but we can make a good guess that Paul explained sin, the Savior, and salvation—the basic good news message Paul had proclaimed in many other cities to many other people. But in that one moment, when everything depended on one thing Paul might say, Paul said transfer your loyalty from all other lords to the lord Jesus. And the man did.

Acts 16:32 anticipates 16:33. Paul spoke to "all those in his house," 16:32. The jailor's household was obviously not in the inner prison with him at 16:31. The jailor removed Paul and Silas from the prison to his house upon hearing Paul's response in 16:31. Removing them from the prison was the demonstration that he had indeed transferred his loyalty from all other lords to the lord Jesus. That was all that was required in that moment in the prison. The jailor's salvation came a little later when "they spoke to him the word of the Lord, and with all those in his house." Then like Lydia, having heard the good news, he was saved; then like Lydia, having believed the good news, he was immersed; then like Lydia he offered his hospitality.

Acts 16:31 is not a formula for salvation. That Scripture is either the closing line to prior testimony concerning the good news message of sin, the risen Savior, and salvation. Or as it is here, the opening line, the topic sentence for later "speaking the word of the Lord," which is the good news message of sin, the risen Savior, and salvation.

Bringing Them Into The House

The jailor brought Paul and Silas into the house where he and his family received the word of the Lord from Paul and Silas. Luke says the jailor "washed the wounds from them." However both actions were coordinated, the end result was the jailor and his household believed and he was "immersed, he and his household immediately." They heard the word of the Lord and then they were immersed, an order that keeps with the biblical standard of saved then immersed.

How were they immersed? Lydia and others had been immersed in a river. Did the jailor and his family accompany Paul and Silas, not long after midnight, outside the city to the river? The scenario is unlikely. Nor would the household have had a bath, let alone a bath filled with water, in which to practice immersion. The only baths were the public baths—think spa with small swimming pools for men and women—and they were not open at midnight.

The most reasonable answer is Luke does not in 16:33 use *baptízō* [Zodhiates, s. v. 907] in its natural meaning of immerse. The means is less important than the reason—a testimony of salvation—and there were several to be *baptízō*. Most likely Paul poured water over the head of each person to *baptízō* that person.

The other answer, of course, is Paul and Silas spoke until daylight, and then took the family to the river or to the public bath.

After being *baptízō*, the jailor brought Paul and Silas into the house. If the means was pouring, then outside the house is a reasonable assumption when one considers pouring water would make a mess in the house. If the means was the river or a public bath, then a trek to and from is assumed. If early enough, then two prisoners outside the prison would not have been noticed. (There is always more going on than the Holy Spirit tells us, allowing us to walk only a little while in the sandals of the people we meet in Scripture.)

The Lord's rescue of Paul and Silas from the prison began at midnight, after which the jailor took them to his house, cleansed their wounds, and the good news was proclaimed, and faith exercised, and instruction necessary to immersion received. Then the new believers were immersed as a consequence of their faith.

After their *baptízō* they all returned to the house. A meal was prepared and all ate. The jailor "rejoiced with all his household having believed in God." Luke probably means all in the household had believed, but he may mean that although not everyone in the household believed, with all those who had believed the jailor rejoiced.

Translation Acts 16:35–37

35 Now day having arrived, the magistrates sent the officers, saying, "Release those men." 36 Now the jailor told these words to Paul: having sent the officers, that you may be let go. Now therefore leaving, depart in peace. 37 But Paul was saying to them, "Having publicly beaten us, uncondemned men, being Romans, they threw us into prison, and now secretly do they throw us out? No! For instead coming themselves, let them bring us out."

EXPOSITION

Scripture often has a discernable "reversal of fortune" theme when relating events. That theme is not created by the writers, but reflects the fact that with those believing in God there often is a sudden reversal of unfortunate circumstances. That is how God works in the lives of his saved people. First the dark night, then the brilliant shining of the dawn.

The magistrates had thought on their earlier actions. They had been swept along with the crowd, and had acted illegally by having Paul and Silas beaten. The best course of action was to pretend the incident had never happened. They would release Paul and Silas, who would probably rejoice at their good luck and leave Philippi, never to be heard from again. But that is not what happened.

The jailor had returned Paul and Silas to the prison. That is where they were supposed to be, and the jailor would suffer greatly if he let them go. Paul would never allow that to happen. Christians follow the law unless the law violates biblical standards. We have an example in the Book of Philemon. Paul had the runaway slave Onesimus return to his master Philemon, to receive whatever punishment Philemon might choose to do. That was the law.

Paul and Silas were legally imprisoned—remember, prison was to hold the presumed guilty until trial—and so to prison they returned, 16:40, probably immediately after eating in the jailor's home. And there they waited to be called to trial. But the magistrates gave the order for them to be released, and sent officers with the message. These officers, *rhabdoúchos* [Zodhiates, s. v. 4465] were like a combination of officers of the court and police. They executed the decrees of the magistrates, including beatings and beheadings. They were the ones who had administered the beating to Paul and Silas.

The officers told the message to the person in charge of the prison: "Release those men." The person in charge of the inner prison, the newly saved jailor, was told. He repeated the message to Paul and Silas and said, "Now therefore leaving, depart in peace." The officers probably waited to watch them go and help them out of town. Paul sent a return message to the magistrates through the waiting officers.

> Having publicly beaten us, uncondemned men, being Romans, they threw us into prison, and now secretly do they throw us out? No! For instead coming themselves, let them bring us out.

I don't know what the punishment might have been for beating "uncondemned men, being Romans." No source available to me (several books and an internet search) had that information. A Roman could be beaten if found guilty by a trial, but not "uncondemned," that is, not without a trial and conviction. As with all Roman laws, punishment depended on social status. Those with a higher social status were considered morally superior to others with a lower social status. The punishment for city magistrates was probably mild, but they also might lose their status and office as magistrates.

Paul may have appealed to his Roman citizenship with the Philippi converts in mind. Philippi was always a poor church—2 Corinthians 8:2

includes Philippi—but also a giving church, 2 Corinthians 8:3–4; Philippians 4:16. Paul may have intended he be seen by the magistrates as the patron of the local church, thus immunizing them against persecution.

Translation Acts 16:38–40

38 Then to the officers the sergeants told these words. Now they were afraid, hearing that they are Romans. 39 And coming, they appealed to them, and brought them out, and asked them to go out of the city. 40 Then leaving out of the prison, they came to Lydia. And having seen them, they exhorted the brethren and left.

EXPOSITION

The soldiers told Paul's words to the officer, the officer told Paul's words to the magistrates, and "now they were afraid, hearing that they are Romans." Various legislation in past and present times gave Roman citizens freedom to travel throughout the empire without fear of local authorities. If necessary a Roman citizen might appeal for a trial by the Emperor, which by law no one could deny. How one proved he was a Roman citizen is unknown, but in this particular case, and in Acts 22:27–28, Paul's word seemed sufficient. Patterson [472] suggests Paul may have carried a document attesting to his birth and registration as a Roman citizen [but erroneously thinks it was removed at 16:22], but there is no way to know if this was so.

The magistrates did what had become necessary, They personally came to the prison and released Paul and Silas, and "asked them to go out of the city." After leaving the prison Paul and Silas went to Lydia's house. Undoubtedly some of the officers followed them to make sure they left the city. This was how the magistrates would know the Christians in Philippi had a Roman patron. They gave a word of exhortation to the believers and left Philippi.

Acts Seventeen

Translation Acts 17:1–4

1 Then passing through Amphipolis and Apollonia, they came to Thessalonica, where was a synagogue of the Jews. 2 Now according to the custom with Paul, he went in to them, and for three Sabbaths he discussed with them from the Scriptures, 3 showing and setting before them that it was necessary the Christ to have suffered and to have risen out from among the dead; and that this Jesus is the Christ whom I preach to you. 4 And some of them were persuaded and joined themselves to Paul and to Silas, with a great many worshiping Greeks, and of the leading women not a few.

EXPOSITION

Luke did not go with Paul and Silas but remained in Philippi. Luke says "they" not "we" passed through, etc. Once again Paul passes through towns without stopping to evangelize. The reason may be no synagogue in Amphipolis and Apollonia, and no Jews discovered meeting for prayer. Even though Paul does evangelize gentiles, he usually begins with Jews in the synagogue, then proselytes, God-fearers, and pagan gentiles.

Paul presented the good news to the Jews in Thessalonica "for three Sabbaths," that is, for three weeks, or three days out of twenty-one. What did he do with the other eighteen days? He evangelized and discipled "some of them [who] were persuaded and joined themselves to Paul and to Silas," 17:4. Paul may have worked at his secular occupation, tentmaking (18:3), to support himself and Silas, 1 Thessalonians 2:9.

The city of Thessalonica, or Thessaloniki as it is known today, had a long history before Paul arrived ca. AD 51. The city was founded in 315 BC by King Cassander of Macedon (later Macedonia) and named after his wife Thessalonike, the half-sister of Alexander the Great. Like several cities Paul visited, Thessalonica was a seaport town on the Aegean Sea. In Paul's time the city was an important trading center on the Via Egnatia. When Paul was there the city had long been part of the Roman Empire, annexed since 168 BC, during the times of the Roman Republic.

In his Sabbath Day testimony Paul majored on three of the four doctrines of the early church: the Christ was prophesied to suffer, die, and resurrect; Jesus of Nazareth is the Christ; there is forgiveness of sins in his Name. His testimony that "this Jesus is the Christ whom I preach to you," may have been supported by Matthew's Gospel. I believe Matthew's Gospel was the first written, ca. AD 42 (see Black), and Paul used Matthew's gospel on his missionary journeys.

The first part, that the Christ must suffer, die, resurrect, was directly from the Hebrew Scripture, as illuminated by the New Testament revelation. In these early days, with only Matthew's Gospel written, Jesus himself was that revelation, i.e., Jesus' life, death, and resurrection, Galatians 1:11–12.

When Jesus talked with the two going to Emmaus, and "beginning from Moses and from all the prophets, he clearly and exactly explained to them in all the Scriptures the things concerning himself," Luke 24:27, Jesus was not saying Moses and all the prophets understood from the Old Testament revelation they had received "the things concerning himself." He was saying that because he was present, because of his birth, life, ministry, testimony, works, death, and resurrection, that the two from Emmaus, and others living during his time on the earth, had been given the revelation—the living, testifying Jesus the Christ—that was necessary to understand "in all the Old Testament Scriptures the things concerning himself."

Paul proclaimed that message: Jesus of Nazareth is the Christ, the Christ had to suffer, die, and resurrect, and "that through this one, to you forgiveness of sins is proclaimed" (Acts 13:38). Paul said he received the good news through the revelation of Jesus Christ, Galatians 1:11–12. But that does not mean Paul did not use written scripture in his proclamation of the gospel. In addition to the Old Testament revelation, if Paul also had (as I believe) a copy of Matthew's gospel, then he had New Testament Scripture in hand that was written with the design of showing to the Jews that Jesus of Nazareth was the Christ, from his conception-incarnation to his death-resurrection.

The result was "some of them were persuaded and joined themselves to Paul and to Silas, with a great many worshiping Greeks, and of the leading women not a few."

Some Jews were persuaded. Some proselytes and God-fearers were persuaded. The proclamation of the Scripture always has a response.

> Isaiah 55:11, My word that goes out from my mouth will not return to me with empty hands, but will do what I desire, and will succeed *in that* which I send it.

Some were persuaded, some were not. In each God's purpose was accomplished, Exodus 33:19; Romans 9:15–18. Among that number of Jews, proselytes, and God-fearers who were persuaded, some were leading women of the city. Unlike other ancient literature of the times, the Scripture does not ignore women. In the synagogues of the times women worshiped beside the men. In Christianity women were valued for their faith and contributions to Christian society and family.

Translation Acts 17:5–9

5 Then the Jews became envious, and taking certain wicked men idle in the market place, and raising a mob, they raised a disturbance in the city. And they suddenly attacked Jason's house, seeking to bring them out to the people. 6 But not finding them, they violently took Jason and certain brethren before the city leaders, shouting, "The ones the world unsettling, these are come here also, 7 whom Jason has welcomed. And all these things are opposed to the decrees of Caesar, saying Jesus to be another king." 8 Then they agitated the crowd, and the city leaders hearing these things. 9 And taking security from Jason and the rest, they let them go.

EXPOSITION

Once again Jews oppose the good news, not on doctrinal grounds, but because they desired to have the success for their religion that Christianity was receiving, and could not attain that success for Judaism. Judaism is a religion of men's traditions and traditional interpretations without spiritual life. May our Lord preserve his church from the same.

Once again, because the Jews could not make a scriptural argument against the good news, they chose to use violence. Violence was against the laws of Judaism, and the Mosaic law, unless against a lying prophet—and then it was through the judicial system, not mob violence. A trial in the synagogue might not have convicted Paul and

Silas of being lying prophets. Knowing this, the Jews also dropped their prejudice against associating with gentiles; the "certain wicked men idle in the market place" were gentiles.

The accusation we read in 17:6–7 is the way they raised a mob, and the mob raised a disturbance in the city. Jews and gentiles did not respect one another, which is why these Jews approached disreputable gentiles to raise a mob and disturbance. The incentive these Jews used to employ the idle men is not important; wicked men are in every time and place; we don't need imagination, we may use our experience to understand how "idle men" were employed to raise a mob. Nor do we need imagination to know how quickly and easily a mob may be raised.

The mob, directed by the Jews, attacked Jason's house. Jason was a fellow Jew with whom the missionary team (Paul, Silas, Timothy) were staying. The missionary team was out doing missionary things, or more likely earning a living to support themselves, 1 Thessalonians 2:9. The mob satisfied their violence by taking Jason, and other Jewish men who had been persuaded by the Scripture, to the city leaders. These leaders were not as easily influenced as those in Philippi. They may have known, or known of, Jason and the others. The mob needed to be satisfied, but not by jailing innocent men. They took security from Jason and the rest—in modern terms a bond to guarantee appearance in court—and let them return home.

The Jews through their gentile mob made two legal accusations of crimes committed by the missionary team. Crime one, disturbers of the peace: "The ones the world unsettling, these are come here also." Jason was guilty of this crime because he had welcomed the missionary team into his home. Disturbing the peace was a serious crime in Roman times. Politicians lost their jobs if they could not maintain the peace. Roman soldiers, if present in the city, might come, beat the mob, make arrests, and the leaders of the disturbance would be severely beaten, or executed, after a brief trial.

The gentile mob knew to make this accusation because the Jewish ring leaders had told the idle men they had hired to say those things, and those men had agitated the crowd with this accusation. In reality— and this could not have been hidden from the city leaders—the missionary team, and Jason and his friends, were innocent; the Jews from the synagogue were guilty. At this point in the history of the New

Testament church, the gentile world they were not unsettling. The local churches Paul was creating were mostly Hebrews plus gentile proselytes, gentile God-fearers, and a few converted pagan gentiles.

There were probably two sources for this accusation. The gentile source would have been official news and gossip of the recent events at Philippi. The Jewish source would have been news and gossip shared from synagogue to synagogue about Jewish men stealing worshipers for a new religion. At this time the Jewish world was being unsettled by the good news. Disturbing the peace was an exaggeration used to good effect, i.e., to achieve the goal: stop the spread of the good news in Thessalonica.

The second accusation was way more serious: incitement to treason. "And all these things are opposed to the decrees of Caesar, saying Jesus to be another king." The source for this accusation was strictly Jewish. Every Jew of the times believed the Messiah was to be the coming king—which was true—of 2 Samuel 7:13–16; Psalm 2:1–12, cf. Luke 1:52, 71, 74. Paul was proclaiming this Jesus of Nazareth was the Messiah, therefore Paul was proclaiming this Jesus of Nazareth was the King of the Jews. In reality Paul was proclaiming this Jesus of Nazareth was the Redeemer of sinners from their sins, the Messiah-Redeemer, also in the Old Testament, and was returning to be king.

Because—follow the logic, it is inexorable and damning. Because this Jesus of Nazareth could not possibly be the Messianic-King—he had been a criminal, he had been executed—the true King of the Jews was Caesar; this same logic was used at Jesus' trial, John 19:12, 15. Of course the gentile mob did not know all this background. They had been told the missionaries were proclaiming Jesus was a king, and therefore speaking against Caesar.

Again the city leaders could not have been ignorant of these things. They knew the missionary team was not fomenting rebellion against Rome; the only disturbance since they came to town about a month of more earlier was this mob. But the city leaders' job was enforcing Roman laws, collecting Roman taxes, and keeping Roman peace. Keeping the peace had just come to the top of the list. Knowing there was no crime, at least by Jason, they did the least legal thing they were required to do. They took a bond from Jason et al., for a trial (that might not happen), and sent them and the mob home. They were probably hoping the situation would resolve itself. And it did.

Translation Acts 17:10–12

10 And the brethren immediately both Paul and Silas sent away by night to Berea, who having arrived, went into the synagogue of the Jews. 11 Now these were more noble-minded than those in Thessalonica, who received the word with all readiness, every day examining the Scriptures, if these things were so. 12 Therefore many of them truly believed, and of the prominent Greek women and men not a few.

EXPOSITION

Notice the progress of faith. The new local Christian church at Thessalonica began with "some of them were persuaded and joined themselves to Paul and to Silas." They became "the brethren." Luke does not mean Jewish brethren, but Christian brethren.

Berea was the next city down the road, west on the Via Egnatia.

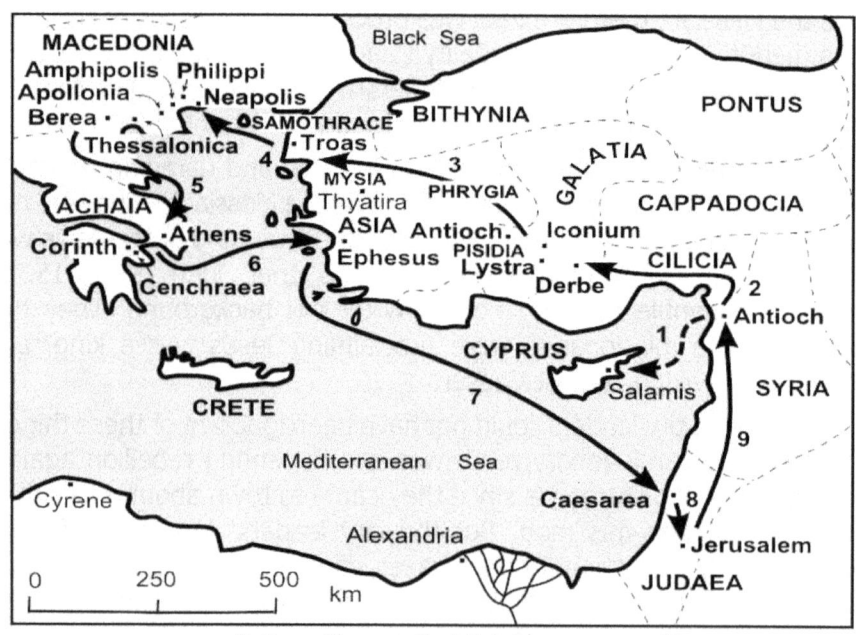

[https://www.thebiblejourney.org/]

The city of Berea was ancient, perhaps as old as the 4th century

BC. Today the ruins of Berea are within the modern city of Veria. The city lay in the plains at the base of Mount Bermius, and drew its water from the Haliacmon and Axios Rivers, supporting extensive agriculture and orchards.

Like Thessalonica, Berea had a Jewish synagogue, to which Paul and Silas went after arriving. Where was Timothy? He may have remained in Thessalonica for a time. Later we discover he came to Berea, 17:14. Timothy seems to have had a close relationship with the Thessalonica believers, 1 Thessalonians 3:1–6.

Luke says the Berean Jews "were more noble-minded that those in Thessalonica." What was the characteristic of this noble-mindedness? They "received the word with all readiness, every day examining the Scriptures, if these things were so." Paul and Silas proclaimed the same message to the Berean Jews as to the Jews of Thessalonica. What can account for the difference? The grace of God.

Sinners do not appreciate the good news. Their spiritually dead state makes them naturally rebel against God and reject his salvation. In Thessalonica "some of them were persuaded" by means of God's grace to hear God's message, and some resorted to violent opposition because they rejected God's message. In Berea they received the good news with "all readiness," and examined the scriptures to see "if these things" Paul and Silas were testifying, "were so," because the grace of God that brings salvation was present and active.

Pause for a moment and notice the goodness of God. The missionary team had been through two difficult seasons, in Philippi and Thessalonica. Now in Berea God gives them a season of rest.

The result of the grace of God and the Bereans searching the scriptures was "many of them truly believed." Those Scriptures were the same Old Testament scriptures we know today. Paul and Silas had given them the key (the same key they had given the Thessalonians) by which to understand "all that the prophets have spoken" about the Christ. That key was the Christ had to die and resurrect, Jesus of Nazareth is the Christ, there is forgiveness of sin in his name.

Was there salvation in the Old Testament scriptures before the Christ was revealed in the New Testament revelation? Yes, of course.

Salvation is when God rescues a sinner out of the state of spiritual death and delivers him or her into a permanent state of spiritual life.

Salvation is the remission of sin's guilt and penalty by the application of Christ's infinite merit, which is gained by receiving God's gift of grace-faith-salvation through the means of personal faith in God's revealed means (way) of salvation.

In every dispensation, in every age of humankind, in the entire history of redemption, a sinner is always saved by God's grace and the merit of Christ's propitiation, through the sinner's faith in God and God's historically current testimony as to the means of salvation, as given by the Holy Spirit in the written progressive revelation of truth. [Quiggle, *Dictionary*.]

Salvation is God by grace forgiving a sinner's sin-guilt and remitting sin's penalty through the application of the limitless merit of Christ's propitiation of God for human sin on the cross. Salvation is gained by receiving God's gift of grace-faith-salvation and applying that gift by means of personal faith in the content of faith (God's historically current testimony in his progressive revelation of truth) that God has revealed at any particular time in any particular age or dispensation, in the written scriptures.

But Judaism had twisted those Old Testament Scriptures into a faith-plus-works-for-righteousness kind of religion. The Old Testament good news was faith in YHWH and YHWH's testimony. Mere obedience to the Law of Moses could not save anyone, Acts 13:38. In this New Testament age salvation occurs when a sinner repents of his or her sins and believes on Christ as their Savior: Acts 2:38; 3:19–20; 11:18; Rom. 3:22–26; 10:9–10, 13; Gal. 3:22; 1 Pet. 1:21; 1 John 3:23.

To summarize, salvation in Old Testament times was by faith in YHWH and his Word; Judaism had distorted God's Word to mean faith by works of the Law; the good news was Jesus is the Messiah-Redeemer—the Christ—who saves from the penalty of sin without works of the Law. That good news has not change since first proclaimed by Peter and Paul. The Christian testimony focuses faith on Christ, because "The one [Jesus Christ] not having known sin, YHWH made to be sin for us, so that we might become the righteousness of YHWH in him [Jesus Christ]," 2 Corinthians 5:21 (I substituted the Old Testament Hebrew word *YHWH*, God, for the Greek word *theós*, God.)

The good news in Berea also had another result. Among the number who believed and were saved were "prominent Greek women and men not a few." Luke has not often mentioned the salvation of pagan gentiles. How did these hear?

Just as local churches today, so then, there were those drawn by the Holy Spirit to the synagogue to seek salvation. They came to church, i.e., to the synagogue, with their gentile friends who were the proselytes and God-fearers of the synagogue, and listened. This time they heard a different message, they heard the good news of salvation in Jesus Christ; and they believed and were saved; and they proclaimed the message to their gentile friends.

As with most of the local churches of the first century, we never again hear about the Bereans. Not to worry. The Holy Spirit provided a letter from Paul about one of those otherwise unknown churches, Colossians, and mentions many more in Paul's letter to Titus. The Holy Spirit always takes care of his saved people, whether we know them or not, whether we know or not. So also the Berean Christians.

Translation Acts 17:13

13 But when those Jews from Thessalonica knew that also in Berea the word of God was proclaimed by Paul, they came there also, agitating and disturbing the crowds.

EXPOSITION

How did Jews from Thessalonica hear about Paul and Silas in Berea? The nature of our own sin and sinning, of our own rejection of the good news before the grace of God intervened, is all we need to inform us that not everyone in the Berean synagogue was happy with the new message. Travel between cities along the Via Egnatia was common. Berea produced fruits and other agricultural products, Thessalonica was the closest trading center and seaport. Some Jews would have travelled to Thessalonica for commerce, attended the local synagogue on Sabbath, and spread the bad news that the good news had come to Berea. What had worked in Thessalonica was imported to Berea: gentiles were agitated to disturb the peace.

Translation Acts 17:14–15

14 Now immediately the brethren sent Paul away to go to the sea. But both Silas and Timothy remained there. 15 Then those responsible for Paul brought him to Athens. And, receiving a command for Silas and

Timothy to come to him as soon as possible, they left.

EXPOSITION

As seems to have become usual in these things, the focus was on Paul. He seems to have been the "preacher" with Silas and Timothy doing the follow up work with those interested. Silas and Timothy were equally as effective as Paul—the Holy Spirit is the source, believers his ambassadors of the good news. Because Paul was the more public person on the missionary team (cf. Acts 14:12), he received the worst part of the opposition.

In response to the violence, the Berean brethren sent Paul away "to go to the sea." The most likely place to find passage was the seaport at Thessalonica. Paul would be safe, one person among the many; he could only be identified if he began evangelizing. There is a proper time and proper place for everything, including silence and anonymity. The other option is a local fisherman or trader operating out of a smaller port, hired for the occasion.

Athens would have been the natural place to take Paul. We see Paul was not alone, "those [Bereans] responsible for Paul brought him to Athens." Silas and Timothy remained in Berea. (Timothy had finally come from Thessalonica to Berea.) The trip away from Berea to Athens happened in such a short time there was no time to make plans. Paul requested "for Silas and Timothy to come to him as soon as possible," and then he was left alone in Athens.

Translation Acts 17:16–17

16 Now in Athens, as Paul was waiting for them, his spirit in him was provoked, seeing the city to be full of idols. 17 Therefore, truly, he continued to discourse in the synagogue with the Jews and those worshiping, and in the market place on every day with those whom he happened to meet.

EXPOSITION

Athens was one of the oldest cities in the region, with an estimated population of 40,000 citizens and 120,000 total residents. The average Greek city had about 3,000 residents. Athens was probably the largest city, by both physical size and population, Paul had ever visited. Luke gives us no details of Paul's living arrangements, but those Berean brethren bringing him to Athens had probably left him at the home of a friend. The city would have had a sizable Jewish population and did have at least one synagogue, 17:17.

Paul was waiting for Timothy and Silas in Athens. Luke never says if they joined him in Athens. However, at 1 Thessalonians 3:1–3 Paul says.

> Therefore, no longer restraining the impulse, we thought it good to be left behind alone in Athens, 2 and we sent Timothy, our brother and fellow worker of God in the good news of Christ, to strengthen and to encourage you to benefit your faith, 3 that no one be disturbed in these tribulations.

Timothy, and one assumes Silas, had come to Athens from Berea. At some point during his stay in Athens, Paul sent Timothy to Thessalonica. Looking to Acts 18:5, Silas went with Timothy to Thessalonica. Then, in Corinth, Paul was reunited with Timothy and Silas.

While Paul was in Athens he divided his evangelistic activities between the synagogue and the agora, i.e., the marketplace. In the synagogue Paul proclaimed the three-fold message of early Christianity: the Christ must die and resurrect; Jesus of Nazareth is the Christ; there is forgiveness of sin through faith in his name.

Toward the gentiles Paul evangelized as the Holy Spirit provided opportunity: "to discourse ... in the marketplace ... with those whom he happened to meet." What was Paul's evangelistic message to the gentiles he met in the agora? "He was proclaiming the good news of Jesus and the resurrection," 17:18. The agora was more than just kiosks selling all manner of products, it was also a gathering place for philosophical, political, and religious discussions. Paul found ways to use the character of the place and its people, 1 Corinthians 9:19–23, to preach the good news.

The city was "full of idols." Athens had for centuries been a center for Greek art, education, philosophy, politics, and religion. Greek religion began about 750 BC and was polytheistic in nature: many gods who could make their lives better and take care of them when they died. However, the Greek gods were also mendacious and capricious, and their worshipers were in many ways victims of their gods. As both a Jew and a Christian the display of idolatry grieved Paul's monotheistic sensibilities.

Translation Acts 17:18

18 Then also some of the Epicureans and Stoics, philosophers, encountered him. And some were saying, "What does this 'babbler' wish to say?" But others, "He seems to proclaim foreign gods," because he was proclaiming the good news of Jesus and the resurrection.

EXPOSITION

Epicureans were essentially the atheists of the times. They followed the philosophy of Epicurus (341–270 BC). He acknowledged the gods, but taught the gods were disinterested in human affairs. He taught: the goal of human life was personal happiness; all that can be known is obtained through human senses; the human soul does not survive the physical death of the body. Epicurean philosophy was a sort of eat, drink, be merry philosophy because this mortal life is all there is. Although some view hedonism as an essential part of Epicureanism (and no doubt it can devolve into hedonism) friendship was essential, sex and marriage were not. "The elimination of the fears [of death and punishment in an afterlife] and corresponding desires [of human nature] would leave people free to pursue the pleasures, both physical and mental, to which they are naturally drawn, and to enjoy the peace of mind that is consequent upon their regularly expected and achieved satisfaction" [Stanford Encyclopedia of Philosophy].

Stoicism was the dominant philosophy of the age. The philosophy came into existence ca. 300 BC. Stoicism is not easy to define in a brief manner because it encompassed physics, logic, and ethics. In some ways, Stoicism was the naturalism of the age. Naturalism is the philosophical belief that everything arises from natural properties and causes, and supernatural or spiritual explanations are excluded or discounted.

The orthodox Stoic position is physics, logic, and ethics must all be mastered for human beings to succeed and prosper in life. Stoicism taught God was a corporeal being. God was characterized as eternal reason (*logos*) or intelligent designing fire or breath (*pneuma*) which structures matter in accordance with its plan. God is "immanent throughout the cosmos" and directs the development of the cosmos to the smallest detail. Stoicism inherited a much more ancient philosophy that god was eternal chaotic matter that created the universe.

An immanent god is not quite the same as an omnipresent god. Immanence may be influence, versus real presence. Omnipresence means God is really present everywhere at once in the time and space of this universe. What immanence does imply is God's presence is felt everywhere, but God is distinct, not part of that everywhere.

Stoicism defined God's immanence differently. "The entire cosmos is a living thing, and God stands to the cosmos as an animal's life force stands to the animal's body, enlivening, moving and directing it by its presence throughout." So when the Paul said, "For in him we live and move and exist," 17:28, the Stoics thought of God's corporeal immanence, whereas Paul was proclaiming God's omnipresence.

The Stoic philosophy brought order in place of the "random and unpredictable" actions of the Greek gods. "The soul and the body it animates are in constant contact," the Stoics hold, "and are later separated from each other at death. Therefore the [human] soul is corporeal." There is no spirit, matter is eternal, and therefore the world is in an endless cycle of destruction and renewal. [Quotes from Stanford Encyclopedia of Philosophy.]

Not to be flippant, but these philosophies are little different from some modern philosophies of life today, which are minus the pedigree of philosophical minds, but rather watered-down versions with little rational or logical strength, having inherited the most godless and extreme parts of both philosophies. In general, setting religions aside, today's Stoics are scientists and educators, today's Epicureans are liberals and progressives.

These were the people who wanted Paul to explain his philosophy. The word "babbler" [Zodhiates, s. v. 4691] was an insult, "someone who picks up and repeats trifling things." This was from the arrogant, who consider all opinions but their own trifling. Those with a more serious frame of mind recognized Paul was proclaiming a different God. Neither philosophy believed in a personal God with an interest in humankind. Resurrection did not fit into either philosophy.

Translation Acts 17:19–21

19 Then taking hold of him they took him to the Ares Hill, saying, "Are we able to know what is this new thing which you are teaching? 20 For some novel things you are bringing to our ears. Therefore we

are willing to know what these things mean." 21 Now all the Athenians and the resident foreigners spend their time in nothing else than to say something and hear something new.

EXPOSITION

Ares Hill, or in English "Mar's Hill" (known today as Areopagus Hill), was where judicial matters were heard and settled by the highest court

of appeals. The Hill was also the place where the Council of Nobles, i.e., the city elders, would meet. The Hill was a high flat-topped rock next to the Acropolis. Apparently it was also where speeches were made and philosophy was discussed. (Photograph, [https://en.wikipedia.org/wiki/Areopagus].)

In 17:21 Luke uses a bit of hyperbole. Most Athenians were like you and me, just trying to make a living. Few had the luxury of time and idleness to "spend their time in nothing else" than discussing politics, philosophy, art, etc.

Translation Acts 17:22–23

22 Then Paul stood in the midst of the Ares Hill, saying, "Men, Athenians, I see in all things you are religiously disposed. 23 For passing through and seeing the objects of your worship, I discovered an altar on which was inscribed, 'To An Unknown God.' Whom therefore not knowing you worship, him I proclaim to you.

EXPOSITION

Polytheism, many gods, is a fluid thing. What is one god more, or less? Most ancient cultures shared more than one god, by function if not by name. [https://historycooperative.org/sun-gods-dieties-of-the-sun/]. For example.

    Ra — The Egyptian Sun God.
    Sol — The Norse Sun Goddess.
    Helios — The Sun God of the Greeks.
    Arinna — The Hittite Goddess of the Sun.
    Surya — The Hindu Sun God.
    Huitzilopochtli — The Aztec God of the Sun.
    Inti — The Incan Sun God.
    Kinich Ahau — Mayan Sun God.

The Athenians had the usual Greco-Roman pantheon. The twelve major gods were Zeus, Hera, Poseidon, Demeter, Athene, Hephaistos, Ares, Aphrodite, Apollon, Artemis, Hermes, Dionysos, sometimes a thirteenth, Hestia, and a plethora of minor gods. For example, the goddess Roma, the personification of the city of Rome, in effect representing the Roman Empire. Each had its duties and interactions with humankind.

The Athenians had an altar to "an unknown god," just in case there was a god unknown to the Greeks, to ensure that particular god would not be insulted by no worshipers and bring disaster upon the city. Their philosophical beliefs allowed an unknown god. For example, the Stoics sometimes identified the universe and god as Zeus, but he might not be Zeus. The website "Modern Stoicism," says of the ancient Stoics, "The Stoic god is wholly impersonal—it is just nature, doing its thing. You can't pray to the Stoic god."

So a god unknown by name was possible, and an altar was raised to the "Unknown God." Paul said, I will make this God known to you.

This introduction immediately defused the criticism Paul was proclaiming "foreign gods," 17:18. The "good news of Jesus and the resurrection" was not about a foreign God but a God they professed not to know.

Translation Acts 17:24–28

24 "The God having made the world and all the things that are in it, he of heaven and earth being Lord, resides not in hand-made temples, 25 nor by men's hands is he served, as needing anything, himself the one giving to all life and breath and all. 26 And he made of one every nation of humankind to live upon all the face of the earth, having determined and set in order seasons and limits of their dwelling place, 27 to seek God, if perhaps truly they might feel their way to him, and might find him—for truly he is not far from each of us. 28 For in him we live and move and exist. As also some of the poets among you have said: 'For of him also we are offspring.'

EXPOSITION

God Having Made The World

Paul begins by opposing their idolatry. At first, Paul's argument might seem contradictory. Paul says God made everything, and therefore God cannot be worshiped through the things God made. Why? Because God as Creator is superior to his works. But why not worship the Creator through his works? Do we not admire and respect the artist or the architect or the builder by admiring their works? But sinful human nature soon substitutes admiration of the work for worship of the person. There is a reason we say a celebrity's fans worship their idol.

The gods of the ancients represented nature, and their idolatry was in essence worship of nature. In modern terms, worshiping the environment—and if you think that is not happening today, I remind you of the goddess "Mother Nature." I remind you that some environmentalists believe "Mother Earth," would be better if there was no human presence. The gods are always superior to human beings, and if the environment is a god, then what interferes must be eliminated.

How can we define a God who is unlimited in every aspect of his being? We cannot, but the world does. Many religions, ancient and modern, have defined God as the universe, and thereby have not only made God corporeal, but limited him in every way to what can be known. That is what an idol does, it makes God corporeal, and limited, and understandable within finite human comprehension.

Sin perverts the God-designed instinct to worship the Creator, by worshiping what is seen, thereby giving form to the unseen God. God designed into human nature the necessity to worship him alone. We see that in Jesus of Nazareth, whose sinless humanity naturally worshiped God (e.g., John 20:17.)

Human beings must respond to that God-designed necessity to worship. If a person does not worship the Creator, then he/she will satisfy that intrinsic necessity by worshiping the creature. Hence, idolatry is born, Romans 1:19–23. Those worshiping representations of a god, an idol, may begin knowing the idol merely represents the god. But the nature of sin is to reject the one true God, and so the idol ceases to be a representation and becomes a substitute.

That is exactly how the God deals with idolatry in the Old Testament. God knows an idol is nothing, but God interacts with idolatry as though an idol is something, because the sinner genuinely believes an idol is something, and worships the idol as though the idol was the god.

Is there something behind the idol? Indirectly an idol represents the fallen angels, who seek human worship as validation of their superiority. But the worshiper does not know that. Even those claiming to worship the fallen angel Satan do so ignorant of his true nature; and ignorant of his true feelings toward human beings. To Satan human beings are flotsam and jetsam floating on the sea of his discontent, tiny, disposable, and easily replaceable cogs in his machinery opposing God.

Paul's argument to the Athenians is God made everything, including you. Why then do you think you can worship God through the things you make? Or the things he has made? None of those things are God.

Of course Paul's argument is based on God's Law, "You will not make to yourself an image: any form which is in the heaven above, which is in the earth under, which is in the water under the earth," Exodus 20:4. But the Athenians are gentiles, not Jews, and so Paul argues from the Law without quoting the Law, because by the Law is knowledge of sin. The world is materialistic, regardless of how much a worldling may protest he or she is spiritual. The world wants to see and feel their god or gods. God's Law also addresses that issue. "You will not bow down to them or serve them."

God Made Humankind to Seek God

Beginning in 17:26, Paul turns to God's purpose in creating humankind. He uses a teaching technique known as apperception: to teach the unknown from the known. God created humankind, "giving to all life and breath and all." From that one creation God formed the nations. God set the places and times of every nation, setting an order of seasons and limits to those times and places. Why? That each in their own order might seek God, and perhaps find God, "for truly he is not far from each of us."

Paul speaks against both Epicureanism and Stoicism. He introduces the concept of omnipresence versus the Stoic simple immanence. Paul also suggests this unknown God is a personal being with a personal interest in human beings. We perceive Paul is familiar with the philosophies of his times, and uses them to suggest they are not correct in their view of God. Paul opposes the Stoic concept of the universe as a living thing, with God as its life force, like the soul in the body.

Here we must be careful to be biblical. God is present everywhere in the time and space of the universe God created, because that which God created exists within God. God is the one and only permanent reality. All other realities were created by God and exist within God because only God has permanent existence: "I exist because I exist," Exodus 3:14. The reality God has created, this present universe, is not part of God, it exists within God, wholly separate from his essence, not created from his essence. This present universe will be destroyed, 2 Peter 3:10; Revelation 20:11, and a new universe created, Revelation 21:1. Therefore what God has created, to date, has no permanent existence. Only God is permanent and all he creates exists within his being.

Paul is saying God is not a life-force animating the universe, as the Stoics teach, nor is God uninterested in humankind, as the Epicureans teach. God is a personal being who created us and is separate from the universe which he created, and that creation, and humankind, exists within God. Therefore God is not far from any of us, that we may seek him and find him, because in him "we live and move and exist."

Paul pulls in supporting evidence from three Greek poets that humankind is an offspring of God (Epimenides, *Cretica*; Aratus, *Phaenomena*; Cleanthes, *Hymn to Zeus*. Longnecker, 476). Of course, Paul does not mean God procreates, but that God creates. Paul uses those poets to support his contention God created human kind to seek him, to feel their way to him, because he is not far from us, 17:26–27. "Your poets," he says, "give evidence that is happening."

Translation Acts 17:29–31

29 "Therefore, being offspring of God, we ought not regard a sculpture of God of gold or silver or stone, of the craft and imagination of man, to be like deity. 30 Truly, therefore, the times of ignorance God bore with, now he commands all persons everywhere to convert, 31 because he set a day in which he is about to judge the world in righteousness, by a man whom he appointed, having given assurance to all, by raising him out from the dead."

EXPOSITION

Paul drives the rational, logical stake through the heart of idolatry. How can the omnipresent God who created all things and orders the affairs of humankind be represented by or worshiped through something he created? Created things are unlike God; they are not God. The unstated conclusion is we should seek after God, find him, and worship him as he is.

God, being a personal being with interest in his creation humankind, is merciful of such ignorance, bearing with it for a time. This is the aspect of God's mercy that delays judgment. Although Paul does not say how God is able to be merciful when confronted by human sin, we may take a moment to explore this aspect of God's character.

God's holy character has an automatic reaction to sin: immediate and just judgment. "God is light and darkness is not in him, none at all," 1 John 1:5. If, as is true, "in him we live and move and exist," Acts 17:28, then how does God tolerate our darkness within his light? The answer is Christ propitiated God for our darkness, i.e., our sin.

Propitiation. The satisfaction Christ made to God for sin by dying on the cross as the sin-bearer, 2 Corinthians 5:21; Romans 3:25; Hebrews 2:17; 1 John 2:2; 4:10, for the crime of sin committed by human beings, suffering in their place and on their behalf. Christ's propitiation fully satisfied God's holiness and justice for the crime of sin. [Quiggle, *Dictionary*.]

Jesus Christ "is propitiation for our sins—but not for ours only but also for all the world," 1 John 2:2. God is able to justly have mercy toward all humankind—delaying just judgment and relieving misery (the two aspects of mercy)—because Christ propitiated God for all human sin. The temporal benefits of that propitiation, God's mercy and goodness, apply to all human beings. The eternal benefits of the propitiation are applied to some human beings according to God's decrees concerning salvation from the penalty of sin.

Paul says, "the times of ignorance God bore with." What does he mean? For that answer, we must consider God's covenants and dispensations. The covenant and dispensation in view here are the Noahic covenant and Noahic dispensation. (From my book, *Covenants and Dispensations in the Scripture*.)

Noahic Covenant

The Noahic covenant began from Noah post-flood.

Associated Dispensation: Noah post-flood.

Type of covenant: unconditional.

Conditions of the covenant: Almost all the conditions of the Adamic covenant continued: worship and have fellowship with God; exercise dominion over the earth and every living thing; to propagate to fill and subdue the earth; dominion is to be exercised as a responsible stewardship.

The conditions of Noahic covenant are seen in the new relationships humankind has with the earth and its creatures: Genesis 8:21–22; 9:2–4; with each other, Genesis 9:5–7; with God, Genesis 9:8–17.

Duration: This covenant remains in effect to the present day for all human beings.

Judgment for unfaithfulness to the covenant. There was a one-time judgment for failure to repopulate the earth, 11:7. The continuing environmental penalties for lack of proper stewardship of the earth and its creatures are well-known. Equally well-known are the failures of many societies and cultures throughout the ages because each rejected worship and fellowship with God.

Noah's Dispensation

Common name: Civil Government

Responsibilities. Genesis 1:28; 2:23–24; 3:16, 20; Genesis 4:3–4, 7a; 5:24a continue. Genesis 9:1, 7 command to reproduce and fill the earth reiterated. Noahic covenant begins, creating human government and capital punishment. The terms and conditions of the Noahic covenant and Noah's dispensation overlap.

Duration. Post flood. The dispensation and covenant are far reaching. There are different durations for different people groups. This dispensation affects all gentiles, and is still in effect for the gentile world, with the exception the content of faith was changed from Christ's resurrection. (Most Dispensationalists end Noah's dispensation at the judgment of the Tower of Babel. See discussion under Noahic Covenant, subheading, "Discussion of Genesis 11:4–7.")

When Abraham was called to leave his home, he and his descendants came under a different dispensation.

Judgment. Genesis 11:7–8. Penalty for failure to repopulate the earth (Genesis 9:1) was humankind's universal language changed to multiple languages, resulting in humankind disbanding as a single group with individuals and families moving to live throughout the earth, thereby fulfilling humanity's responsibility to reproduce and fill the earth.

Content of Faith. Faith in God the Judge and the promises of the Noahic covenant (exampled in Acts 17:27–29). After the crucifixion-resurrection-ascension of Jesus Christ: believe on the Lord Jesus Christ and you will be saved, Acts 16:31; 17:30–31.

The gentile world was under the Noahic covenant and dispensation until Christ's crucifixion-resurrection-ascension. The covenants and dispensations intervening between Noah and Christ were directed toward national ethnic Israel.

The gentile world, like Israel, failed in their covenantal and dispensational responsibilities. Paul, about seven years after this moment in Athens, said something about God bearing with the "times of ignorance," Acts 17:30.

> Romans 3:24–25, being freely justified by his grace through the redemption that is by Christ Jesus. 25 Whom God set forth publicly as a propitiation, through faith in his blood, for declaring his righteousness—because of the passing over of the sins that are past because of the temporary long-suffering of God.

God passed over the sins in those times of ignorance—his justice did not enact immediate judgment—because of the eternal and limitless merit of Christ's propitiation of God for human sin. God could act in mercy because of the limitless merit of the propitiation.

Christ's propitiation, accomplished at a specific moment in time, was and is efficient to completely and fully and comprehensively save any sinner at any time since the creation of the world, according to God's eternal decree. The decree of salvation, which was made *before* time was created, Ephesians 1:4, is not bound by time, but applies to all sinners to save them (by grace through faith) at any moment in their particular time. God calls those things which do not exist as though they did exist, Romans 4:17. When God in eternity past decreed Christ's propitiation was the only merit for salvation, the act that accomplished the propitiation was set for a particular moment in time, but having been decreed before time, it was efficient to completely save throughout all time.

That same limitless merit that saved before the historic act of the propitiation also provided temporal benefits to all humankind before the historic act of the propitiation. For many it is impossible that they should see temporal benefits to all humankind in Christ's propitiation. That is because, having been raised on Reformed soteriology, they consistently have the view propitiation = redemption. That the only purpose of the propitiation is the redemption of sinners. The Scripture is not so man-centered. The primary purpose of Christ's propitiation was to satisfy God's holiness and justice: propitiation = judicial satisfaction. The application of that judicial satisfaction is temporal benefits to all, eternal benefits to the elect.

That "temporal benefits" aspect of the propitiation, and God's mercy because of that propitiation, is what Paul refers to in Acts 17:30 (as well as the eternal benefit of saving any gentile who believed in God and God's testimony).

But now, says Paul, those times have ended. The Noahic covenant and dispensation that regulated gentile faith and behavior has been superseded by a new covenant made in Christ's death and resurrection, and a new dispensation, the New Testament church.

The New covenant for the New Testament church is described at Hebrews 10:16–18, and supported by Hebrews 7:22; 8:6; 9:15; 12:22, 24. Christ's propitiating death has made him mediator of a New covenant for those saved by his propitiating death during this New Testament church dispensation, Hebrews 9:16–18; 10:8–17.

(There is a New covenant for national ethnic Israel, waiting for the second advent, Jeremiah 31:33–34.)

The New Testament church dispensation.

> Common name: Grace.
>
> Responsibilities. Believe on the Lord Jesus Christ as Savior, Acts 16:31; worship the God-man Jesus Christ, Acts 2:36; 42; 7:56; Colossians 2:9; evangelize and disciple, Matthew 28:19–20; the person claiming to abide in Christ is obligated, even as Christ lived his life, also to behave in the same manner, 1 John 2:6; make a "sacrifice" of confession and repentance after committing an act of sinning, 1 John 1:9–2:2, cf. Psalm 38:18; 51:17.
>
> Duration. Christ's resurrection to rapture of the church. Initiated when Holy Spirit began indwelling believers, John 20:22. Ending with the Rapture of the New Testament church, 1 Thessalonians 4:13–18; 1 Corinthians 15:51–53; 2 Thessalonians 2:1.
>
> Judgment. The Bema (Judgement) Seat of Christ. 2 Corinthians 5:10; Romans 14:10; 1 Corinthians 3:11–15. This is not the Great White Throne judgment of Revelation 20:11–15, at which only the unsaved are present, but judgment of the New Testament church for rewards for post-salvation works. (I

believe each believer faces the Bema upon his or her physical death, or rapture, but most Dispensationalists believe all the New Testament church faces the Bema at the same time at the rapture.)

Content of Faith.

Acts 2:38, "Repent," he said, "and be baptized, each of you, in the name of Jesus Christ, for the forgiveness of your sins, and you will receive the gift of the Holy Spirit."

Acts 13:38–39, Therefore be it known to you, men, brethren, that through this one, to you forgiveness of sins is proclaimed. 39 And from all things from which you were not able in the Law of Moses to be justified, in him everyone believing is justified.

Acts 16:31–32 (NKJV), So they said, "Believe on the Lord Jesus Christ, and you will be saved, you and your household." Then they spoke the word of the Lord to him and to all who were in his house.

Romans 10:12, 13, The Lord is rich to all, Jew and Gentile, who call on his name, for whoever calls on the name of the Lord Jesus Christ as savior shall be saved.

Acts 15:14, God is taking out a people for his name. Ephesians 2:15; 3:6, the New Testament church.

In Athens, Paul is calling the gentiles to the New covenant and New Testament church dispensation of saving faith in Christ.

> Now God commands all persons everywhere to convert, because he set a day in which he is about to judge the world in righteousness, by a man whom he appointed, having given assurance to all, by raising him out from the dead.

Paul knows, and here teaches, there is no propitiation without the resurrection; there is no Redeemer without the resurrection. Why? Because the wages of sin is death, Romans 6:23. Death is the "calling card" of sin. The fact physical death affects all human beings from the moment of conception is proof all are sinners, Romans 5:12. There is but a small step from these facts to the resurrection of Jesus Christ. If Jesus had remained in the state of physically dead, that would mean he had not fully satisfied (propitiated) God for the human sin imputed to him, Isaiah 53:6, 10; Ephesians. 5:22 Corinthians 5:21; Hebrews 9:14. If payment in full had not been received for the judicial debt due the crime of sin, then Jesus would not have resurrected out from the dead.

But he did resurrect, because he propitiated God, and now God commands all persons everywhere to convert from sinner to saved through faith in God and God's testimony that salvation is through faith in the risen Jesus Christ.

This Jesus, God has given the authority to "judge the world in righteousness, by a man whom he appointed," Acts 17:31. Did not Jesus say the same?

> John 5:25–29, I tell you the truth, that an hour is coming, and now is, when the dead will hear the voice of the Son of God, and those having heard will live. 26 For as the Father has life-in-himself, so also to the Son he gave life to have in himself, 27 and he gave to him authority to execute judgment, because he is Son of Man. 28 Do not marvel at this, because an hour is coming in which all those in the grave will hear his voice 29 and will come forth: the ones having practiced good, to resurrection of life; the ones habitually doing evil, to resurrection of judgment.

The one who saves is also the one who judges the unsaved.

Translation Acts 17:32–34

32 Now having heard of a resurrection of the dead, some truly began to mock him. But some said, "We will hear you about this again also." 33 Then Paul left them. 34 But some persons, joining themselves to him, believed; among whom also Dionysius the Areopagite, and a woman named Damaris, and others with them.

EXPOSITION

The good news did what it always does: winnowed the chaff from the wheat. Some mocked. These were those where the seed of the word fell on the wayside. Some said they wanted to hear more, and only time would tell if they were like the seed on the stony places, or among the thorns, or were good ground. Some were the good ground, and joined themselves to Paul. Luke names two of those believers, who when he wrote the Acts, about ten years later, were remembered, and may have become prominent in the local church at Athens. We never hear about Athens again, but knowing the names of two, and that there were "others with them," tells us Paul did establish a local church at Athens before he left.

Acts Eighteen

Translation Acts 18:1–3

1 After these things, having left out of Athens, he came to Corinth. 2 And he found a certain Jew named Aquila, of Pontus by birth, having lately come from Italy, and Priscilla his wife—because Claudius had commanded the Jews to leave Rome—he came to them. 3 And because they were of the same occupation he stayed with them and worked; for they were tentmakers by trade.

EXPOSITION

Paul would have remained in Athens a sufficient time to establish and strengthen the local church he had founded. Apparently neither Silas nor Timothy came to him in Athens, 17:15, because they come from Macedonia to Corinth, 18:5.

The city of Corinth was ancient, perhaps dating to 3,000 BC. The city developed as a commercial center between 800–700 BC. Corinth had a unique location. The city was located on a narrow isthmus between the Saronic and Corinthian gulfs, allowing it to have two seaports, a short distance east and west of the city. The location gave Corinth great strategic value and made it an important commercial and trading hub. In 44 BC Julius Caesar made Corinth a Roman Colony, and it became the administrative center of Achaia. Today the ancient city is ruins, destroyed by an earthquake. Modern Corinth lies about three miles northwest, founded in 1858 after the earthquake. [https://www.britannica.com/place/Corinth-Greece].

Luke dates Paul's arrival in Corinth using two historical markers. The first is in 18:2, "Claudius had commanded the Jews to leave Rome." The second is in 18:12, "Gallio being Proconsul of Achaia." The date or year when Emperor Claudius expelled the Jews from the city of Rome is unknown. Claudius reigned AD 41–54. The Roman historian Seutonius, in his *Life of Claudius* (AD 121) wrote, "Since the Jews constantly made disturbances at the instigation of Chrestus, he expelled them from Rome." This Chrestus is not Jesus Christ, who is identified in Roman histories as Christus.

What is known of Gallio is he was proconsul of Achaia probably between AD 50–54, although a shorter time, AD 51–52, has been proposed. What is known of Gallio, in addition to Luke's testimony in Acts, is from the *Gallio Inscription*, issued ca. AD 52 by Emperor Claudius, a copy of which was recorded in stone at the oracle at Delphi. The inscription was recovered from nine fragments. It is a copy of a letter from the Emperor Claudius to the city, addressing the problem of their sparse population.

> Tiberius Claudius Caesar Augustus Germanicus, 12th year of tribunician power [AD 52], acclaimed emperor for the 26th time, father of the country, sends greetings to [...]. For long have I been well-disposed to the city of Delphi and solicitous for its prosperity, and I have always observed the cult of the Pythian Apollo. Now since it is said to be destitute of citizens, as my friend and proconsul L. Iunius Gallio recently reported to me, and desiring that Delphi should regain its former splendour, I command you [singular] to invite well-born people also from other cities to come to Delphi as new inhabitants, and to accord them and their children all the privileges of the Delphians as being citizens on like and equal terms. For if some are transferred as colonists to these regions....

[https://biblearchaeologyreport.com/2019/10/31/gallio-an-archaeological-biography/]

Proconsul Gallio is also know from other Roman historians, such as Seneca (his brother), Cassius Dio, and Tacitus.

Paul spent about eighteen months in Corinth. After the Gallio incident Paul stayed in Corinth "many more days." Paul's second missionary journey began ca. AD 51, after the Jerusalem Council. Putting it all together, Paul probably arrived in Corinth in AD 52, and remained in the city until mid-to-late AD 53.

Aquila and Priscilla were tentmakers by trade, as was Paul. Jewish custom required a scholar such as Paul to have a skill, other than teaching, by which to support himself.

Translation Acts 18:4–7

4 Then he was reasoning in the synagogue on every Sabbath, persuading both Jews and Greeks. 5 Now when both Silas and Timothy came down from Macedonia, Paul was pressed with the word, earnestly bearing witness to the Jews the Christ to be Jesus. 6 But they opposed

him and slandered him, so he shook out his clothing and said to them, "Your blood be on your head. I am clean. From now on I will go to the gentiles." 7 And leaving from there, he came to the house of a certain one worshiping God, named Titius Justus, whose house was next to the synagogue.

EXPOSITION

Proclaiming The Good News In Corinth

Luke does not explain Paul's Sabbath messages in 18:4, because he has previously explained them. Paul's synagogue messages incorporated three truths. One of those truths was the Old Testament revelation tells us messiah must die for the sins of the people.

Passages such as Daniel 9:26, Isaiah 52:13–53:12, Psalm 22, and others, when illuminated by the New Testament revelation of Jesus Christ, teach the Messiah must die. These are Psalms the four gospels use to describe the crucifixion.

> Psalm 16:10 — John 20:9
> Psalm 22:1 — Matthew 27:46; Mark 15:34
> Psalm 22:7; 109:25 — Matthew 27:39; Mark 15:29; Luke 23:35
> Psalm 22:8 — Matthew 27:43
> Psalm 22:18 — Matthew 27:35; Mark 15:24; Luke 23:34; John 19:24
> Psalm 25:19 —John 15:25
> Psalm 31:5 — Luke 23:14
> Psalm 38:11; 88:8 — Luke 23:49
> Psalm 34:20 — John 19:36
> Psalm 41:9; 109:8 — John 13:18; 17:12
> Psalm 42:5 — Matthew 26:38; Mark 14:34
> Psalm 69:21 — Matt 27:34, 48; Mark 15:36; Luke 23:36; John 19:28
> Psalm 110:1, 2 — Matthew 26:64; Mark 14:62; 16:19

The Jews were expecting a Messiah-King to redeem the nation from gentile oppression, not Messiah-Redeemer to redeem them from the penalty due sin.

> The older Messianic hope virtually moves within the boundary of the then present circumstances of the world, and is nothing else than the hope of a better future for the *nation*. That the nation should be morally purified from all bad elements, that it

should exist unmolested and respected in the midst of the Gentile world, whilst its enemies were either destroyed or forced to acknowledge the nation and its God, that it should be governed by a just, wise, and powerful king of the house of David, and that therefore internal justice, peace and happiness would prevail, nay that all natural evils would be abolished and a state of unclouded prosperity would appear—this may be said to have formed the foundation of the future hope among the older prophets. [Schurer, Division 2, 2:129–130.]

Paul opened the Old Testament Scriptures to reveal Messiah must die. Compare Luke 24:26–27. This was a very unpopular and very unbelievable message. How could the Messiah-king die and still be king? We see the same disbelief at Matthew 16:21–23.

The second truth was Jesus of Nazareth was the Old Testament Messiah-Redeemer. To reveal this truth Paul depended on what Jesus had revealed to him, Galatians 1:11–12, and both (then) oral and (later) written information concerning Jesus, such as Peter's Pentecost Day sermon (which through Luke became written Scripture), and Matthew's gospel.

The third truth was through faith in Jesus the Messiah-Redeemer there was forgiveness of sin which could not be achieved through the Mosaic Law. Compare Acts 13:38–39.

Apparently Paul was not preaching all three points as he reasoned in the Corinth synagogue every Sabbath.

> he was reasoning in the synagogue on every Sabbath, persuading both Jews and Greeks.
>
> Now when both Silas and Timothy came down from Macedonia, Paul was pressed with the word, earnestly bearing witness to the Jews the Christ to be Jesus.

Paul had apparently been presenting only point one, the Messiah must die. He had been persuading "both Jews and Greeks," i.e., Hebrews, gentiles proselytes, and gentile God-fearers. He was laying the basis for the points two and three, but so far had not presented those two points.

Why Paul had limited his good news presentation cannot be known. We might speculate Paul was trying to avoid the persecution he knew would come when he declared Jesus of Nazareth was the Messiah-Redeemer, and the Mosaic Law was useless for redemption from sin. But it might also be true Paul's progress in persuasion was going slowly, so he was still in that first step process. Regardless, we cannot know why Paul had limited the message as he was reasoning in the synagogue on every Sabbath. We also do not know how many Sabbaths; at least two, perhaps three. We know in Thessalonica Paul,

> for three Sabbaths he discussed with them from the Scriptures, showing and setting before them that it was necessary the Christ to have suffered and to have risen out from among the dead; and that this Jesus is the Christ whom I preach to you. Acts 17:2–3.

Whatever the reason or reasons, "when both Silas and Timothy came down from Macedonia, Paul was pressed with the word, earnestly bearing witness to the Jews the Christ to be Jesus." That phrase, "pressed with the word," seems to be explained in 1 Corinthians 9:16, "... for I am compelled; for woe be to me if I should not preach the good news."

Now having with him his two fellow missionaries, the missionary team was complete, and Paul was pressed to present points two and three of the good news. Luke only gives us point two, "earnestly bearing witness to the Jews the Christ to be Jesus," but without point three it is not the good news of salvation in the risen Jesus Christ. There is no reason to accuse Paul of not completing the proclamation.

> Acts 13:38–39, Therefore be it known to you, men, brethren, that through this one, to you forgiveness of sins is proclaimed. 39 And from all things from which you were not able in the Law of Moses to be justified, in him everyone believing is justified.

And probably with the same warning, "Be aware, therefore, so that what is said in the prophets might not come upon you," see 13:40–41.

Reactions To The Proclamation Of The Good News In Corinth

"But they opposed him and slandered him." Having labored on several Sabbaths to persuade "both Jews and Greeks" the Messiah must die, Paul now gives the complete good news, requiring faith in the risen Jesus of Nazareth, the Christ of God. The fruit of his arguments on previous Sabbaths is revealed. The Holy Spirit was not working in the Corinthian synagogue to widely bless the good news with salvations. Instead, the good news was allowed to have its negative effect: rejection and condemnation of those rejecting.

In response to their opposition and slander Paul "shook out his clothing." There is biblical precedent.

> Nehemiah 5:13 (ESV), I also shook out the fold of my garment and said, "So may God shake out every man from his house and from his labor who does not keep this promise. So may he be shaken out and emptied.

> Matthew 10:14, And whoever may not receive you, nor will hear your words, when going out of that house or the city, shake off the dust of your feet.

Tearing clothing was a sign of anger, great distress, or mourning, but Paul may have substituted grabbing and shaking his clothing as the sign of his frustration or anger. However, it is more likely he shook out his clothing as a sign of judgment. He may have used it to symbolize he was no longer responsible for those rejecting the message.

Paul then said, "Your blood be on your head. I am clean." Blood is often a symbol of physical death. For example, when the apostle John wrote, 1 John 1:7, "the blood of Jesus Christ his Son is continually cleansing us from every sin," by "blood" he meant the limitless merit of Christ's propitiating death, 1 John 2:2, "Jesus Christ ... is propitiation for our sins." A most reasonable meaning of Acts 18:6 is "You bear the guilt of rejecting God and the salvation God offers you through faith in the risen Jesus Christ."

Paul was probably thinking of this scripture passage.

> Ezekiel 3:18–20 (ESV), If I say to the wicked, "You shall surely die," and you give him no warning, nor speak to warn the wicked from his wicked way, in order to save his life, that wicked person shall die for his iniquity, but his blood I will require at your hand.

> 19 But if you warn the wicked, and he does not turn from his wickedness, or from his wicked way, he shall die for his iniquity, but you will have delivered your soul.

> 20 Again, if a righteous person turns from his righteousness and commits injustice, and I lay a stumbling block before him, he shall die. Because you have not warned him, he shall die for his

sin, and his righteous deeds that he has done shall not be remembered, but his blood I will require at your hand.

The watchman on the wall is not responsible to warn all in the city, but only those within the sound of his voice. His opportunity is to sound the warning to those able to hear. The one hearing and believing the watchman is not responsible to warn all, but only those who can hear him, that is his responsibility and duty.

The Holy Spirit gives each of his saved people opportunities within their own particular circumstances of life and living to proclaim warning and deliverance from the penalty of sin. The Spirit brings into our life those he wants to hear through us. That is not every person we know without exclusion, but every person to whom the Spirit gives us opportunity to warn the wicked from his wicked way. Not every conversation with the unsaved must be the gospel or include the gospel. To each as the Holy Spirit allows.

When a believer is given an opportunity to proclaim the good news, but does not, that is a sin, and he or she will bear the judicial guilt of that act of sinning (as with any act of sinning). The one failing to give warning is not guilty of the unsaved death, that falls on the sinner for rejecting salvation. Paul is saying to those opposing and slandering, "I have warned you. Now you bear the judicial guilt for rejecting God's Christ."

Therefore, said Paul. "I am clean," which is to say, "your blood—your death for your sins—is not my responsibility." They were not his responsibility to save—God alone is the Savior—but to warn. He had fulfilled his responsibility, and they had rejected the way of salvation.

The believer's responsibility is to "proclaim the good news," Mark 16:15, "warning every person and teaching every person," Colossians 1:28, that all who believe may be complete in Christ. Obviously Paul did not mean he was responsible to warn every single person without exclusion. There is a balance in life, one may do only what he or she is able to do. It is like the command to "pray without ceasing." If all one does is pray, there would be no opportunity for family, friends, or labor for life's necessity. To literally pray without ceasing would be to withdraw from all other activities of life. The command means pray at every suitable opportunity or occasion. So also the command to warn every person by proclaiming the good news.

The Holy Spirit gives his saved people opportunities to proclaim the good news of salvation. No believer is responsible to warn every person who crosses their path. Paul did not wander through Corinth and stop every person passing by that he might warn them. He used the opportunities given to him by the Holy Spirit to fulfill his duty. Let us be the same and pray and act to fulfill our duty, as the Holy Spirit brings opportunities into our life.

"From now on I will go to the gentiles." Paul had already been speaking to gentiles, those who were proselytes to Judaism and God-fearers attending the synagogue. He means he will go to pagan gentiles. Paul had previous experience with pagan gentiles at Athens. And he had proclaimed the good news to pagan gentiles in other cities. In fact, this same scenario had worked itself out in Antioch of Pisidia.

> Acts 13:46–48, Paul, and also Barnabas, speaking boldly said, "To you [Jews] it was necessary the word of God first be spoken. But because you reject it, and you judge yourselves unworthy of eternal life, look, we are turning to the gentiles. 47 For so the Lord has commanded us: 'I have set you for a light of the gentiles, for you to be salvation to the uttermost part of the earth.'"
>
> 48 Then hearing this, the gentiles were rejoicing and glorifying the word of the Lord, and believed, as many as were ordained to eternal life. 49 Then the word of the Lord was published throughout all the region.

In Corinth was neither the first nor the last time Paul turned away from the Jews and proclaimed the good news to the pagan gentiles.

Paul left the synagogue and went to "the house of a certain one worshiping God, named Titius Justus." This man was not a pagan gentile but either a proselyte or God-fearer. Luke says his house was "next to the synagogue." Paul may have already been lodging with Titius. Whether he was or not, Paul would not have invited himself, Titius would have invited the missionary team to lodge at his house.

We know nothing more about Titius Justus than what is said here. He is one of many in Scripture who are mentioned one time because they faithfully serve the Lord all the time. Even so, seek not to be honored, but let God honor you as he will.

Translation Acts 18:8–11

8 Now Crispus, the ruler of the synagogue, believed in the Lord, with all his household. And many of the Corinthians hearing believed and were immersed. 9 Now the Lord said to Paul in the night, in a vision, "Fear not, but keep on speaking, and do not be silent 10 for this reason: I am with you; and no one will lay a hand on you to harm you for this reason: there are to me many people in this city." 11 Now he continued a year and six months, teaching among them the word of God.

EXPOSITION

Many Believed And Were Immersed

Crispus is mentioned again in 1 Corinthians 1:14. Through mention of Titius and Crispus, Luke and the Holy Spirit assure us God's word did not return only opposition, but also salvation. Crispus was "the ruler of the synagogue." The position was administrative. There is no analogous position in the New Testament church.

> The ruler's duty was silent one. When the congregation had assembled, it was his duty to select the various persons who should for that time take the leading part in service, and to send the *Chazzan* to notify them what part they were to perform. For the Sabbath morning service some ten persons or eleven were required. [Burton, *the Ancient Synagogue Service*, 144.]

In vol. 1, *Acts 1–14*, I gave the order of a synagogue service, which I will repeat here. [Burton, 148].

1. Benediction I. Sheliach, Congregation responding.
2. Benediction II. Sheliach, Congregation responding.
3. Shema (the creed).
4. Prayer.
5. Eulogy I. Sheliach, Congregation responding.
6. Eulogy II. Sheliach, Congregation responding.
7. Reponses.
8. Eulogy III. Sheliach, Congregation responding.
9. Other prayers, including extempore prayers might be added here.
10. Eulogy XVII. Sheliach, Congregation responding.

11. Eulogy XVIII. Sheliach, Congregation responding.

12. Priestly Benediction.

13. Eulogy XIX. Sheliach, Congregation responding.

14. Reading of the Law, by seven readers appointed from the congregation by the ruler, and notified by the *chazzan*; the *methurgeman* interpreting.

15. Reading of the Prophets, by one reader, appointed from the congregation as above.

16. Sermon (likewise by a member of the congregation, not by an ordained or permanent officer).

17. Benediction (?).

As I stated in vol. 1, Paul's opportunity came at item 16. Some were persuaded to believe on Jesus as the Christ, and were saved from the penalty for their sins. When Luke says, "many of the Corinthians hearing believed and were immersed," he means Hebrews and gentiles.

Luke's account does not directly mention the consequences of Crispus' belief in Jesus Christ. He would have been dismissed from his position as ruler of the synagogue (cf. Acts 18:17). A significant and important part of his life would have been taken away. Friends were no longer friends. The respect he had gained from his synagogue position was gone, and he was most likely held in contempt by his Jewish brethren.

But what the world takes away, God replaces, cf. Mark 10:28–30. The Holy Spirit may have used Crispus' administrative abilities to organize the local church at Corinth. Certainly the Holy Spirit would not have allowed Titius, and Crispus, and "many of the Corinthians" to continue without a place for fellowship and worship. The Holy Spirit seldom mentions local churches in the Book of Acts, but we know from scriptures such as Acts 14:23 that Paul founded local churches wherever the Spirit provided believers. So too at Corinth. Someone— more than one someone as the church grew in numbers—guided by the Holy Spirit, offered his home for fellowship and worship.

In addition to Tertius and Crispus, "many of the Corinthians hearing believed and were immersed." Where they were immersed is unknown—they could not use the synagogue *mikvah*—but a Roman public bath is likely. From 1 Corinthians we know Paul immersed

Crispus, Gaius, and the household of Stephanus. Silas and Timothy would have immersed others. As the church grew in numbers Paul would appoint elders, and one or more of the elders would have immersed new believers. That is how a local church begins and grows: one saved soul at a time.

I Am With You

Soon after Paul had been rejected and ejected from the synagogue, Christ spoke to Paul "in the night." Paul had not been waiting for this word from the Lord. He and his missionary team members had kept on proclaiming the good news, and organizing the Corinthian local church. That is what believers do, they keep on obeying the Lord and doing their duty toward Christ. Opposition sharpens, it does not defeat, the desire to work for the Lord. Paul knew what he was supposed to do and did his duty.

"Duty" is one of those good words that has disappeared from modern Christianity. Perhaps because it seems to imply servitude, or lack of choice. Too many Christians, especially in Western churches, are confused by the cultural imperatives of independence, autonomy, becoming self-made, pulling ourselves up by our own bootstraps. Those concepts are foreign to genuine Christianity. "Duty" is the moral obligation to do what one is supposed to do. Duty is the responsibility to perform what one is required to perform. The Christian has many duties: to the Lord, to fellow believers, to seekers and sinners.

God did not create humankind to be autonomous: to act on one's own values and interests. That was Adam's crime. He chose to be governed by self, not by God. God created humankind to be dependent upon and in submission to God. Adam and his descendants were to be stewards of God's creation by living and acting according to God's moral values. Adam and his descendants were to depend on God to supply their needs and allowable desires. Adam chose a different path: to live his life and make his way in the world apart from God. That hasn't worked out very well for his descendants, all of whom are infected with Adam's sin.

As Paul was doing his duty, Christ spoke to him in the night (a dream or vision; the Greek word allows either) to encourage him. Encouragement implies its opposite. Perhaps Paul anticipated his Jewish opponents might raise a gentile riot against him, as had happened before. Paul had repeatedly had to leave other cities. Actions repeated build habits and expectations. Whatever the reasons, the Lord addressed his discouragement: "Fear not."

Did Paul have fear? Of course. Let us not put the pedestal so high Paul does not have normal human emotions. Constant and consistent opposition in every city he had visited over the past several years would discourage anyone. The word "fear" translates *phobéō* [Zodhiates, s. v. 5399], "to put in fear, terrify, frighten." The word has several shades of meaning, and the best meaning here is fear in the sense "apprehension" as to what might happen.

When the Lord tells Paul "keep on speaking, and do not be silent" the implied action is "keep on speaking the good news, and do not be silent because of those opposing." There is little doubt if Paul kept on speaking he would be the focus of opposition, and that opposition would spread to those under his care. While he might have been considering himself, his little flock was probably uppermost in his thoughts. If he himself was silent, i.e., was not proclaiming the good news, then the infant local church would have less persecution. The good news would still be proclaimed by Timothy and Silas and those newly added to the church. Others could proclaim the good news, Paul would disciple the believers.

The Lord had different plans, and encouraged Paul to "keep on speaking." Christ gives Paul two encouragements.

> I am with you; and no one will lay a hand on you to harm you.
>
> There are to me many people in this city.

Paul's safety, and the safety of the local church, was because "there are to me many people in this city." The Lord intended Paul and the missionary team to stay and give people the good news. This is the only time such is said of any city, so it would be unwise to apply this to other circumstances. However, there is an application. No place is so morally or religiously opposed to Christianity that the Lord does not have some people in that place; perhaps many.

Corinth was not known as a nice place to live. I have read (long ago, and so cannot recall the source) that to say someone was "Like a Corinthian" was an insult to their moral character. Located as it was on an isthmus, so that it had two seaports, the city's culture was heavily influenced by all manner of visitors and residents, from farmers to sailors, from businessmen to soldiers, from politicians, to priests, to philosophers. Every vice and every religion had a presence in Corinth. We need only look at Paul's two letters to the local church to see the many worldly influences. Some would have said Corinth was an unlikely place for salvations. The Lord said, "There are to me many people in this city."

The outcome was, Paul "continued a year and six months, teaching among them the word of God." In Christianity, to be taught, which is to say to be discipled, is the natural and expected outcome of salvation. The Lord has appointed some to be teachers, and gives his spiritual gift of teaching. The Lord had told the apostles and others prior to his ascension, "disciple the peoples," Matthew 28:19. Not "make disciples," because the Greek word for "make" is absent, but disciple all those whom the Lord saves. Paul "teaching among them the word of God," indicates there were some to teach, which indicates salvation was the result of the proclamation of the good news.

Paul remained in that city for eighteen months (Luke is rounding up or down). I once lived ten months in a particular city, the reason being it was where the Lord saved me, in the seventh month, and had me discipled for three months, and then sent me elsewhere. Paul's itinerant evangelistic lifestyle had probably seen him in and out of cities quickly. Some estimate Paul spent three months in Thessalonica; less in Philippi, and Berea, and Athens. In Corinth the Lord gave him an opportunity to see the fruits of his labors in sinners saved and discipled.

Translation Acts 18:12–17

12 Now Gallio being Proconsul of Achaia, the Jews rose up against Paul with one accord, and led him to the judgment seat, 13 now saying, "Against the law, this man earnestly persuades men to worship God." 14 Then Paul, about to say something, Gallio said to the Jews, "Truly if this was some unrighteousness or evil crime, O Jews, I would have born patiently with you according to reason. 15 But if it is a dispute about a word, and names, and according to your law, you will see to it yourselves. I choose not to be a judge of these things." 16 And he drove them from the judgment seat. 17 Then all having taken hold of Sosthenes, the ruler of the synagogue, began beating him before the judgment seat. And nothing about these things mattered to Gallio.

EXPOSITION

The Lord had told Paul, "no one will lay a hand on you to harm you." Luke now gives an example. The Lord's assurance of safety did not mean there would not be opposition.

> 1 Corinthians 10:13, God is faithful who will not allow you to be tempted beyond what you are able, but will cause with the temptation also the escape, to be able to endure.

In Corinth, the "escape" was "no one will lay a hand on you to harm you." Therefore Paul endured opposition, knowing the Lord always provides the grace to endure through opposition and persecution, until the "escape" arrives.

I have previously spoken of Gallio, in comments at 18:1–3. At some moment in time during the eighteen months Paul lived in Corinth, "the Jews rose up against Paul with one accord, and led him to the judgment seat." In saying "Jews" Luke makes a distinction common in the New Testament. The word "Jews" does not mean ethnicity but religion. A "Jew" was a Hebrew or a gentile practicing Judaism.

The word "jews" began as an identification of ethnicity. The Hebrews living in Babylon city during the Captivity were known as the "captives of Ju-dah," or "Jews." The name stuck. Their religion became known as Jew-daism. (Which is not the YHWH-ism God gave through Moses. Judaism is a religion of traditions.) The Hebrew people became identified by their religion: Jews. In the New Testament the identification Jews means those of Judaism opposed to Christ. When a Hebrew Jew is saved he becomes a Hebrew Christian.

These Jews persecuting Paul did not involve the gentiles, which may indicate the isolation of the Jewish population in Corinth from interaction with gentiles. Either the Jews were an insignificant number within the gentile population, or they were numerous enough to form a self-sufficient community.

This action by the Jewish community also shows the effect Paul and the local church was having on the Jews in Corinth. One suspects many God-fearers had become Christians, as well as not a few gentile proselytes, and some Jews. Paul may have enjoyed popular support from the gentile community, or at least was not perceived as a threat to gentiles ways and worship.

The latter possibility is supported by the Corinthians letters, to wit, the behavior and lifestyle of the Corinthian saved was not much different after salvation than before salvation. Ecstatic utterances, i.e., "tongues" was not unknown in pagan religions. I am not speaking of the spiritual gift of speaking a language, but the nonsense utterances self-generated, and therefore susceptible to any interpretation. Pagans used such "utterances" in the same way they are used today, to "declare a word from the gods." Sexual immorality was also in the local church; and divisions over teachers; and attendance at pagan temples. From that last arose the argument over eating meat sacrificed to idols.

The Jewish community stood apart from the gentiles, and therefore acted without gentile help. For that reason they, the Jews, "led Paul to the judgment seat." They probably came upon him *en masse* as he was preaching the good news, took him by the arms, and as a group surrounded him and led him to the judgment seat.

The words "judgment seat" translate *bēma* [Zodhiates, s. v. 968]. The word literally means a step, as in a footstep, e.g., Acts 7:5, Abraham was not given even a single footstep (*bēma*) in the promised land to call his own. The word came to mean an elevated place reached by steps. From there the meaning changed to a stage, or pulpit, or a judge's bench. In Paul's times *bēma* had come to mean a tribunal held by a judge or magistrate. The judge sat on a special chair or throne set on an elevated place, such as a stage.

The Jews took Paul to the place where Proconsul Gallio held court. Court was in session at specific times, most likely in the morning hours, per Roman custom. Gallio was aware of Jewish customs and the basics of Judaism. As the representative of Roman jurisprudence in Corinth, he was aware of the customs and religions of all the peoples under his jurisdiction. His duty as a judge was to apply and enforce Roman law. As we will see, he refused to get involved in what was obviously a strictly Jewish matter. The same was true of Pilate, John 18:31, "Therefore Pilate said to them, 'Take him [Jesus] yourselves and judge him according to your Law.'" Pilate became involved when he was told the Jews wanted Jesus put to death, a sentence only Roman jurisprudence could command.

The Jews in Corinth were not asking for execution. The crime was described to Gallio as, "Against the law, this man earnestly persuades

Acts Eighteen

men to worship God." Now I have capitalized "god" because the Jews meant YHWH. Gallio knew this because they used the Greek word *theós*, god, in the singular form, and he understood the basics of Judaism. What the Jews were saying was Paul was persuading gentiles to worship YHWH.

Gentiles worshiping YHWH not a crime under Roman law; nor was proselytizing. Why? Because the Jews had a treaty with Rome that made worship of YHWH legal for Jews and proselytes. There were two legal religions under Roman law. Worship of the Roman goddess Roma (the city of Rome deified) and worship of the Jewish God YHWH. Roman law did not care whoever or whatever else you might worship, as long as Roma or YHWH was worshiped. Indeed, there is a large helping of hypocrisy in the Jews' accusation, as they were also persuading gentiles to worship YHWH.

(An aside. Christianity became illegal once it was distinguished from Judaism. The Christian profession was they worshiped Christ only. They might have worshiped other gods also and been safe from Roman law, but the Christian worship of Christ only was not protected by Roman law or the Roman treaty with the Jews. The Christians were considered traitors to the Roman state, because they would not pray to Roma and other gods and goddesses for the protection of the Roman Empire. A simple test, an act of devotion to the deified Roman Emperor, outed them as Christians.)

Gallio was not a fool. Worship of YHWH was not a crime. Now, if the Jews had specified Jesus Christ, then Gallio might have become involved; at the least an interrogation of the accused. In such an interrogation Paul would have told Gallio, "I confess to you that according to the way they call a sect, so I serve the God of our fathers," YHWH, Acts 24:14. Gallio would have dismissed the charges.

Gallio answered as Roman law required him to answer. Paul was not fomenting a riot: the peace was not being disturbed, except by these Jews. Paul was not fomenting a rebellion: he was not accused of telling people Christ not Caesar was king. Gallio told the Jews, "see to it yourselves." That verdict prohibited any legal action under Roman law. A fight between two Jewish factions was not outside what was allowable, as long as no one was injured or killed, and property was not damaged, and it did not evolve into a riot.

Gallio gave them a legal decision.

> Truly if this was some unrighteousness or evil crime, O Jews, I would have born patiently with you according to reason. But if it is a dispute about a word, and names, and according to your law, you will see to it yourselves. I choose not to be a judge of these things.

Indeed, he was not required to judge these things. There was peace, not riot or rebellion, and he exercised the legal discretion afforded him by Roman law to dismiss the charges. Gallio had the officers of the court remove the Jews and Paul from the presence of the court.

That was not quite the end of these matters. When Gallio dismissed the matter, "all" took hold of "Sosthenes, the ruler of the synagogue" and "began beating him before the judgment seat." The "all," which is in the plural form, would be gentiles, for it seems unlikely the missionary team would beat Sosthenes. Gallio did not care, The Jews had troubled him with a non-issue. The Gallio incident probably occurred toward the end of the eighteen months.

Translation Acts 18:18–23

18 Now Paul, after staying many more days, then taking leave of the brethren, sailed to Syria, and with him Priscilla and Aquila—he had shaved his head in Cenchrea, for he had taken a vow. 19 Then they came to Ephesus, and he left them there. Now Paul himself went into the synagogue and reasoned with the Jews. 20 Then they entreated him to remain a longer time, and he did not consent, 21 but leaving he said, "I will return again to you, God willing," sailing from Ephesus, 22 and landing at Caesarea. Then having greeted the church, he went to Antioch. 23 And after staying some time, he left, passing successively through the Galatian region and Phrygia, strengthening all the disciples.

EXPOSITION

Cenchrea To Ephesus

How many days Paul remained in Corinth after the Gallio incident cannot be known. Luke says, "many more days." When those days were completed he decided to return to Antioch of Syria, his home church, or as we might say today, the sending church. Luke does not say, but

Acts Eighteen

one supposes Silas and Timothy left Corinth with Paul. Timothy was from Lystra, and it may be he went home after a brief stop in Antioch of Syria. Priscilla and Aquila left Corinth with Paul, but 18:19 tells us they remained in Ephesus.

Why did Paul shave his head in Cenchrea, and what was the vow? No one can say for certain. A Nazirite vow, Numbers 6:19, required the person to shave his head when the vow was completed, but nothing indicates Paul had previously taken a Nazirite vow. Nor was Paul a cleansed leper, Leviticus 14:8. No one suddenly died beside him, Numbers 6:9. Nor was Paul of the tribe of Levi, Numbers 8:7 (Paul was a Benjamite, Philippians 3:5). Those are all the commandments of the Law requiring the head be shaved. Why Paul shaved his head and the vow he had taken cannot be known.

Most suppose a Nazirite vow. The head was to be shaved when the time of the vow was completed. The purpose of a Nazirite vow was for the person "to separate himself to YHWH" for a specific period of time. The means of separation was not to consume alcohol, vinegar, grape juice, grapes, or raisins, to let the hair grow, and not to go near a dead body, even a close relative.

However, the end of the Nazirite vow also required the following offering to the Lord, on the altar in the temple in Jerusalem: one male lamb in its first year without blemish as a burnt offering, one ewe lamb in its first year without blemish as a sin offering, one ram without blemish as a peace offering, a basket of unleavened bread, cakes of fine flour mixed with oil, unleavened wafers anointed with oil, and their grain offering with their drink offerings (Numbers 6:14–15). In addition, the hair must be shaved off at the door of the temple, and put on the fire in the altar when the peace offering was being offered.

Because of these additional requirements, it seems unlikely the vow Paul took was a Nazirite vow. Paul may have taken a vow to dedicate himself to YHWH in some way, for some unknown period of time, and ended that separation by shaving his hair off his head. (OR perhaps Paul took a vow and then shaved his head as a symbol of that vow.) As I said above, why Paul shaved his head and the vow he had taken cannot be known. It also seems unlikely that Paul, preaching to both pagan gentiles and Jews that faith in Jesus the Christ saved "from all things from which you were not able in the Law of Moses to be justified," would take on a vow from the Law.

The best interpretation is to say only what Luke says: at Cenchrea and Paul shaved the hair off his head because he had taken a vow.

Cenchrea is the modern seaport of Kechries. In Paul's times Cenchrea was the eastern seaport of Corinth, located about seven miles east of the city, see map. Paul sailed from there with a final destination of Syria. The ship from Cenchrea went to Ephesus. From there Paul booked passage to a ship going to Caesarea. Then he went to his home church in Antioch of Syria. Paul did not go direct from Cenchrea to

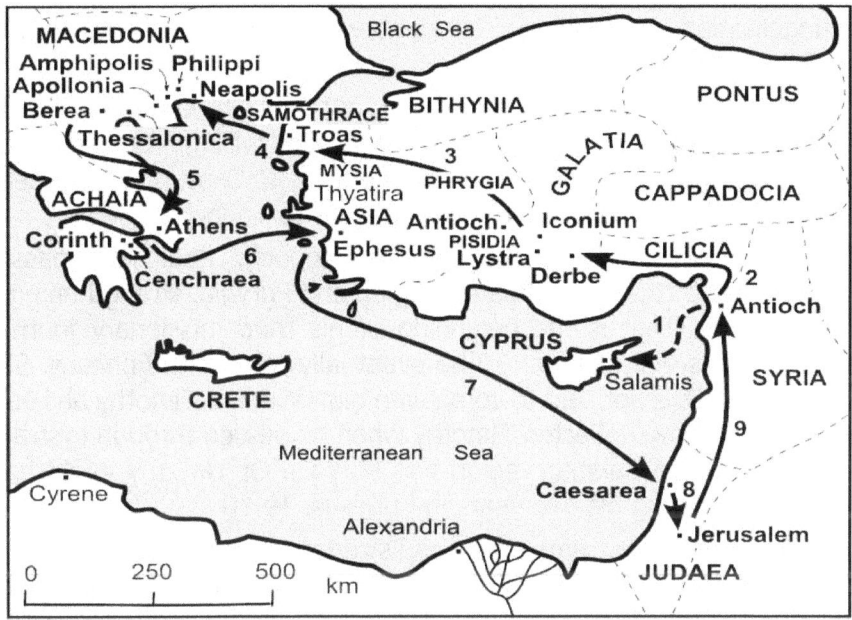

Antioch of Syria because the ship, or ships, on which he and his missionary team booked passage were not going to Syria. The map shows him going to Jerusalem, but Luke does not say that. Paul probably booked passage on a ship from Caesarea to the seaport of Seleucia in Syria, and then walked to Antioch of Syria. Luke does not say how Paul traveled from Caesarea to Antioch.

In Ephesus

Paul arrived in Ephesus with Priscilla and Aquila, and continued his journey home from Ephesus. He had time between arriving and departing to visit the local synagogue and "reason with the Jews."

Although these days we might suppose a departure hours after arriving, the sailing vessels were trading and cargo ships that also carried passengers. Offloading and/or loading trade goods was neither easy nor quick.

Again, the subject of Paul's synagogue message would have been the three points of the good news proclaimed by the early church: the Messiah must die, Jesus of Nazareth is the Messiah; faith in his name remits the penalty of sin from "all things from which you were not able in the Law of Moses to be justified." (The fact those three points were focused on Jews later led Paul to have Luke write a gospel for evangelization of gentiles. The gentile message was simpler, Acts 16:32; Romans 10:9–11.)

Those Jews wanted to hear more, but Paul's time was limited. He promised them, "I will return again to you, God willing." The rest of the story is quickly told. Paul sailed from Ephesus to Caesarea. He greeted the local church in Caesarea and then went to Antioch of Syria.

After staying for some time in Antioch, Paul left, passing successively through the Galatian region and Phrygia, strengthening all the disciples. That is the beginning of his third missionary journey, because we see in chapter 19 he eventually returns to Ephesus. Silas and Timothy are not said to come with him. We find Timothy at 19:22, so Paul may have collected Timothy when he passed through Lystra on his way into the Galatian region and Phrygia. Or Timothy might have joined Paul during his two years in Ephesus, 19:10.

This is the third time Paul has "strengthened all the disciples" in the regions of Phrygia and Galatia. His first missionary journey ended in Phrygia and Galatia, Acts 14:21–23. His second and third began there, Acts 16:1; 18:23. Why would the Holy Spirit tells these things? All but two of Paul's letters to local churches are to those in Macedonia and Achaia. One is to the Romans ca. AD 58 and one is to the Galatians ca. AD 50-51. Paul's third journey is ca. AD 54–58. The Holy Spirit wants us to know Paul paid attention to all the local churches he founded. What was it Paul said? "The pressure on me every day, the concern for all the churches," 1 Corinthians 11:28, written ca. AD 57.

Translation Acts 18:24–28

24 Now a certain Jew named Apollos, born in Alexandria, an

eloquent man, came to Ephesus, being able in the Scriptures. 25 He was taught in the way of the Lord. And being zealous in spirit, he was speaking and was earnestly teaching the things concerning Jesus, knowing only John's immersing. 26 He then began to speak boldly in the synagogue. Now Priscilla and Aquila having heard him, they took him and more exactly expounded to him the way of God. 27 He then deciding to pass through into Achaia, having been encouraged, the brethren wrote to the disciples to welcome him, who when arriving, greatly helped those having believed through grace. 28 For he powerfully disputed the Jews publicly, showing according to the Scriptures Jesus to be the Christ.

EXPOSITION

The events Luke describes happened before Paul returned to Ephesus. Apollos is mentioned in the books of Acts, 1 Corinthians, and Titus. Luke gives us a mini-biography. Apollos was a Jew. Luke means ethnicity and religion. Apollos was born in Alexandria, Egypt. Jeremiah 44:24–28 speaks of Jews in Egypt (the Book of Jeremiah was written ca. 628–580 BC). Alexandria was founded in 331 BC by Alexander the Great.

Luke says Apollos was "an eloquent man," meaning he was taught in and practiced rhetoric, the art of effective or persuasive speaking or writing. Why he had come to Ephesus cannot be known, except in that way the Holy Spirit has of placing people where he wants them to be.

Apollos was "able in the Scriptures" being "taught in the way of the Lord." In modern terms, Apollos had a PhD in Old Testament studies. More than that, he had applied the scriptures to his life and conformed his life to the ways of the Lord. His was an academic achievement plus the practical application of being conformed to YHWH's moral principles and values. Was he saved? Yes, his content of faith was in YHWH the Savior, and he believed Jesus of Nazareth was YHWH's promised Messiah.

(Luke later, Acts 19:2ff., gives an example of the effect of teaching about Jesus through John's immersion. At Acts 19:1–4 Luke is not saying those men had listened to Apollos, but it is an example of the Old Testament message, Messiah-King is coming. These men were saved, but not indwelt by the Holy Spirit. Their content of faith was John's message, they had believed YHWH had sent Jesus as the

Messiah-King, and on the basis of that content of faith God had saved them. Their salvation and regeneration was complete, but like all Old Testament salvations the Holy Spirit did not indwell.)

Apollos had one other characteristic: he was "zealous in spirit." His disposition (his spirit) was to teach others the Scripture, and through the Scripture persuade others to know and live the way of the Lord. I understand that disposition, having long ago taken as my guide and prayer for Christian service 2 Timothy 2:2, "And those things you have heard from me among many witnesses, these commit to faithful persons, such as will be competent to teach others also." I am no eloquent Apollos, but I am zealous in spirit to speak and earnestly teach the things concerning the Scriptures, the way of the Lord, and Jesus.

Apollos was applying the Old Testament to Jesus through John's immersing, that being all he knew of Jesus. Apollos knew at least one of the three basics of the good news to the Jews, that Jesus of Nazareth was the Messiah. That was John the Immerser's message, the Old Testament message of a coming Messiah-King, fulfilled in Jesus of Nazareth. Apollos had placed his faith in Jesus as YHWH's Messiah.

The Old Testament clearly promised a coming Messiah-King, e.g., 2 Samuel 7:13–16; Psalm 2, and that was the message of John the Immerser. The Messiah-King would redeem the nation from gentile oppression. We see that particular understanding in Mariam and Zecharias, Luke 1:52–54, 71–74. John the Immerser's message was repentance for sin as the sign of faith in the coming Messiah-King. Repentance prepared the believer for entrance into the kingdom.

(When Jesus did not redeem the nation from gentile oppression, as Psalm 2 indicated he would, John asked Jesus if he was indeed the coming One, i.e., the Messiah-King. Matthew 11:2–3, "Now John, having heard in the prison the works of the Christ, having sent two of his disciples, 3 he said to him, "Are you the Coming One, or are we to look for another?" Jesus pointed John to himself as fulfilling prophecy, Matthew 11:4–6, as Redeemer, Isaiah 61:1–2a, not as King, Isaiah 61:2b.)

The message of Messiah-Redeemer was not as clear in the Old Testament. Yes, today that message is clear, because like the Ethiopian eunuch we have been given the New Testament revelation of Jesus the Messiah-Christ-Redeemer, by which we now understand the Old

Testament witness of a coming Redeemer. But the Old Testament peoples did not have that New Testament revelation.

Had Apollos heard John's message that Jesus of Nazareth was God's lamb "who takes away the sins of the world?" Perhaps. But that also might have been understood as "that the nation should be morally purified from all bad elements" [Schurer, Division 2, 2:129–130,] see full quote at comments on 18:4–7.

After Priscilla and Aquila heard Apollos in the synagogue, they "more exactly expounded to him the way of God." The most reasonable interpretation is they taught him the rest of the good news to the Jews: Jesus the Messiah had died and resurrected, through faith in his name one could be saved from the penalty due sin and be given that justification before God the Law could not give. Priscilla and Aquila expanded and completed Apollos' content of faith.

Through the New Testament revelation Priscilla and Aquila taught Apollos that Jesus was the Messiah-Redeemer revealed in the Old Testament revelation, as understood by the New Testament revelation. What is that you say? There was no New Testament revelation at this time? Of course there was. Through the written scriptures of Matthew, Mark, Luke, and John we see all that Jesus taught the Twelve. Through Acts we see all that the Twelve and Paul taught. Through Paul's letters we see what Paul had taught during his missionary journeys. When the Holy Spirit had those men put those things in writing, wasn't what they put in writing an accurate report of what Jesus, the Twelve, and Paul said and did before the written record was creaed? Yes it was, an inspired and accurate account of what had been said and done.

Apollos, now knowing the way of God more exactly, decided to travel to Achaia. Luke does not say why, but the most reasonable view is Priscilla and Aquila had told Apollos about local Christian churches in Macedonia and Achaia. From Ephesus Apollos went to Corinth, see Acts 19:1; 1 Corinthians 1:12 (Apollos did not create the divisions in the Corinthian church). Priscilla and Aquila wrote a letter of introduction and recommendation for Apollos, a common practice.

In Corinth Apollos "greatly helped those having believed through grace." He himself, having been instructed in the way of God more exactly, taught others what he had been taught. He also continued his synagogue ministry, "for he powerfully disputed the Jews publicly, showing according to the Scriptures Jesus to be the Christ."

The story of Apollos was given to us for a reason. His story answers the question, how did the good news spread throughout the world? The Twelve and Paul were appointed to that duty. They trained others to help them in that duty. But Apollos was outside that environment; undoubtedly there were others, such as disciples trained through the ministries of the Twelve and Paul, and the next generation (Apollos is an example) trained through those disciples. Through Apollos the Holy Spirit shows us he works through all believers, not merely a select few.

Acts Nineteen

Translation Acts 19:1–4

1 Now it happened while Apollos was in Corinth, Paul passed through the inland parts to come to Ephesus. And finding certain disciples, 2 he said to them, "If you did receive the Holy Spirit having believed?" Then they said to him, "We did not even hear that there is a Holy Spirit." 3 Then he said, "Into what then were you immersed?" And they said, "Into John's immersing." 4 Then said Paul, "John immersed an immersion of repentance, telling the people they should believe in the one coming after him, that is, in Jesus."

EXPOSITION

Before Paul reached Ephesus, he found "about twelve" Jewish men (Acts 15:7). Twelve Jewish men would have been sufficient to start a synagogue, but perhaps Paul met them in a manner similar to meeting Lydia and her group of Jews. Apparently Paul was proclaiming the good news as he passed through the inland parts on his way to Ephesus. These men were disciples of John the Immerser, so they may have been excluded from the synagogue in their area. Paul would have been able to identify them as Jews by their appearance; Jews dressed differently than gentiles. Or he may have heard them speaking Hebrew. In whatever way, the Holy Spirit identified these men to Paul, leading Paul to speak with them about Jesus.

These men were saved, but not indwelt by the Holy Spirit. Their content of faith was John's the Immerser's message. They had believed YHWH had sent Israel the Messiah-King, and on the basis of that content of faith in YHWH, he had saved them. Their salvation and regeneration was complete, but like all Old Testament salvations the Holy Spirit did not indwell. However, their understanding was incomplete for this New Testament church age. Paul gave them that missing information, 19:4.

Luke does not record a specific response to Paul's message in 19:4. That is because they had already believed, 19:1. Like Priscilla and Aquila did with Apollos, "more exactly expounding to him the way of God" so Paul to these men. Their content of faith, which had already saved them, was expanded to know the way of God more exactly. Like Apollos, like many in the first days of the New Testament church, like the apostles themselves after Jesus' resurrection, these men were transformed from Old Testament saints to New Testament saints, by being given a full understanding of the New Testament message concerning salvation through Jesus of Nazareth. That they did believe Paul's good news "in the one coming after John the Immerser, that is, in Jesus," is known by the events in 19:5–7.

Translation Acts 19:5–7

5 Then having heard, they were immersed in the name of the Lord Jesus. 6 And Paul, laying hands on them, the Holy Spirit came upon them. Then they were speaking in foreign languages and prophesying. 7 Now there were in all about twelve men.

EXPOSITION

Fuller understanding required a new immersion to symbolize their faith in Jesus as Messiah-Redeemer. Then, as with other New Testament believers, they received the Holy Spirit. We may look to gentile proselytes to Judaism as an example of a new immersion. Those persons had been immersed upon their conversion from paganism to Judaism. When they believed on Jesus Christ as Redeemer, they were immersed as a public testimony of their conversion from Judaism to faith in Jesus the Christ.

The Holy Spirit provided these twelve Jews (Luke says, "about twelve men"), and Paul, with visible testimony they had received the Holy Spirit: "they were speaking in foreign languages and prophesying." This is the last time "speaking in foreign languages and prophesying" is mentioned in Acts.

Translation Acts 19:8–10

8 Now entering into the synagogue, he was boldly speaking, for three months reasoning and persuading about the kingdom of God. 9 But when some were hardened and were unbelieving, speaking evil of the Way before the many, he left them, separating the disciples, and daily publicly teaching in the lecture hall of Tyrannus. 10 This then continued for two years, so that all those living in Asia heard the Word of the Lord, both Jews and Greeks.

EXPOSITION

Acts Nineteen

The Synagogue

Paul arrives in Ephesus, and on the succeeding Sabbath he begins the process of reasoning and persuading the Jews about the kingdom of God. Depending on the time of the year, he continues for about twelve to thirteen Sabbaths. During this time some believed (re: disciples, 19:9) and some did not. Luke does not elaborate because he has told that story in other cities; everywhere the story is the same.

There are always some who believe, and always some who reject. Those rejecting are always the greater number. We know that fact because the opposition of those who do not believe requires Paul stop testifying in the synagogue. The good news hardens those who are unbelieving. They become hardened against the good news, not because the purpose of the good news is to harden hearts, but because their sinful human nature naturally rejects the message. The message is accepted by the efficacious action of God's grace, then faith.

> Grace, efficacious. God's grace working effectively with the sinner's human nature to free the will from the dominion of sin, and inform the sinner of his or her spiritual guilt and spiritual need, so that the sinner is able to choose to act in agreement with the command to believe and be saved. Efficacious grace is the work of the Holy Spirit in applying God's gift of grace-faith-salvation to effect salvation. Efficacious grace enlivens the sinner's faculty of spiritual perception (2 Thessalonians 2:13; 1 Peter 1:2), infallibly leading to the exercise of saving faith. [Quiggle, *Dictionary*.]

When the good news is rejected, what remains is the same bad news that was there before the good news came to their hearing. All human beings are sinners from conception. The good news reveals that corruption, saying also how that corrupt nature may be redeemed. If the good news of redemption is rejected, the sinner continues in that same corrupt state he had before the good news was heard. In that sense the good news hardens the person when it is rejected.

Sinners are already hard against God, and when they hear and reject the good news that hardness becomes stronger. Only God can change a heart of stone, Ezekiel 36:26–27, and we submit to his choices of the where and when and who of salvation. Some receive God's grace and believe.

The Lecture Hall Of Tyrannus

Paul left the synagogue and took those believing (the disciples), with him. To use a modern term, he "split the church." There may come a point when separation is required. The Christian is always practicing some kind of separation, whether from the sinful practices of others, his own sinful practices, or false beliefs and doctrines. When his or her local church turns to sinful practices or false beliefs and doctrines, and cannot be turned back to the Lord, then it is time to separate from that local church. Thirteen Sabbaths of reasoning, and who can tell how many private sessions with members of the congregation during those ninety days, was sufficient to make separation necessary when the majority continued hardened and unbelieving, and were publicly speaking evil of the Way before the many.

The disciples, or what has now become the local church in Corinth, gathered in other places to worship; probably a member's house, and as they grew more than one house. Elders would have been appointed in the passage of time, deacons selected, an order of service created. Preaching and teaching would have occurred regularly, and probably more than once a week. "The Way" is how the early Christians distinguished their "sect of the Nazarenes" from Judaism (see Acts 24:5, 14; 28:22).

Paul began "daily publicly teaching in the lecture hall of Tyrannus." Most likely this was both evangelizing the lost and discipling the saved. The words "lecture hall," translate *scholē* [Zodhiates, s. v. 4981], a school, a place of learning for a teacher and his disciples. The word is used only here.

The word I have translated "publicly teaching" and others translate reasoning or discussions is *dialégomai* [Zodhiates, s. v. 1256], converse, reason, intelligent discourse. I have given a contextual translation. Tyrannus may have been a philosopher, or he may have owned the building, or both. He apparently rented space for philosophers to teach their disciples and anyone who wanted to attend. Thus it was public teaching. An ancient philosopher was a teacher of a particular philosophy, that is, a way of life. Paul and Christianity fit right into the environment.

To the Greeks, Christianity was just another philosophy, and its evangelists were philosophers. Every philosophy requires of its disciples to effect a change in their life that agrees with the philosophy. The difference from other philosophies is Christianity is not just a change on the outside, but a real change on the inside that effects a change on the outside. From the outside Christianity can look like the normal reformation effected by self-discipline. Reformation seeks to change the inside by changing the outside. Genuine Christianity is just the opposite. An investigation by those seeing the outer change will reveal the outside has been affected by a real change on the inside: the regeneration of human nature, aka: born-again.

Paul and members of the local church would meet daily in the lecture hall of Tyrannus and discuss the Way and the Scripture. The local church probably had rented the hall for a specific period of time each day. Others coming in and out of the building would see and hear. By that natural means testimony, evangelization, and discipleship took place. This continued for two years.

When Luke says "all those living in Asia heard the Word of the Lord, both Jews and Greeks," that may be hyperbole. The Roman

province known as Asia was huge [Map: https://www.freebibleimages.org/]. However, what is not shown on the map are other cities in Asia, which we read about in Revelation 1:11; 2; 3. These were the cities of Ephesus, Smyrna, Pergamum, Thyatira, Sardis, Philadelphia, and Laodicea.

These cities were connected by a Roman roads that began in Ephesus, then went north to Smyrna, then Pergamum, then turned south until Laodicea. At Laodicea the road became two roads, one going east into Phrygia (eventually coming to Antioch of Syria), the other going west to Ephesus. See below.

So "all of Asia," is possible, meaning all parts of Asia heard the Word of the Lord. Paul did not found those churches. They were founded by converts from Ephesus and churches to the east. The Holy Spirit has given us an example of a New Testament local church not founded by Paul, the local church at Colosse (on the map above, below the "R in "Phrygia"). The city of Colosse was a few miles southwest of Laodicea. Paul may have passed through Colosse and Laodicea on his way to Ephesus, on the Roman road running through Colosse and

Laodicea to Ephesus. [Map: https://biblemapper.com/].

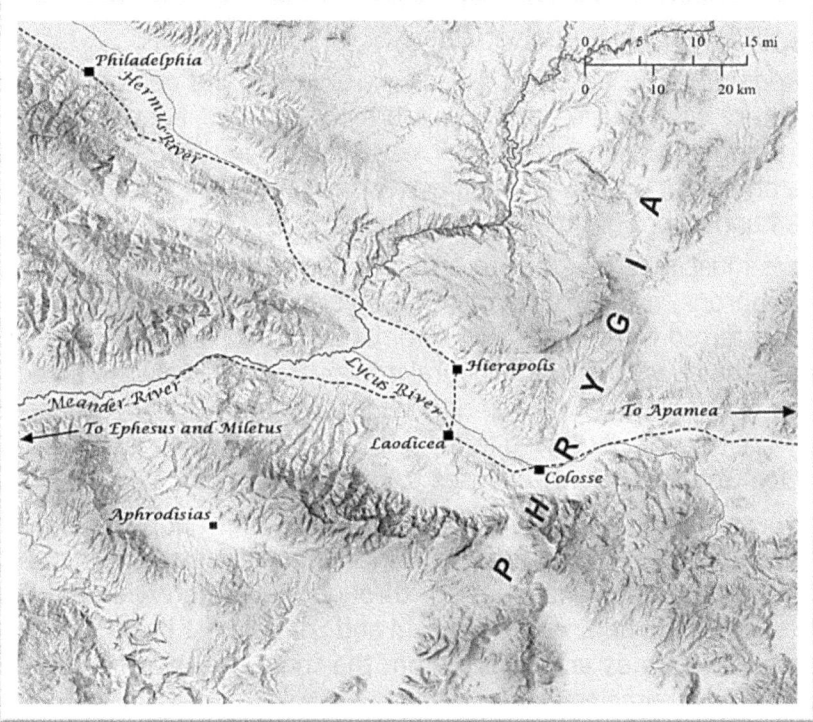

Translation Acts 19:11–12

11 Then God was mightily working not ordinary works through Paul's hands, 12 even so that to the ill his handkerchiefs or aprons were brought from his skin, and the diseases left them; also evil spirits left.

EXPOSITION

Paul was a tentmaker, laboring for the financial means to support himself and the public assemblies held in the school of Tyrannus. We should not assume Paul was proactive in the miracles Luke reports. People may have been taking his handkerchiefs (literally a sweat cloth worn around the neck) and his aprons. If so, the continuing cost of replacement must have been frustrating for Paul.

These works are extraordinary. Something similar was seen at Acts 5:15, "so as even into the streets, to bring out the sick and to put them on cots and mats, that Peter coming, at least the shadow might overshadow some of them." Whether or not being touched by Peter's shadow healed the ill is not said. I think not, as Luke does not say, and the act itself seems like superstition.

Regardless, in Corinth diseases were healed and demons cast out by contact with articles of Paul's clothing that had been touched by Paul. Whether or not Paul himself was involved in these things cannot be determined. God "was mightily working not ordinary works through Paul's hands," but did that include objects worn by Paul?

We must take care not to attribute supra-natural power to sweat cloths, aprons, or any other material object. Supra-natural power was not transferred from Paul's skin to objects he had worn, because Paul was not the source of supra-natural power. Healing is always an action by the omnipotent and sovereign God, and is always a response to faith—not necessarily saving faith, but faith in the power of God to heal, to which God sovereignly chooses to respond, or not.

These events are also extraordinary in that they happen in a gentile environment. We should recall the incident at Lystra, Acts 14:8–18, where a lame man was healed through Paul's intervention. That particular miracle had resulted in Paul and Silas almost being worshiped as gods (as Hermes and Zeus). From that time Paul had been careful in distributing miracles among gentiles.

Because the Holy Spirit is the source of healing, one must bow in reverence and submission and say "Amen, Lord, for it was good in your sight." Luke makes no further comment, and seems to use his report of miracles as an introduction to 19:13–20. It is an isolated incident, never mentioned or referred to again.

Translation Acts 19:13–16

13 But also some of the itinerant Jews, exorcists, tried to name over those having evil spirits the name of the Lord Jesus, saying, "I adjure you by Jesus whom Paul proclaims." 14 Now there were certain of Sceva, a Jew, a chief priest, sevens sons, doing this. 15 But the evil spirit responding said to them, "Jesus I know; and Paul I recognize; but you, who are you?" 16 Then the man in whom was the evil spirit assaulted them, overpowering them, overcoming them so that nude and wounded they ran out of that house.

EXPOSITION

Jewish exorcists were not uncommon. An extract from my commentary on Mark's Gospel, p. 80.

> "In the age in which Jesus ministered, unclean spirits were assumed to be everywhere. Abnormal or violent behavior, or some serious disease, were often thought to be caused by unclean spirits. Acts 19:13 indicates there were people making a living by expelling, or attempting to expel, demons. The word translated exorcists by most versions is *exorkistēs* [Zodhiates, s. v. 1845], 'one who by adjuration and incantation professes to expel demons.'
>
> "Bock and Herrick [72] give examples 'from the magical papyri, which date from after the time of Jesus,' of incantations the *exorkistēs* of Jesus' time may have used. Nine such texts are exampled. I repeat one here.
>
>> I conjure you, daimon, whoever you are, by this god, SABARBARBATHIOTH SABARBARBATHIOUTH, SABARBARBATHIONETH SABARBARBAPHAI. Come out daimon, whoever you are, and stay away from him . . .. Come out, daimon, since I bind you with unbreakable adamantine fetters, and I deliver you into the black chaos in perdition.
>
> "Apparently these *exorkistēs* had limited success. Demons reluctantly came out, or argued with the exorcists, or ignored their commands."

Such were Sceva and his sons. The fallen angel was not impressed. "Jesus I know; and Paul I recognize; but you, who are you?" The fallen angel may have met or seen Jesus; more likely he had a report from others of his kind who had seen or met Jesus. He had heard of Paul, he knew who he was.

Why did invoking "Jesus whom Paul proclaims" not work? Because it is not the name that does the work. God does the work. The exorcist must have a salvific relationship with God through Jesus Christ. The authority to cast out demons, but not the power, is delegated from Jesus Christ to his saved people. The authority and the power belong to Jesus Christ to use as he wills.

Luke's purpose in relating this incident is not for our entertainment, but to show Paul's ministry in Ephesus was effective and had become well known. Of course, some worldlings tried to make money off the good news, even as today.

Translation Acts 19:17–20

17 Now this became known to all, both Jews and Greeks, living in Ephesus. And fear came upon all, and the name of the Lord Jesus was praised. 18 Then many of those having believed were coming, confessing, and declaring their works. 19 Then many of those practicing the black arts, bringing their books, burned them before all. And they reckoned the prices of them and found it to be five thousand pieces of silver. 20 Thus with the Lord's power the word continued to increase and prevail.

EXPOSITION

The miracles through Paul's sweat cloths and aprons, and the incident with the exorcists and the demon, were the sensational news of the day. But they had an effect beyond mere sensational news. "Fear came upon all, and the name of the Lord Jesus was praised." The word translated "fear" is the same as used at 18:9, where Christ told Paul, "Fear not." The word is *phobéō* [Zodhiates, s. v. 5399], "to put in fear, terrify, frighten." There I said the context made the sense apprehension. Here the context agrees with the fear of the Lord that is reverence.

> The fear of the Lord is a profound awe of God incorporating devout reverence, unhesitating trust, complete dependence, and a cautious attitude toward displeasing him, resulting in worship and respectful obedience.
>
> The Hebrew word is *yārē'*. This word is used in five ways in the Old Testament: 1. The emotion of fear; 2. The intellectual anticipation of evil without emphasis upon the emotional reaction; 3. Reverence or awe; 4. Righteous behavior or piety; 5. Formal religious worship. (Harris et al., s. v. 907).
>
> The Greek word is *phóbos* [Zodhiates, s. v. 5401] from which *phobéō* is derived. The meaning of the Greek words is the same as the Hebrew word; reverence or awe resulting in righteous behavior or piety.

Luke seems to be describing two kinds of persons. In those who believed, the miracles and the incident with the demon invoked reverence or awe resulting in righteous behavior or piety. These "were coming, confessing, and declaring their works."

In others, those who were "practicing the black arts" (whatever passed for magic in those days), the response was different. Their fear was the emotion of fear. They burned their books in response to their fear.

I do not want to unintentionally lessen the impact of the Lord's work through the miracles and the incident with the demon. There were undoubtedly some burning their books because they had become believers. Those who were already believers became serious about their Christianity. Those whom the Father was drawing to Christ were found by the One they were seeking.

Luke brings the sensational news to a close. The value of the burned books was estimated at "five thousand pieces of silver." If Luke meant the Greek stater, the value today would be $435,000.00. If Luke meant the Roman denarius, the value today would be $217,500.00. [https://testamentpress.com/ancient-money-calculator.html]. The books would have been papyrus or parchment scrolls, and perhaps a few in codex form—pages bound on one side, as we know books today.

(The codex was invented in the third century BC, but did not become popular until used by the Christians following the first century AD. Finding a verse in a codex was easier than finding a verse in a scroll. By the fourth century AD the codex had replaced the scroll.)

Translation Acts 19:21–22

21 Now after these things had taken place, Paul purposed by the Spirit to pass through Macedonia and Achaia then go to Jerusalem, saying, "After having been there, it is necessary for me to also see Rome." 22 Then sending into Macedonia two of those serving him, Timothy and Erastus, he stayed for a time in Asia.

EXPOSITION

Paul's two years in Ephesus are coming to a close. He has been in Ephesus since late AD 54. From 1 Corinthians 16:8–9 we see Paul intended to remain in Ephesus until late May, until the Day of Pentecost, most likely the AD 57 Pentecost. The "great and effective" door in Ephesus (1 Corinthians 16:9) may refer to the events related in Acts 19:17–20. That would date the Corinthian letters to early AD 57, and the events in Acts 19:23–41 to just before Pentecost, AD 57.

The widespread acceptance of the Way paved the way for Paul to move on to other cities. His plan was to visit the churches he had founded in Macedonia and Achaia. After visiting the churches, Paul intended to go to Jerusalem. Most believe he arrived in Jerusalem AD 58.

Some historical perspective may be helpful. Before leaving Ephesus Paul wrote the first letter to the Corinthian believers, AD 57, and possibly the second. Their content suggests why Paul was eager to return to Macedonia and Achaia. He sent Timothy and Erastus to Macedonia and Achaia about the same time. Of the Four Gospels, only Matthew had been written (ca. AD 42, as I believe). Of the letters, James, AD 44; Galatians, AD 50–51; the two Thessalonian letters, AD 49–53, had been written. (The letter to the Roman believers was written AD 58 from Corinth. Luke would write his Gospel AD 58–62, when Paul was imprisoned in the governor's house, and write the Acts AD 62–63 during Paul's first Roman imprisonment.)

Paul sent Timothy and Erastus ahead to Macedonia. Erastus is mentioned again at Romans 16:23; 2 Timothy 4:20. Timothy was also to go to Corinth, 1 Corinthian 4:17, and 16:10 indicates someone else took the first letter to Corinth.

The order seems to be this. In late AD 56 Paul gets a letter from the Corinthian church, 1 Corinthians 5:1; 7:1. At about the same time the events of Acts 19:17–20 occur. Paul writes 1 Corinthians and sends it back with the person who brought him the letter from Corinth. Paul sends Timothy and Erastus to Macedonia. The incident of Acts 19:23–41 occurs. Paul leaves Ephesus for Macedonia, Acts 20:1.

Translation Acts 19:23–27

23 Now it happened at that same time not a small commotion concerning the Way. 24 For a certain man named Demetrius, a worker in silver, was making silver shrines of Artemis, which was bringing to the artisans no little business. 25 Then gathering the workmen in such things, he said, "Men, you know that from this business is our

prosperity. 26 And you see and hear that not only in Ephesus, but almost all of Asia this Paul has persuaded a great many people who have turned away, saying that they are not gods which are made by hands. 27 But not only this is a danger to us, refuting the business to come, but also the temple of the great goddess Artemis accounted for nothing, and also her glory to be cast down, whom all Asia and the world worship."

EXPOSITION

"At that same time" refers to 19:17–20. But not the exact same time. Paul left Ephesus after the events of 19:23–41, and we know from 1 Corinthians 16:8 Paul intended to remain in Ephesus until May (Pentecost). The incident created by Demetrius the silversmith may have altered his plans, but probably not significantly.

The "Great is Artemis of the Ephesians!" riot most likely occurred mid to late spring, AD 57. Demetrius had seen his profits drop as more people believed on this Jesus whom Paul preached, Acts 19:17–20. After some time Demetrius decided to publicly oppose Christianity. The incident may have caused Paul to leave Ephesus for Macedonia earlier than Pentecost, before he had written 2 Corinthians, but probably after receiving the Corinthians' second letter. (Internal evidence reveals Paul's second letter to the church in Corinth was written in Macedonia, 2 Corinthians 2:12–13; 7:5–9.) Considering travel time by ship and foot between Ephesus and Corinth—Ephesus to Corinth for the first letter; time in Corinth for opposition to grow against Paul; a messenger from Corinth to Paul in Ephesus to report more problems; the second letter written and sent from Macedonia—a mid to late spring date before 2 Corinthians 2:12–13 is reasonable for the "Great is Artemis of the Ephesians!" riot.

Demetrius and his friends made idols: "silver shrines of Artemis." Not all were made of silver, which was only for the rich buyer. Worship of Artemis was widespread in Asia (much of modern Turkey, see map above). Artemis was known as Diana by the Romans. She was the goddess of wild animals, the hunt, vegetation, and of chastity and childbirth.

The Temple of Artemis in Ephesus was renowned for "that fallen from the sky," Acts 19:35, a large fragment of a meteor. The city of Ephesus called itself "the temple warden of the great Artemis," 19:35.

Technically, for a city to be a temple warden, it had to have a temple dedicated to the Roman Emperor. Ephesus wanted to be a temple warden. But Emperor Augustus had appointed Pergamum and Smyrna as temple wardens because Ephesus was too involved in the worship of Artemis. Having lost the honor of temple warden for the Roman Emperor, they honored themselves as "the temple warden of the great Artemis." [https://www.mq.edu.au/, "Ephesus as temple-warden"].

By AD 57, conversion to Christianity had affected the profits of the silversmiths making silver shrines to Artemis. The silver shrines were expensive and were bought only by the wealthy. Other tradesmen used materials of lesser values to make the shrines for the common people. Maintaining a business and purchasing materials, whether silver or terra cotta, required a large capital outlay, so Demetrius and others making shrines had heavy investments in their business. Ramsey says [278], "Vast numbers of these shrines were offered to the goddess by her innumerable votaries," who were not only residents of Ephesus, but came to the temple from throughout the entire region.

Demetrius makes his case to his fellow idol-makers. Collectively they were one of the trade guilds in Ephesus. An ancient trade guild was similar to the modern trade union, but heavily involved in religion, and more like a big family. They held feasts, supported one another financially, and marched in religious parades together.

Demetrius succinctly states the problem.

> Men, you know that from this business is our prosperity. And you see and hear that not only in Ephesus, but almost all of Asia this Paul has persuaded a great many people who have turned away, saying that they are not gods which are made by hands.

Then he makes the appeal for action.

> But not only this is a danger to us, refuting the business to come, but also the temple of the great goddess Artemis accounted for nothing, and also her glory to be cast down, whom all Asia and the world worship.

Appealing to religion rather than profit makes their cause noble. "We are not really protesting for ourselves [as I am sure they said to one another], but for all who worship Artemis.

Translation Acts 19:28–32

28 Then having heard, and becoming full of indignation, they were crying out, saying, "Great is Artemis of the Ephesians!" 29 And the whole city was filled with an uproar. And with one accord they rushed to the theater, seizing Gaius and Aristarchus, Macedonians, fellow travelers with Paul. 30 But Paul, deciding to go in to the people, the disciples would not let him. 31 Then also some of the Asiarchs, being his friends, sent to him, urging him not to venture himself into the theater. 32 Truly others some thing were crying out; for the public assembly was confused, and most did not know for what cause they had come together.

EXPOSITION

The appeal works: "Then having heard, and becoming full of indignation." A slogan justifying their cause spontaneously comes to their lips: "Great is Artemis of the Ephesians!" They form a parade through the town to the amphitheater. I can imagine them making appropriate placards to carry. They quickly go to the amphitheater, and along the way seize "Gaius and Aristarchus, Macedonians, fellow travelers with Paul." Paul's missionary team had grown since the early days in Ephesus.

Paul wanted to reason with the demonstrators. His friends stopped him. Others in a leadership position, being "Asiarchs" also spoke against the idea. The title essentially means leaders in Asia. The position was both civil and religious. They presided over public games and religious festivals. The office was held by wealthy men, and they contributed financially to the public games. The reach of Christianity is not inhibited by wealth or social position.

Paul may have referred to this incident at 1 Corinthians 15:32. If so, that would date this incident before that letter was written in Ephesus. "Beasts" is metaphorical of evil men, not a literal fight with animals.

As does happen, then and now, many people joined the excited protestors, without really knowing why they were there. The large crowd made for an unruly mob, and they yelled loud slogans and milled about as mobs do. However, they were not destroying property as has become common in the modern age. That may be why the riot's leaders directed the rioters to the amphitheater.

Everyone was aware of the Roman soldiers stationed in Ephesus, no one wanted to interact with them. As the city clerk said, 19:40, "we are in danger of being accused of an insurrection for this day." No one wanted to be crucified for rebellion, nor prosecuted for disturbing the peace. So the riot was noisy, but not destructive. If the local Roman garrison did respond, it was only to contain the mob inside the amphitheater.

Translation Acts 19:33-34

33 Now out of the crowd the Jews together thrust forward Alexander. And Alexander, having beckoned with the hand, was wanting to make a defense to the people. 34 But knowing that he is a Jew, there was a one cry from all, continuing about two hours crying out, "Great is Artemis of the Ephesians!"

EXPOSITION

Why did the Jews, who were certainly not involved with the Way, want to make a defense. One wonders why there were even present, because they were not making or buying shrines to Artemis. And that may have been the reason. The Jews did not support the temple of Artemis, nor the idolatry intrinsic to the shrines. They may have feared being identified with the Christians. As I have mentioned before, at this time in the history of the New Testament church, the Christians did not themselves and were not by gentiles distinguished from the Jews. The Jews wanted to declare that distinction, to declare their opposition to Paul and his disciples.

Drawing attention to themselves was a futile effort to divert attention to the Christians. Immediately the crowd recognized Alexander as a Jew and thought him to be part of the problem they were protesting. Had not Paul begun in the synagogue? Was he not proclaiming a message based on Jewish beliefs? Did not the Jews speak against Artemis? Yes, yes, and yes.

The tumult must have been dying down for the Jews to think they might be allowed to speak and proactively defend themselves. Their efforts ramped it up again. "Knowing that he is a Jew, there was one cry one from all, continuing about two hours crying out, 'Great is Artemis of the Ephesians!'" Crowds take on a personality. As a group they would yell out their slogan and then it would die down as voices tired. Then someone somewhere in the crowd would yell it again, others would join in, and soon the majority were yelling. Then it would die down, only to be sparked again. This up and down cycle continued for about two hours. The town clerk wisely let everyone become tired before acting.

Translation Acts 19:35–41

35 Then the clerk, having calmed the crowd, says, "Men, Ephesians, for what man is there who knows not the city of the Ephesians as being the temple warden of the great Artemis, and of that fallen from the sky? 36 Therefore these things being indisputable, it is necessary for you to be calm, and to do nothing rashly. 37 For you brought these men, neither sacrilegious nor slandering our goddess.

38 "If therefore truly Demetrius and the artisans with him have a matter against anyone, courts are conducted, and there are Proconsuls; let them accuse one another. 39 But if anything more than this you demand, it will be determined in the lawful public assembly. 40 For we are in danger of being accused of an insurrection for this day, there being not one cause for which we are able to give a reason for this public tumult." 41 And having said these things, he dismissed the public assembly.

EXPOSITION

The town clerk was not as worried of Roman intervention as his threat, 19:40, implied. He knew if the soldiers were going to act, they would have already acted. As long as the crowd kept to the amphitheater they were safe. He waited for everyone to tire of yelling slogans. Then he calmed the crowd—probably like Alexander the Jew beckoning for attention with a raised hand. He had probably sent his officers into the crowd with instructions to direct attention to him when he acted.

This clerk knew how to manage a crowd. First he supported them.

What man is there who knows not the city of the Ephesians as being the temple warden of the great Artemis, and of that fallen from the sky?

Then he appealed to them.

Therefore these things being indisputable, it is necessary for you to be calm, and to do nothing rashly.

Then he accused them of acting improperly.

> You brought these men, neither sacrilegious nor slandering our goddess.

Then he accused them of acting illegally, and suggested a legal solution.

> If therefore truly Demetrius and the artisans with him have a matter against anyone, courts are conducted, and there are Proconsuls; let them accuse one another.

Then he reminded them their gathering was illegal, with an implied promise to take action if necessary.

> But if anything more than this you demand, it will be determined in the lawful public assembly.

Then he threatened them with legal action.

> For we are in danger of being accused of an insurrection for this day, there being not one cause for which we are able to give a reason for this public tumult.

Then, having made his case, he dismissed them to their homes and businesses.

All riots eventually end and mobs disperse. Calming and dispersing this particular crowd was made easier because "most did not know for what cause they had come together." The threat of military and legal action against them was genuine; the people knew the clerk could summon the soldiers with but a word. The soldiers would violently subdue them: some would be injured, some would die, some would be imprisoned. Very few would escape unscathed. Better to go home.

Acts Twenty

Translation Acts 20:1–3

1 Now after the uproar had ended, Paul called the disciples, and encouraged them, and saying farewell, left to go to Macedonia. 2 Then passing through those regions, and exhorting them with many words, he came to Greece. 3 He continued three months. A conspiracy was made against him by the Jews. He being about to sail into Syria, he decided to return through Macedonia.

EXPOSITION

Luke shortens his description of Paul's travel to Corinth. We know from 2 Corinthians 2:12 that on his way out of Asia Paul stopped at Troas for a while, "Now I came to Troas for the good news of Christ, and a door opening to me in the Lord." After ministering to that local church he went to Macedonia. Then he went to Greece, probably stopping for a little time to visit the local church in Athens. Then he came to Corinth. From Corinth he returned to Macedonia, and from Philippi he began his journey to Jerusalem.

Acts 20 is the voyage home. Paul's family home was Tarsus of Cilicia. His church home was Antioch of Syria. His home was Jerusalem, where he had lived for years, and had been trained in the Scripture by Gamaliel, and from which he began his journey to salvation and apostolic office.

Paul left Ephesus not long after the riot. He had completed his task. The good news had been proclaimed, people were saved, disciples were taught, a local church was established. With a final sermon and some personal farewells, he left Ephesus for Macedonia. There may have been a ship going northwest to Neapolis, but he went to Troas (walked or a ship), and from there made the short voyage across the Adriatic Sea to Neapolis. From there he visited the local church at Philippi, then the local churches at Thessalonica and Berea. Passing from there he may have stopped to see the local church in Athens. From Athens he went to Corinth, where he stayed for about three months.

What did Luke mean when wrote, "A conspiracy was made against Paul by the Jews?" Possibilities come to mind: to have him arrested?

Imprisoned? Killed? A conspiracy with other synagogues, or with gentiles? We cannot know. Whatever the reason might have been, Paul had intended to sail for Syria from Corinth, but decided to return to Asia the way he had come, through Macedonia.

Translation Acts 20:4–6

4 Now Sopater Phyrrus, a Berean, went with him; and of the Thessalonians, Aristarchus and Secundus; and Gaius of Derbe and Timothy; and the Asians Tychicus and Trophimus. 5 But these having gone ahead waited for us in Troas. 6 Then we sailed away from Philippi after the days of Unleavened, and we came to them at Troas in five days, where we stayed seven days.

EXPOSITION

In this passage we have confirmation Paul had visited the local churches in Berea and Thessalonica on his way to Corinth. Gaius of Derbe and Timothy (of Lystra, 16:1–4) must have come with Paul to Ephesus, he collecting them on his way to Ephesus, 18:23. We know Paul had sent Timothy ahead from Ephesus into Macedonia before leaving Ephesus, 19:22. Erastus, who had went to Macedonia with Timothy, came with Paul to Corinth, and remained in Corinth, because he was the steward (city manager?) of Corinth, Romans 16:23. Tychicus and Trophimus came with Paul from Ephesus. Tychicus is mentioned again at Ephesians 6:21; Colossians 4:7; 2 Timothy 4:12; Titus 3:12. Trophimus continued with Paul to Jerusalem, Acts 21:29, and is later mentioned in 2 Timothy 4:20.

Luke says "these" went ahead and waited for "us" at Troas. The "us" means Luke joined the group. Most likely, they all, except Luke who was in Philippi, traveled with Paul from Corinth, to Athens, to Berea, to Thessalonica, to Philippi. At Philippi Luke reconnected with Paul and decided to go with Paul to Jerusalem. The others left Paul at Philippi and continued on to Neapolis and then Troas, where they waited for Paul.

Then "we," Paul and Luke, "sailed away from Philippi after the days of Unleavened." Luke gives a time marker. The "days of Unleavened" are the eight days of Passover-Feast of Unleavened Bread, which in AD 58 occurred April 26–May 3. Luke and Paul left Philippi on May 4. The walk to Neapolis, securing passage on a ship to Troas, and the two day voyage across the Adriatic Sea took five days. The entire group—Paul, Sopater Phyrrus, Aristarchus, Secundus, Gaius, Timothy, Tychicus, Trophimus, and Luke—then stayed in Troas for seven days, meeting with the local church.

Translation Acts 20:7

7 Then at the first day of the week, as we came together to break bread, Paul spoke with them, intending to leave the next day. He continued speaking until midnight.

EXPOSITION

On the seventh day after their arrival, they met with the local church in Troas to "break bread," intending to leave the next day. That seventh day was Sunday, day 1 of the week. Luke does not mean they had not been meeting with church members during the preceding six days, but that the first day of the week was the regularly scheduled day for the local church at Troas to meet as one body in one place. Part of that meeting was to "break bread," i.e., to celebrate the Lord's Supper (so named by Paul at 1 Corinthians 11:20). As part of that meeting, Paul did what must have been his usual and common practice. He spoke to the church, most likely teaching the scriptures, perhaps also giving a report of his activities since he had last visited Troas.

We do not know what time of the day the local church met on Sunday, but I would suppose in the evening after the regular work day. Unlike much of the world's population in modern times, there was no "weekend" or "days off" in the ancient world. The Jews were the only people group that practiced a day of rest from productive labor (sundown Friday to sundown Saturday). Sunday was not the "Lord's Day," it was not a day of rest, but it was on that day the local church at Troas met to worship as one people.

(Compare 1 Corinthians 16:1. Together these two passages may indicate in those churches Paul founded, he established the first day of the week as a regular day for the local churches to meet as one body. No New Testament scripture commands a certain day, so we must consider meeting on Sunday a long-standing church tradition.)

Paul had a lot to say. He continued speaking until midnight. The common practices of Christianity today are not the same as first century Christianity. Christianity adapts to each culture in which people are saved. Not adaptations that change doctrine, but adaptations in how worship is expressed and teaching-discipleship is done.

The only written Scripture in the early church was the Old Testament. The Old Testament scriptures any local church may have had on hand was not a group of scrolls or a codex containing the thirty-nine books we know as the Old Testament. They knew the same books, but no one could have afforded the cost of that many scrolls; nor was it likely the Jews would sell them a copy.

The Old Testament books they had on hand were the ones Paul and other Jews, now become Christians, had memorized in their youth, or perhaps had personal copies of portions of books they had copied. If there were any former Jews or gentile proselytes in the Troas church, there was knowledge of the Old Testament Scripture.

Whatever copies of the Old Testament the church at Troas may have had on hand, they had all (virtually a certainty) been dictated and written out for use in the local churches. We know Paul had a set of books and parchments, 2 Timothy 4:13. A common practice in those times was to record, in writing, speeches given by notable persons. The Book of Mark originated as recorded from Peter's teaching, according to Papias (AD 70–150), *Fragments*, VI. (The Gospel According to Mark is really The Gospel According to Peter.)

"Speaking until midnight," Paul explained the Old Testament in its relationship to Christ. He also taught Christian practices and moral values and behavior, based on the moral values and principles in the Old Testament. Most likely many things we see in Paul's letters originated in times of speaking, such as at Troas, duplicated many times in the many local churches he had founded, and visited, and visited again. Eventually the things spoken became the things written, the New Testament Scripture.

Translation Acts 20:8–12

8 Now there were many lamps in the upper room where we were gathered. 9 And a certain man named Eutychus was sitting by the window, overcome by deep sleep as Paul spoke at length. Having been overcome by the sleep, he fell down from the third story; and was taken up dead. 10 But Paul, having went down, took him in his arms and embraced him, saying, "Do not lament, for his life is in him." 11 Then

he went up, and they broke bread, and ate, and having spoken for a long time, until daybreak, he left. 12 Now they brought the young man alive, and were not a little comforted.

EXPOSITION

One of the great questions an expositor may ask himself is, "Why is that in the Scripture?" This is one of those places, because if absent nothing is missing from the narrative of Paul's journey. One might jump from 20:8 to 20:11 and leave out 20:12, without materially affecting the historical narrative.

Some wit somewhere has said this story is to warn preachers not to preach too long, a dubious application, at best. Certainly it is in the narrative because it happened, and Luke is a careful historian. Having brought us to Troas for seven days, Luke may have felt the need to report any interesting or unusual events. What else may we glean from this account?

The place where they gathered had three stories, so certainly at least one of the members of the local church was a person of some wealth. The Lord saves out of every social strata. The meeting place is described as "the upper room." The room was large because it had "many lamps," which may speak to the size of the church at Troas. An "upper room" was usually built as a guest room, an "inn," or as the British say, a "holiday let." An upper room could also be a room to rent for special occasions or visitors. Using the room as a place for the whole church to meet would have been natural.

The certain man named Eutychus might have been a young man or an old man; both age groups are prone to napping during sermons, (I speak from experience at both ends of life). He may have been by the window avoiding the smoke from the many lamps. He was probably a young man, late teens or early twenties, because an older man is wiser than to sit so close to open window, through which one might fall out and down to the ground. Windows were not covered with glass as today, but at most were covered with a fabric curtain.

While Paul spoke at length, Eutychus was "overcome by deep sleep," and fell out the window to the ground. Having fallen about twenty feet, he was killed and "taken up dead." (A house "story" is about eight to ten feet floor to ceiling, Eutychus fell from the floor of the third story.)

Someone saw Eutychus fall out the window (he may have awoken mid-fall and screamed). Paul, and undoubtedly others, went down to see how he was, alive or dead. He was dead. Luke says he was "taken up dead." Paul took him in his arms and embraced him, saying, "Do not lament, for his life is in him." Then they went back to the upper room and ate (this particular breaking of bread was also a meal, an early New Testament church tradition, 1 Corinthians 11:20, discontinued because of abuses, 11:21). Paul continued speaking "until daybreak," and then he left Troas. The young man was brought to the upper room and everyone was greatly comforted.

Luke does not always tell a story in chronological order. Here is a more natural order of events.

> Eutychus falls out the window.
>
> Others see him fall out the window and run downstairs.
>
> When they arrived at the scene, they discovered Eutychus was dead.
>
> One of those finding Eutychus dead went back upstairs and told the others.
>
> Paul came down, and having arrived, took the body in his arms, hugged him, and revived Eutychus.
>
> Then Paul and the others, including Eutychus went back upstairs. Everyone was "not a little comforted" the young man was alive.
>
> The group took time for a meal, "they broke bread and ate." This was not the Lord's supper. The Lord's Supper was the reason the whole church had gathered on Sunday, and the meal was part of that event.
>
> Paul resumed his lecture and spoke until daylight. Paul left, everyone was tired, everyone went home, and those outside the home went to work.

That is the order of events as I understand these things. Reviving Eutychus was a healing not a resurrection, which requires bodily transformation from mortal to immortal.

Resurrection. God reforms the physically dead decomposed

body from existing materials and gives that body endless immortal physical life, and God causes the disembodied soul originally propagated with that body to unite with it and animate it. The united soul and resurrected body will continue endlessly in that reunited state.

Paul healed Eutychus of the physical condition death.

Translation Acts 20:13-16

13 But we, having gone ahead to the ship, sailed to Assos, there to pick up Paul. For so he had arranged, intending to go on foot. 14 Then he met us at Assos and we picked him up; and we came to Mitylene. 15 From there we sailed away, arriving on the next day opposite Chios. Then the next day we came to Samos. Then the following day we came to Miletus. 16 For Paul had decided to sail past Ephesus, so that he might not spend time in Asia. For he hurried, if it was possible for him to be in Jerusalem on the Day of Pentecost.

EXPOSITION

Luke and the others go to the seaport and hire passage on a ship. On the map [https://www.ccel.org/], the journey we want begins at

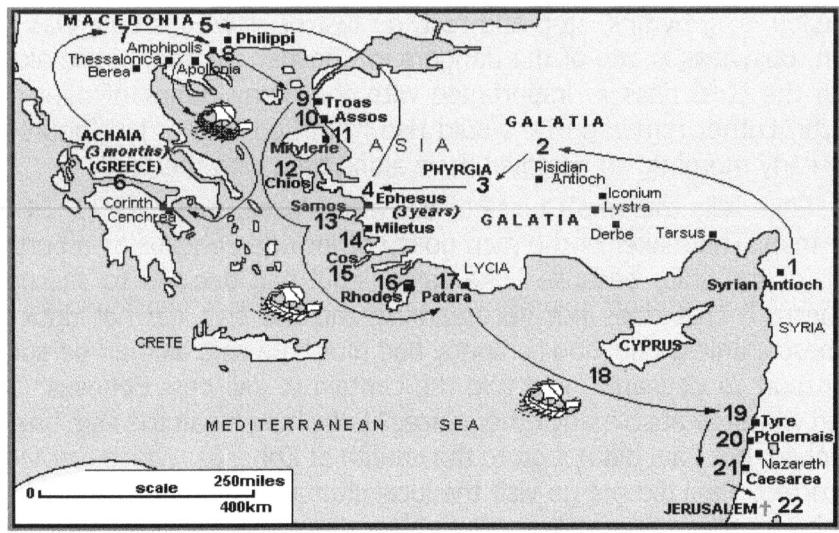

number 9, Troas, continuing to number 22, Jerusalem. Ships in Paul's times, cargo and trading ships also carrying passengers, usually sailed within sight of the coast. Only when necessary did they venture out into the open sea. The particular ship on which Paul had hired passage was going to Patara (map number 17), Acts 21:1. The ship would stop at almost every town along the way to load or unload cargo and passengers. That is why Luke mentions every little town on the way. At Patara, Paul and friends would find another ship and continue their voyage to Phoenicia (number 19), Caesarea (21), and then walk to Jerusalem (22).

Paul decided to walk from Troas to the ship's first stop, Assos (number 10) where he would board the ship. The straight line distance is about twenty-one miles, the Roman road was about thirty-one miles. For a people used to walking, thirty miles can be done in a day: three miles per hour for ten hours. Paul is now in his fifties, so we will give him a day and a half to walk the distance. Why did Paul choose to walk?

Men like Paul, with important positions in the world, are seldom alone. Everyone wants a piece of their time. Paul was an older man, and roads could be dangerous with thieves preying on travelers. Paul probably had to persuade some in the group to let him go alone. The value of walking alone for a day and a half (or so) should not be underestimated. Paul could, without interruption, think, meditate, pray, worship, sing hymns, stop and rest, go fast or slow—his time was his own. Busyness is one of the dangers in Christian ministry. Time alone with the Lord rises in importance with the many duties of ministry. Martin Luther remarked he would rise from bed in the dark hours of the early morning, so he could have alone time with the Lord.

Luke tells the ship's ports of call after Assos, numbers 11–14 on the map. The maker of the map does not include Ephesus as a port of call for the ship, because Luke says, "Paul had decided to sail past Ephesus." That does not necessarily mean the ship did not dock at Ephesus, unless Paul and company had hired the ship as their personal transport to Caesarea, and told the captain to sail past Ephesus; but then why stop at so many other places? Luke may mean the ship briefly stopped, but Paul did not go to the church at Ephesus. Whichever view is correct, Paul did not go visit the local church at Ephesus "so that he might not spend time in Asia." But unless this ship was passengers only, which would be very unusual, the ship needed to stop at many ports for cargo and passengers.

Paul's intent was to "be in Jerusalem on the Day of Pentecost." There are fifty days between the last day of the Feast of Unleavened Bread and the Day of Pentecost. Paul had spent twelve of those days between leaving Philippi and leaving Troas; thirty-eight days left. His walk to Assos was another day and a half (or so), but perhaps two days, for the ship might not have left Assos until the dawn after the day he arrived; thirty-five days to Pentecost. A day from Assos to Mitylene, a day to Chios, a day to Samos, a day to Miletus; thirty-one days left until the Day of Pentecost.

Translation Acts 20:17–21

17 Then from Miletus he sent to Ephesus, calling for the elders of the church. 18 Then when they had come to him, he said to them, "You know from the first day on which I arrived in Asia, how I was with you the entire time, 19 serving the Lord with all humility, and tears, and trials coming upon me by the schemes of the Jews. 20 How in nothing did I hesitate not to declare that which was profitable to you, and to teach you publicly and from house to house, 21 repeatedly testifying to both Jews and to Greeks, repentance toward God and of faith in our Lord Jesus Christ.

EXPOSITION

After Paul arrived in Miletus, he sent for the elders of the local church in Ephesus to come to him at Miletus. Miletus was one of the major seaports in Asia. Miletus is about 36 miles south of Ephesus. A messenger walking three miles/hour could travel the distance in about 12 hours, less if he walked faster. A day from Miletus to Ephesus, then a day and a half for the Ephesian elders. There are now twenty-nine (perhaps twenty-eight) days until the Day of Pentecost.

I will assume the Ephesian elders arrived in Miletus about midday and immediately met with Paul at the prearranged place. The elders of the church of Ephesus having arrived, Paul makes a farewell speech, summarizing his two years in Ephesus, his anticipated future, and a warning for their future. He begins with these words.

> You know from the first day on which I arrived in Asia, how I was with you the entire time, 19 serving the Lord with all humility, and tears, and trials coming upon me by the schemes of the Jews.

By "first day" Paul means the day he arrived in Ephesus. He was with them from the first, although they had not been with him from the first. They had come to be with him through their salvation. But Paul, in his heart and mind, in his intent to serve the Lord in Ephesus, was with them from the first day. From when he arrived in Ephesus he continued to declare the truth. When they believed he began to teach them from house to house (as well as in the school of Tyrannus).

Paul describes his time with them as "with all humility, and tears, and trials." Surely there were also good times in the Lord. But Paul focuses on his attitude. He had not come to lord it over them. Nor had he taught them academically, or by lecturing them as a teacher might his disciples. He had been humble among them.

> Humility means valuing myself as God values me, and valuing others as equal or better than myself. Humility means knowing my relationship with God: created in his image, chosen to salvation, rescued from sin by the Savior. Humility means knowing my importance to others arises out what God has given me to be used for the material and spiritual benefit of others. Humility recognizes that my worth to others is because of my relationship with Christ. If, as is the case, I can do through Christ all the things God requires of me, then humility means I realize that in myself I cannot do all things. In Christ I am exalted by what he can do through me, his willing friend and servant, for the best interests of myself and others. [Quiggle, *Dictionary.*]

He had served the Lord "with tears." Paul had sorrowed with them, and Paul had rejoiced with them. He had been among them as one of them. His tears, whether literal or figurative of his emotions, indicated he had the deepest concern for them. He desired their salvation when he preached the good news, He desired they lead a life pleasing to the Lord as he discipled them in and by the scriptures. He desired them as a New Testament church to oppose the false and cling to the true.

We get some idea of the structure of the local church at Ephesus. Paul was renting the lecture hall of Tyrannus, 19:9, but he still discipled the church, "from house to house." Local churches were house churches, which is to say, divided into small groups, each led by an elder, meeting in the homes of those willing to use their home for that purpose. From time to time, according to an agreed upon schedule, e.g., Acts 20:7; 1 Corinthians 16:2, they would meet as one body. That meeting place was often outdoors on the outskirts of the city, or a building large enough to accommodate all, such as a large upper room, 20:7, or a lecture hall at a school, 19:9.

Paul taught them "that which was profitable to you" so well and so in depth, over the two-plus years he spent with them, that his later letter to them has been characterized as instruction for advanced Christians. In 20:21 Paul summarizes his constant teaching in Ephesus as repentance and faith. The phrase "Jews and Greeks" is used as a merism to mean all who practiced Judaism and all who practiced pagan religions. Not all Jews and Greeks without exception but without distinction. Whoever would listen, Jew or Greek, Paul taught.

Translation Acts 20:22–24

22 "And now, look, I go bound in the Spirit to Jerusalem, not knowing what will happen to me there, 23 except that the Holy Spirit in every city repeatedly testifies to me, saying that bonds and tribulations await me. 24 But I do not say I make my life dear to myself, so as to complete my course and the ministry I received from the Lord Jesus, to earnestly testify of the good news of the grace of God.

EXPOSITION

Paul tells them what awaits him in Jerusalem, in order to "cut the apron strings" so to speak. They had depended on him for much; he would have them depend on Christ. He knows only "bonds and tribulations await me," and they should be prepared for his death, as indeed he is prepared.

Let us not misunderstand. The Holy Spirit is sending Paul to Jerusalem. The Holy Spirit is telling Paul he will endure bonds and tribulations in Jerusalem. (Thus we see something of Paul's mind as he walked from Troas to Assos.) The Holy Spirit is not telling Paul he will die in Jerusalem. That is Paul's opinion, not the Spirit's declaration; at the least Paul is prepared to die.

Paul has accepted what will happen: "bonds and tribulations"; and what might happen: in Jerusalem he might "complete my course," i.e., come to the end of "the ministry I received from the Lord Jesus." He knew that up to that time he had fulfilled the requirements of that ministry, "to earnestly testify of the good news of the grace of God." The Ephesians were one proof of that ministry fulfilled. (But Jesus was not yet finished with Paul, Acts 23:11.)

Translation Acts 20:25-28

25 "Now, look, I know that never again will you see my face, among whom you all I have gone about preaching the kingdom. 26 Therefore, I testify to you in this day, that I am clean of the blood of all. 27 For I have not hesitated from not declaring all the counsel of God to you. 28 Attend to yourselves and to all the flock among which the Holy Spirit has set you as overseers, to shepherd the church of God which he acquired through his own blood.

EXPOSITION

Verses 25-26

One must separate opinion from inspired declaration. Paul's expectation was that he would die in Jerusalem. He was prepared. Therefore he assumed "that never again will you Ephesians see my face." But about five to six years later he did see them again. With many I believe Paul was released from his Roman imprisonment ca. AD 63. I discuss this in full in my commentary on Paul's Pastoral Letters (see Introduction). Between his imprisonments Paul traveled to these places [Hollingsworth, 201].

> Macedonia, Philippians 2:24
> Crete, Titus 1:5
> Asia Minor, Philemon 22
> Troas, 2 Timothy 4:13
> Perhaps Spain, Romans 15:22-29

The cities listed *are not* given in a particular or suspected order of travel and visitation. His other obligations probably make Spain last on the list. If Paul did travel to Spain, then it was between his two imprisonments.

> Released from prison ca. AD 63
> Promised visits, as listed above, ca. AD 63-64
> Missionary journey into Spain, ca. AD 64-66
> Travel back to Asia Minor from Spain, ca. AD 66

1 Timothy and Titus written, ca. AD 66–67

Visit to Nicopolis, Titus 3:12, ca. AD 66–67

Second Roman imprisonment, ca. AD 67–68

Second Timothy written from prison in Rome, ca. AD 68

Paul Executed by Nero, ca. AD 68.

Paul could have visited Ephesus as early as AD 63–64, or about five to six years after meeting with them at Miletus.

Preaching The Kingdom

The "kingdom" concept is well-defined in Scripture, but means different things to different Christians. When some, those holding to a postmillennial eschatology, think of the kingdom, they think of the New Testament church and Holy Spirit creating a kingdom for Christ on the earth, then Christ returns to receive that kingdom, then the final judgment in Revelation 20:11–15. Others, holding to amillennial eschatology, look for Christ to return, the final judgment, and then the kingdom, Revelation 21–22. A Dispensationalist, a premillennial eschatology, looks for the Davidic-Messianic-Millennial kingdom that Christ will establish at his second advent immediately following the Tribulation, and then after the thousand years has ended final judgment, and a new heavens and earth.

The same as all believers in the early church, Paul expected the return of Christ at any moment. Upon his return Christ would establish his kingdom. That Davidic-Messianic Kingdom was the one promised to King David, 2 Samuel 7:13–16, and which David wrote about in Psalm 2. I have every confidence Paul told every church he founded about the coming Davidic-Messianic Kingdom.

> The Davidic-Messianic Kingdom: based on the Davidic covenant (2 Samuel 7:11b-17; 1 Chronicles 17:10b-15) promised to national ethnic Israel through King David's heir, who is Christ. The ruler is Christ through national ethnic Israel. The ruled will be all the inhabitants of the earth. The resurrected church will reign with Christ in this kingdom (Romans 8:17; 2 Timothy 2:12; Hebrews 10:12–13 (cf. Psalm 110:1–2); Revelation 5:10; 20:6).

However, there is a kingdom, which Christ is building right now, and which Paul proclaimed. Christ is building a kingdom during this current New Testament church age. That kingdom may be characterized as the Spiritual Kingdom, because composed of those persons Christ has made spiritually alive. It is opposed by a kingdom characterized as the Mystery Kingdom.

> The Spiritual Kingdom: the kingdom between Christ's ascension and the rapture, composed only of believers, entered by the new birth. This is the New Testament church that is the body of Christ.
>
> The Mystery Kingdom: the kingdom between Christ's ascension and the rapture, composed of the saved and people professing but not possessing saving faith. This is the church the world sees

The Spiritual Kingdom and Mystery kingdoms end with the rapture of the New Testament church to heaven. Those of the Mystery Kingdom who were professing but not possessing salvation continue into the Tribulation age. The Spiritual and Mystery kingdoms are explained by Christ in several parables, most notably in Matthew 13. See my book, *A Private Commentary on the Bible: Matthew's Gospel*.

All The Counsel of God

Believing he might not see them again, Paul gives them some parting counsel, 20:26–31.

Paul first declares they know all they need to know to manage the church and themselves. He begins by saying, "I am clean of the blood of all." By this he means he had been faithful to the charge the Lord Jesus had given him as an apostle. He had declared all the counsel of God to them. He had warned them of sin and given them the remedy through salvation from sin. After they had believed he had warned them of judgment to come. The nature of the judgment facing every believer we find in 1 Corinthians 3:11–15; 2 Corinthians 5:10. Surely he had also taught the Ephesians concerning the Judgment Seat of Christ.

As elders of the church, they were responsible to "shepherd the church of God." First they were to "attend to yourselves" and then attend to "all the flock among which the Holy Spirit has set you as overseers." They were to "attend to yourselves" because an empty cup has nothing to give. They needed to be full of the Spirit and the Scripture. They needed to be living habitually righteous lives. Those under their care needed not just to hear knowledge but to see the example of understanding applied. As John said, 1 John 2:6, "The person claiming to abide in Christ is obligated, even as Christ lived his life, also himself to behave in the same manner."

As they attended to themselves, they would naturally attend to "all the flock among which the Holy Spirit has set you as overseers." One of the natural consequences of living a godly life is to help others live a godly life: by proclaiming the good news of salvation; by teaching the Scripture; by presenting an example of godly living. Some definitions and discussion follow.

> Godliness. God living and active in humanity, humanity acting and living according to God's values. [Quiggle, *Dictionary.*]

Godliness may be described as thought, will, and action that conforms the believer's manner of life to the moral, holy, and righteous standard set by God's own character. In simpler terms, to be Christ-like. God takes delight in those whose character and actions reflect his character and actions. God's character defines the worth of the actions performed by all beings: they are godly or ungodly.

Godliness is not naturally generated by the believing soul, but depends on the work of the Holy Spirit through the grace he gives to all believers to live a godly life pleasing to God. While it is true a life of faith is the product of God's grace, it is also true that a lot of personal effort must be expended in order to live a godly and righteous life. There is a cost to living a life of faith: denying the temptations of sin in the mind and flesh; alienation from the world and worldly practices; separation from sinning and sinners engaged in sin; caution in one's relationships with sinners.

As elders some were teachers, some were pastors, some ruled. Teaching is "the Spirit-given ability to understand and explain doctrine in a practical way to show others its sense and relevance (meaning and significance; interpretation and application)." [Quiggle, *Spiritual Gifts.*]

> Teacher. The believer who has an irrepressible motivation to instruct others in the things which the divine will has revealed to him or her (John Owen).

Scriptures associated with this gift are: 1 Corinthians 12:7–11; 2 Chronicles 1:7–12; Colossians 2:2–3; 2 Corinthians 11:6; Daniel 2:20–21; Proverbs 2:6; Proverbs 9:10; Psalms 119:66; Jeremiah 3:15;

Ephesians 4:11–16; Romans 12:6–8; 1 Corinthians 12:28–31; Hebrews 5:12–14; Acts 18:24–28.

To "shepherd the church of God" is to be a pastor [Quiggle, *Spiritual Gifts*].

> Pastor. The Spirit-given ability to lead, discipline, provide watch-care for, and spiritually feed believers gathered together in a New Testament church. To assume a long-term personal responsibility for leadership and the spiritual care, protection, guidance, and feeding (teaching) of a group of believers. The divine enablement to nurture, care for, and guide people toward on-going spiritual maturity and becoming like Christ.

Because the position of pastor/shepherd is of great importance to the local church. An extended explanation of the gift is required.

A pastor is Christ's representative to the Lord's congregation. Christ loves his congregation by loving each individual person. The pastor is to have the same attitude of love and exercise the same care for Christ's people which characterized Christ. A pastor is a man who leads the congregation of the Lord as the faithful servant who pays attention to, cares for, feeds, defends, and disciplines his Master's people to promote their physical and spiritual well-being.

A pastor is one spiritually gifted believer among a congregation of spiritually gifted believers. The pastor's spiritual gift is to be a steward managing Christ's household. The pastor-as-steward is to use his Master's goods to ensure everyone is spiritually fed, clothed with righteous works, active in the congregation, able to protect themselves against spiritual evil, and growing and prospering in the Lord, to the end that everyone in the church can use his or her spiritual gifts to accomplish all the necessary work of his Master's household and business, in the church and in the world.

Christian leadership is not supposed to imitate the world. The pastor is an equal among equals. In the local church he is the servant of Christ, and practices ministry as a shared duty and privilege. His greater honor does not come from being the leader, but from the burden of a greater responsibility.

The skills associated with this gift are:

A pastor is to be a steward managing Christ's household.

A pastor will experience joy over the growth, development, and ministry of even one Christian in the church he leads, knowing that the good of the individual tends to the good of all.

A pastor is part of the church he leads. He leads the church to serve their common Lord and Savior. His professional training is used to mentor some and guide others into effective ministry. He shepherds individual Christians for the good of the whole flock.

A pastor recognizes each Christian in the church he leads is important. He helps the individual Christian discover, develop, and use his or her spiritual gifts in harmony with other Christians in the church.

A pastor mentors, trains, spiritually feeds, and disciplines the Christian under his care for that person's individual good, taking responsibility to nurture the whole person in their walk with God.

A pastor provides guidance and oversight to the local church he leads. He oversees the functioning of the church as a living organism and as a living organization.

A Pastor leads church members to work together to accomplish the ministries of the church.

A pastor models with his life what it means to be a fully devoted follower of Jesus.

A pastor establishes trust and confidence through long-term relationships.

A pastor leads and protects those within his span of care.

A pastor loves and cares for the lovable and the sinning, irregular, or un-lovable believers under his spiritual watch-care.

Scriptures associated with this gift are: John 10:1–16; Acts 20:28; Ephesians 4:11–15; 1 Timothy 3:1–7; 2 Timothy 4:1–2; 1 Timothy 4:11–16; 1 Peter 5:1–4.

To be an "overseer" in the church of God is to be a leader. The word translated "overseer" is *epískopos* [Zodhiates, s. v. 1985]. The Greeks used this word of "magistrates sent to outlying cities to organize and govern them." Paul adapted this word for the leaders of the New Testament church.

The Spiritual gift of leadership-ruling [Quiggle, *Spiritual Gifts.*]

Leadership-Ruling. The Spirit-given ability to set goals in accordance with God's purpose, clearly communicate these goals to others, and serve others in such a way that they voluntarily and harmoniously work together to accomplish these goals for the glory of God. The divine enablement to cast vision, motivate, and direct people to harmoniously accomplish the purposes of God. To serve others in such a way that they are led by you to accomplish their goals.

The skills associated with this gift are:

Mentor, train, spiritually feed, and discipline the Christian for his or her individual good.

Lead Christians to work together to accomplish the ministries of the church.

Provide direction for God's people or ministry.

Motivate others to perform to the best of their abilities.

Present the "big picture" for others to see.

Model the values of the ministry.

Take responsibility and establish goals.

Scriptures associated with this gift are: Romans 12:6–8; Hebrews 13:7; Hebrews 13:17.

In today's world, the spiritual gifts of shepherd and overseer are often assumed to exist in one person, the pastor of the local church, and he is made to perform both duties. The wise pastor and church understands this is seldom true or wise. The church functions best with a plurality of elders: some teach, some rule, some pastor. Some churches have adopted an "elder council," to manage their church.

Acquired Through His Own Blood

Paul makes a singular statement: "the church of God which he acquired through his own blood." God does not have blood. God is a self-existent, unique, spirit being. What Paul expresses here is the duality that exists in the person Jesus Christ.

Jesus Christ is a union of human being and deity. In a union each part retains its individual properties. In my garage, in my toolbox, I have a hammer. That hammer is a union of metal and wood: a steel head attached to a wood handle. In this union the steel does not take on properties of the wood; the wood does not take on properties of the metal. A union is the joining of dissimilar things to create a new thing. Metal and wood are dissimilar things, that when joined together in a union create something new: a hammer.

Jesus Christ, the God-man, is a union, not a unity. Jesus Christ, the God-man, is composed of dissimilar things: human nature (body and soul) and deity nature (one essence).

> The human nature, Luke 1:31, "Look now, you [Mariam] will conceive in your womb, and will bear a son, and you will call his name 'Jesus.'" The human nature began in Mariam's womb.

> The deity nature, Colossians 2:9, "For in him [Jesus Christ] dwells all the fullness of the deity in bodily form." The deity nature has no beginning. Exodus 3:14, "I exist because I exist." John 5:26, "For as the Father has life-in-himself, so also to the Son he gave life to have in himself." John 8:58, "before Abraham came into existence, I existed."

At that moment when the human being came into existence, i.e., at the exact moment Jesus of Nazareth was conceived in Mariam's womb, Luke 1:31, 38, at that moment the self-existent God the Son joined in union with the newly conceived Jesus of Nazareth. God the Son joined in permanent union with the newly conceived, just-come-into-existence, genuine human body and genuine human soul of Jesus of Nazareth.

That act of deity joining with humanity was a union of dissimilar things: deity in union with humanity. That particular union of those two dissimilar things is known as the incarnation. Just as metal and wood are brought into union to form a hammer, even so the deity and humanity were brought together into union by the omnipotent power of God to form the God-man, who is the Christ of God. The same as any other union, each part retained its own properties: the deity did not take on properties of the humanity, the humanity did not take on properties of the deity.

That union of deity with humanity, the incarnation that formed the God-man, Jesus the Christ, has certain characteristics peculiar to that one and only union. The person who is the God-man is simultaneously, at-the-same-time, eternal and finite; knows everything (omniscient) and learns things (Luke 2:52); is omnipotent and is limited in power; is everywhere at once in time and space (omnipresent) and is confined to one place at any one moment in time; has life in himself and was mortal and died. He is the eternal God who created the universe and he is a finite limited creature living in the universe he created.

How then did God purchase the church with his own blood? Because the Scripture treats the God-man as a whole person with two natures: the human nature had blood; the deity nature purchased the church; God with his own blood who purchased the church. Therefore it is scriptural to speak of his mortality and his eternity in the same breath; in the same scripture.

Translation Acts 20:29–31

29 "I know that after I leave, fierce wolves will come in among you, not sparing the flock. 30 And out from your own selves men will rise up speaking perverse things, to draw away disciples after them. 31 Therefore be mindful, remembering that three years, night and day, I did not cease with tears warning each one.

EXPOSITION

Apostasy And Heresy

Paul warns of two kinds of dangers to the New Testament church. The first are from the outside. Those attacking the New Testament church from the outside are apostates.

> Apostate. An unsaved person who has mentally subscribed to the doctrines of the Christian faith and who then rejects those doctrines while still remaining within the visible church and posing as a Christian (Wuest). Apostates remain within the visible church teaching false doctrine with the goal of converting others to their false doctrines. Apostates are great pretenders, mixing a little truth with substantial error.

I defined an apostate as "remaining within the visible church" but Paul seems to imply they are outside the church. They are outside the true church, but because they pose as believers they must remain within the visible church to prey on the members of the true church. I am speaking of the Mystery form of the New Testament church. They pretend to be Christians and draw both professors and possessors of genuine faith away from the true church. They also deceive those looking for the true church. The true church is within the visible church. Apostates usually attract those professing but not possessing salvation, for example, the many today attending "prosperity gospel" churches.

Those who are Christ's, whether being drawn to salvation or already saved, may be drawn away by apostasy, but the Holy Spirit will not allow his sheep to remain outside the true church for long.

Here are the characteristics of apostates.

> "There is an objective, well-understood, and previously believed standard of truth from which the apostates depart. The departure is willful. The very word implies it and the actions and life of apostates show it (particularly 1 Timothy 4). Thus, apostasy involves both the mind and the will" (C. C. Ryrie).

> Apostates start out looking like believers. They use the correct language, recite Scripture, may even preach and teach in the church, and are careful to be seen to perform good works. On the outside they resemble the true wheat of the believer, but they are really darnel, false wheat (Matthew 13:24–30), working to separate the believer from his faith.

> An apostate was never saved, despite any seemingly outward evidences. This does not mean an apostate cannot be saved. Unbelief, not sin, disqualifies a person from salvation. Should an apostate reject his false doctrines and believe the testimony of Scripture concerning the risen Jesus Christ as Savior, then he or she will be saved. Only salvation reveals who has been called to salvation, therefore, continue to witness to an apostate.

Paul also speaks of those out from your own selves who attack the church. These are heretics.

> Heretic. A person using heresy to establish a sect or religion in competition with Christianity, within or without the professing church.

> Heresy. A deliberate denial of truth as revealed in the Scripture, development of an alternative belief, and teaching that alternative belief as though it was Scripture.

Heretics do "draw away disciples after them." Some heretics become apostates, some do not.

Apostates are easy to identify and defend against. They deny one or more of the essential doctrines of the New Testament church. Heretics are less easy to identify. They deftly mix true with false. The doctrinal errors are more subtle. Satan is neither apostate nor heretic, but his temptation of Christ provides examples of both apostasy and heresy.

> Example of apostasy, Matthew 4:9, "And Satan says to Jesus, 'These things, to you I will give all, if falling down you will worship me.'"

The apostasy is easily detected. An essential doctrine is violated. The believer is to worship God alone.

> Example of heresy, Matthew 4:5–6, Then the devil takes him to the holy city and sets him upon the highest point of the temple, 6 and says to him, "If you are God's son, throw yourself down. For it has been written: 'To his messengers he will give command concerning you,' and 'In their hands they will bear you so at no time may you strike your foot against a stone.'"

The error is more difficult to detect. There is no particular essential doctrine at stake, but there is a principle of one's relationship with God in danger. Satan quotes Psalm 91:11–12, but he leaves out part of that scripture.

> Psalm 91:11–12 (ESV), For he will command his angels concerning you to guard you in all your ways. On their hands they will bear you up, lest you strike your foot against a stone.

Do you see what Satan left out? He left out this part, "to guard you in all your ways." What is the way of the Christian? Jesus gave the answer, Matthew 4:7, "You will not put to the test the Lord your God." Genuine faith does not put God to the test.

The way to guard against apostasy and heresy is to know and understand the Scripture. The elders of a local New Testament church have the responsibility to "attend to yourselves and to all the flock" in ways that teach the flock to protect itself. But each believer is also responsible to learn the Scripture not only through what is taught by the elders, but to also read and study and learn through his or her own reading and studies.

Three Years

Acts Twenty

Here Paul says he was in Ephesus three years. In Acts 19 Luke gives two time markers for Paul's stay in Ephesus.

> Acts 19:8, Now entering into the synagogue, he was boldly speaking, for three months reasoning and persuading about the kingdom of God.
>
> Acts 19:9–10, But when some were hardened and were unbelieving, speaking evil of the Way before the many, he left them, separating the disciples, daily publicly teaching in the lecture hall of Tyrannus. 10 This then continued for two years, so that all those living in Asia heard the Word of the Lord, both Jews and Greeks.

Luks says Paul spent two years and three months, or twenty-seven months, in Ephesus. Here in 20:31 Paul says three years, or thirty-six months in Ephesus. What has happened? Times and dates are always rounded up or rounded down in Scripture.

The ancient world did not have the means to determine the "down-to-the-second" accuracy the modern world expects. For example, Luke says Mariam stayed with Elizabeth for "about three months," Luke 1:56. If, as I believe, Mariam arrived at Elizabeth's house in December, after Hanukkah, and returned to Jerusalem with Zecharias at Passover, that is about three months, but not exactly ninety days. Luke says when Jesus began his public ministry he was "about thirty years of age," Luke 3:23. Luke does not mean Jesus was exactly thirty years of age, and there are good reasons for believing Jesus was at his baptism about thirty-five years of age (See my commentary on Luke's Gospel, volume 1.)

There is another reason dates and times were approximate. Just about everyone in the ancient world counted months and years using the lunar cycle, usually new moon to new moon. But a new moon itself (a new moon is when the moon is not visible in its monthly cycle) may be a calculated value, depending on weather and visibility. A lunar calendar year is about 354 days, versus a sidereal (solar) year of about 365 days. The difference in any particular year is about eleven days, but over three years it is about twenty-nine days.

For those reasons, a lunar calendar "floats" against a solar calendar, and every few years the lunar calendar must be adjusted, by about a month, to keep calendars and harvests and yearly feasts on the same schedule as the orbit of the earth around the sun. What that means is both Paul and Luke were estimating the time Paul was in Ephesus.

Another issue is years were determined by rulers. I and others use AD 54–58 to date Paul's third missionary journey. But to everyone in the Roman empire the years were determined by who was Emperor, Claudius or Nero, see Acts 11:28; 18:2. By our reckoning Claudius reigned AD 41–54, Nero AD 54–68. Claudius was Emperor when Paul began his third missionary journey and Nero was Emperor when Paul came to Ephesus. Perhaps Paul was counting from Claudius to Nero.

Paul may have used the recurring Jewish feasts to estimate his time in Ephesus. For example, if he arrived in Ephesus close to one of the feasts, and then estimated his time in Ephesus by remembering that feast and others, he may have estimated his time from the feasts.

In Paul's memory he spent *about* three years in Ephesus. Luke's investigation determined Paul spent *about* two years and three months in Ephesus. Paul is remembering his experiences and rounding up. Luke has gathered information from Paul and other sources who knew Paul in Ephesians and has rounded down. We must also consider Luke's three months and two years probably does not include the time leading up to the riot by the Artemis idol artisans, and the time after the riot before Paul left Ephesus. The exact duration of Paul's time in Ephesus is somewhere in the middle between Luke's documented twenty-seven months and Paul's estimated thirty-six months.

Translation Acts 20:32–35

32 "And now, I entrust you to God and to the word of his grace, able to build and to give you an inheritance among all those having been sanctified. 33 I did not wrongfully desire any person's silver or gold or clothing. 34 You yourselves know that my needs and those with me, these hands served. 35 In all things I plainly taught you that by thus laboring it is necessary to help those who are weak, and also to remember the words of the Lord Jesus, how he himself said, 'It is more blessed to give than to receive.'"

EXPOSITION

Their Relationship With God

Paul tells the Ephesian elders, "I entrust you to God and to the word of his grace." They were always entrusted to God and his grace, because a believer belongs to Christ, not to the evangelist or pastor or teacher or anyone else. Paul means his time of responsibility for the church at Ephesus has come to an end. Of course he has not abandoned them, we see that in his letter to them. But as a parent with a child, so here also, the child has matured and it is time for the parent to step away.

He reminds them that God's grace is the foundation of their life of faith. God is the one who builds up the believer by his grace. But he has required our cooperation. To know the Scripture we must read it. To understand the Scripture we must study it. To apply the Scripture we must live it out in our everyday life. To be in fellowship with God we must fully cooperate in submission to and dependence upon God Father-Son-Spirit.

The believer has "an inheritance among all those having been sanctified." The inheritance is Christ himself, the relationship and fellowship the believer has with God in Christ. The believer is an heir with Christ in the kingdom Christ inherits from the Father. The believer, having been placed by the Father in the status "adult son," Ephesians 1:5, has an inheritance from God and is God's inheritance, Ephesians 1:11 (see my commentary on Ephesians for an exegesis of this verse).

When Paul says "an inheritance among all those having been sanctified" he is not marking out a special group among believers. All believers are sanctified once and for all in Christ, Hebrews 10:14, "For by one offering he has completed continually those being sanctified." Paul says "sanctified" to remind the Ephesians that by salvation they have been separated from the world and dedicated to God.

Paul Warns Against Materialism

Paul uses his own behavior as an example against the inordinate desire for material possessions.

> Example one: Paul was content with all that God provided. "I did not wrongfully desire any person's silver or gold or clothing."
>
> Example two: Paul worked to provide for his needs and the needs of those ministering with him. "You yourselves know that my needs and those with me, these hands served."

Example three: Paul gave of his own substance to help those needing help. "In all things I plainly taught you that by thus laboring it is necessary to help those who are weak."

Example four: Paul exemplified love toward others. "Remember the words of the Lord Jesus, how he himself said, 'It is more blessed to give than to receive.'"

Those who place their heart's desire into having more will perish with their possessions. The Christian is to take care for himself and care for others. There may be times when the Christian is or becomes one of those whom others must care for, but in the normal course of his or her life, the Christian is to take care of himself and care for others.

Where did Paul come up with this saying of Jesus? Some supposed Paul developed this saying from one of the known sayings of Jesus in the four gospels (Luke 6:38 has been suggested). The fact is, this is a previously unknown saying of Jesus, which is to say, not found in the gospel accounts. As John 20:30 says, not everything Jesus said or did is in the four gospels. There are two previously unknown sayings of Jesus in the New Testament, here and Hebrews 13:5.

Translation Acts 20:36-38

36 And having said these things, bowing his knees, with all of them he prayed. 37 Then there was much weeping among all. And falling upon Paul's neck they were kissing him, 38 especially distressed over the word that he had spoken, that no more are they about to see his face. Then they accompanied him to the ship.

EXPOSITION

Prayers are made, farewells are said, love expressed in much weeping, hugging, and kissing. The kissing was the traditional touch of lips on the cheek. They believed what Paul has said, that they would not see him again. That seems impossible in the modern world, but in Paul's world seeing required a personal visit. They walked with Paul to the ship, he sailed away, and they walked home.

Acts Twenty-one

Translation Acts 21:1–3

1 Then after, it happened our sailing, drawing away from them, sailing a direct course, we came to Cos, and the next day to Rhodes, and from there to Patara. 2 And finding a ship passing over to Phoenicia, going on board, we set sail. 3 Then, sighting Cypress, and leaving it on the left, we kept sailing to Syria and landed at Tyre; for there the ship unloaded its merchandise.

EXPOSITION

Please consult one of the maps above for the location of these cities. The port of Patara was the last port of call for the ship on which Paul and his companions were passengers. How many days passed before finding a ship on the way to Phoenicia Luke does not say. There were twenty-eight days to Pentecost when Paul sailed from Miletus. Three more days had passed sailing to Patara. Let us say a day to book passage on another ship, leaving the next day. There are now twenty-three days to Pentecost.

Luke does not say the time to sail from Patara to Tyre in Phoenicia. They did not make port in Cypress, thereby saving a day or two. The distance by ship from Patara to Tyre is about 400 miles. A wind-driven ship, a sailing ship, has an average speed of six to eight miles per hour. The ship Paul was on was a cargo ship, probably heavily laden with fruits, vegetables, and grains. Sailing a distance of 400 miles at six miles per hour takes sixty-six hours; at eight miles per hour about fifty hours. When Paul landed at Tyre there were about twenty days to Pentecost. At Tyre the ship "unloaded its merchandise," and probably loaded new merchandise. That gave Paul and his companions a few days wait in Tyre.

Translation Acts 21:4–6

4 Then seeking out the disciples, we stayed there seven days. They kept on saying to Paul through the Spirit not to go up to Jerusalem. 5 Then after we had completed the days, leaving, we traveled. All joined us, with wives and children, as far as outside the city. And on the shore bending the knees, we prayed, 6 and said farewell to one another. Then we went into the ship, and they returned to their own.

EXPOSITION

The ship was in Tyre for seven days. Unloading the old cargo and taking on new cargo also required selling and delivering and buying and receiving. Doing business takes time. Paul and those with him made good use of the time by visiting with the local church in Tyre.

When Paul arrived at Tyre there were twenty days to Pentecost. When he left there were thirteen days to Pentecost. Paul might have spent those seven days walking to Caesarea, which is about nine days walking distance (280 miles at 3 miles/hour). By water it is about 2 days sailing distance (280 miles at 6 miles/hour). Paul and his companions knew these things, and wisely spent those seven days in Tyre, and then two days by ship to Caesarea.

While visiting with the local church, certain disciples kept on telling Paul "through the Spirit not to go up to Jerusalem." But we know Paul was going up to Jerusalem "bound in the Spirit," Acts 20:22. Those disciples had learned from the Holy Spirit what Paul knew, that "bonds and tribulations" awaited Paul in Jerusalem. Their response was to tell Paul not to go.

The entire local church turned out to bid Paul farewell. Before they boarded the ship, everyone prayed. There are now thirteen days to Pentecost.

Translation Acts 21:7–9

7 Then the voyage from Tyre being completed, we came down to Ptolemais, and greeting the brethren, we stayed with them one day. 8 Then we left on the next day and came to Caesarea, and entered the house of Philip the evangelist, he of the seven, and stayed with him. 9 Now this man had four daughters, virgins, prophesying.

EXPOSITION

The ship stopped at Ptolemais; twelve days to Pentecost. While the ship was docked at Ptolemais they visited the local church. The ship continued the next day to Caesarea, which was the last stop for Paul and those with him. Eleven days to Pentecost. The distance from Caesarea to Jerusalem is about 55 miles, or about a day and one-half walking distance.

They stayed with Philip the evangelist for "many days," Acts 21:10.

This is the Philip who had been one of the seven, Acts 6:5; had evangelized Samaria, Acts 8:5, and the Ethiopian eunuch, Acts 8:35. He had four unmarried daughters (in those times virgin = unmarried), who prophesied. Whether that means teaching or foretelling the future Luke does not say; perhaps both. If they taught the Scripture, which seems the most likely meaning, it was because they had been well-taught by their father. Philip and his family had an impact on their community and in their local church.

Translation Acts 21:10–12

10 Then continuing there many days, a certain one came down from Judea, a prophet named Agabus. 11 And having come, he took Paul's belt, bound his feet and hands, and said, "Thus says the Holy Spirit, 'The man whose belt this is, in this way the Jews in Jerusalem will bind and will deliver him into the hands of the gentiles.'" 12 Then when we heard those things, both we and those in that place exhorted him not to go up to Jerusalem.

EXPOSITION

When Paul and the others came to Philip's house, there were eleven days to Pentecost, and a day and one-half walk to Jerusalem. They might have stayed with Philip for seven or eight days, thereby arriving in Jerusalem a day or two before the Day of Pentecost. (Oddly enough, Luke never mentions Pentecost after 20:16.)

Paul again receives a warning about what awaits him in Jerusalem. Many commentators have interpreted this warning as the Holy Spirit telling Paul not to go to Jerusalem. But that is not what the Holy Spirit told Agabus. The prophet says nothing by the Holy Spirit that the Holy Spirit had not already told Paul, which he had told the Ephesian elders, Acts 20:22–23.

> And now, look, I go bound in the Spirit to Jerusalem, not knowing what will happen to me there, 23 except that the Holy Spirit in every city repeatedly testifies to me, saying that bonds and tribulations await me.

Why, then, does the Holy Spirit continue to warn Paul of those things he had previously told Paul? Not for Paul's sake, but for the sake of those with Paul. They should have joined with Paul in his resolution to go to Jerusalem, and his preparedness to meet with whatever awaited him. But instead they "exhorted him not to go up to Jerusalem." Trying to persuade Paul not to obey the Holy Spirit reminds me of this conversation between Jesus and Peter.

> Matthew 16:21–23, From that time Jesus began to show to his disciples that it is necessary for him to go away to Jerusalem, and to suffer many things from the elders and chief priests and scribes, and to be killed, and on the third day to be raised. 22 And having taken him aside, Peter began to rebuke him, saying, "Far be it from you, master; no, this will never be to you." 23 But having turned he said to Peter, "Get behind me, Satan! You are an offense to me, because your thoughts are not of the things of God, but the things of men."

The esteem and affection Paul's friends had for Paul mistakenly led them to try and persuade Paul not to do the things of God but the things of men.

A believer should always look for counsel from others whom he trusts in the faith. However, when convinced in his own mind the Holy Spirit has convicted and committed him to a certain course of action, then the believer must stay the course, despite friendly and well-meaning persuasion from others to do the opposite.

Again I am reminded of an example, this time from the history of the New Testament church.

> If, then, I am not convinced by proof from Holy Scripture, or by cogent reasons, if I am not satisfied by the very text I have cited, and if my judgment is not in this way brought into subjection to God's word, I neither can nor will retract anything; for it cannot be right for a Christian to speak against his conscience. Here I stand; I cannot do otherwise. God help me. Amen.

Martin Luther at the Diet of Worms. Paul also knew he could not do otherwise."

Translation Acts 21:13–16

13 Then Paul responded. "What are you doing, weeping and breaking my heart?" For I am ready not only to be bound, but also to die at Jerusalem, for the name of the Lord Jesus. 14 Then, not having persuaded him, we were silent, saying, "The Lord's will be done." 15

Now after these days, we packed the baggage and began our way to Jerusalem. 16 Then also disciples from Caesarea came with us, bringing one with whom we would lodge, Mnason of Cyprus, a disciple from the beginning.

EXPOSITION

Paul speaks his mind and convictions. Not being able to dissuade him, they delivered him to the Lord's will, where he had always been. When their visit was completed, they packed their bags and left for Jerusalem. Some from Caesarea came with them, including "Mnason of Cyprus, a disciple from the beginning." He may have been a friend of Philip from their early Jerusalem days. Regardless, he was a resident of Jerusalem and offered the guest room in his home for Paul and his eight companions (Acts 20:4).

One of the more remarkable things about Paul's voyage and his times in local churches along the way is some of his companions were gentiles. Yet, none of the Hebrews in the local churches or the homes they all stayed in as guests thought anything of it. The local churches outside of Jerusalem had fully adjusted to gentiles and Hebrews living and working and worshiping together.

Only the Jerusalem church had remained divided. Why? "You see, brother, how many thousands there are among the Jews who have believed, and all are zealous for the Law," Acts 21:20. The days of the Jerusalem church were numbered with the days remaining to the nation and city. And rightly so.

The New Testament church cannot allow racial and ethnic divisions. Christ saves sinners out of every nation, tribe, people, and language. The New Testament church is a one family under one Father, one Savior, and One Spirit, erasing worldly distinctions and divisions.

There were about twelve years remaining until Jerusalem and the Jerusalem church were destroyed by the Romans. So all churches and organizations naming Christ, but dividing the body of Christ, will not find success but troubles and destruction.

Translation Acts 21:17–20a

17 Now arriving at Jerusalem, the brethren gladly received us. 18 Then on the next day, Paul went with us to Jacob, and all the elders

were present. 19 And after greeting them, he told one by each the things God had done among the gentiles through his ministry. 20 Then those hearing glorified God.

EXPOSITION

Of those with Paul, only Mnason and Paul were known to the Jerusalem church. The others were Hebrews and gentiles from gentile lands. The "brethren" are most likely those who were Christian friends of Mnason. The next day Luke and others, including Paul, went to see Pastor Jacob, the leader of the Jerusalem church, and the church elders. I notice Luke is quite exact, saying "Paul went with us to Jacob," not "we went with Paul to Jacob." Paul respected no man's person, see Galatians 2:6–9.

What Paul's intent was in going first to Jerusalem and then to Rome is not stated in Acts, but in the letter to the Corinthians. Certainly when Paul was in Ephesus, and later Macedonia and Corinth, he was better positioned geographically to go to Rome. Paul's letter to the Romans was written from Corinth in AD 58, and it certainly seems he was then prepared to follow the letter with a visit to Rome. But in Acts 19:21, while he was still in Ephesus, Paul had laid out his plans: first to Macedonia, then Achaia, then Jerusalem and then to Rome.

> Now after these things had taken place, Paul purposed by the Spirit to pass through Macedonia and Achaia, then go to Jerusalem, saying, "After having been there, it is necessary for me to also see Rome."

Why was Paul going to Jerusalem before going to Rome? Paul had asked the local churches to take up a collection for the Jerusalem church.

> 1 Corinthians 16:1–4, Now concerning the collection which is for the saints. As I have appointed the churches of Galatia, so also you are to do. 2 Every first of the seven *days*, each of you put beside him, storing up what if you may be successful[aa] *in the collection*, so that not when I may come then there should be collections. 3 Now when I might arrive, whoever if you might approve, these I will send with letters to carry your benevolence to Jerusalem. 4 Now if it is suitable for I also to go, they will go with me.

2 Corinthians 9:1–2, For truly concerning the ministry that *is* for the saints, it is superfluous for me to write to you. 2 For I know your readiness, which about you I boast to the Macedonians, that Achaia has made ready from last year, and that your zeal has stimulated the many.

Paul's trip into Macedonia and Achaia was not only to visit the local churches, but to gather the collection for the Jerusalem saints.

Perhaps Paul also wanted to visit his sister and nephew (and other relatives?), Acts 23:16. However, it does not seem Paul went to Jerusalem to report to the church elders. But that is what happened.

Having agreed to go and see Jacob and the elders of the church, Paul then "told one by each the things God had done among the gentiles through his ministry." The idiom "one by each," means Paul gave an account of his work among the gentiles—what God had done among the gentiles through Paul—in a reasonable order, not leaving out any important events.

Those hearing gave God the glory for the salvation of gentiles. There were probably no gentiles in the Jerusalem church, except former proselytes to Judaism now saved by faith in Christ. But their appreciation of God's works among the gentiles was genuine. However, their attitude toward evangelizing pagan gentiles had not changed from the earliest days.

> Galatians 2:7, … they having seen I had been entrusted with the good news of the uncircumcision, just as Peter of the circumcision….
>
> Galatians 2:9, … Jacob and Cephas and John, those esteemed to be pillars, gave right hands to me and Barnabas, of fellowship, that we to the gentiles, but they to the circumcision.

That division, begun ca. AD 46 (Paul's first missionary journey), was probably ratified at the AD 50 Council of Jerusalem. That division was still in place in AD 58 when Paul came to Jerusalem on his way to Rome. No progress had been made in transitioning the Jerusalem church to evangelize pagan gentiles and include those saved gentiles as members equal to Jews in the Jerusalem church, as not under the Law.

Translation Acts 21:20b–22

Then they said to him, "You see, brother, how many thousands there are among the Jews who have believed, and all are zealous for the Law. 21 Now they have been told about you, that you teach all those Jews among the gentiles to depart from Moses, telling them not to circumcise the children, nor to live according to the customs. 22 What then to do? Assuredly they will hear that you have come.

EXPOSITION

In order to keep the peace, the church elders propose a compromise. Paul will show he is zealous for the Law. Now certainly Paul had respect for the Law. Paul's letters reveal he understood that the moral principles and values he taught the churches came from the Law. We should not be surprised at this. God's moral values originate in God's immutable character. The morality, righteousness, and holiness taught in the Old Testament is the same as taught in the New Testament.

Paul's argument against the Law was not against the Law itself, but the use Judaism had made of the law. Paul's view of the Law is clear.

> Romans 7:7, What then shall we say? The Law is sin? Never may it be!
>
> Romans 7:12, So that truly the Law is holy, and the commandment holy and righteous and good.

Paul's issue was that Judaism thought they could use the Law to gain the righteousness necessary to have a salvific relationship with God. Galatians 2:21, "I do not set aside the grace of God. For if righteousness is through the Law, then Christ died for no reason."

In what way the "many thousands there are among the Jews who have believed," were "all are zealous for the Law," is not explained, but is exampled here and in 21:23–25.

Here, we see those Jewish Christians zealous for the Law did not depart from Moses, did circumcise their children, and did keep the customs. The word "Moses" is used as a metonym (a substitution) for the entire Law. These Hebrew Christian were still Jewish in thought and practice. They were still sacrificing, still following dietary rules, still following the rituals and ceremonies of Moses, i.e., of the Law YHWH gave to Moses, still supporting the Levites and priests with their tithes.

They had compromised their Christianity with the Law.

What the Jerusalem church had done is known as religious syncretism: combining different religions to form one religion. Their ancestors had done the same, combining parts of the Law with worship of pagan gods. The Jerusalem Christians thought they were on safer ground by worshiping Christ through the sacrifices and offerings and rituals of the Law. Were they wrong?

> Matthew 9:16–17, no one puts a piece of unshrunk cloth on old clothing; for the patch tears away from the cloth, and a worse tear is made. 17 Nor do they pour new wine into old wineskins; but if it is, the wineskins burst and the wine is spilled and the wineskins ruined. But rather they pour new wine into new wineskins, and both are preserved."

Judaism and the Law were the old, Christianity was the new. As both Paul and the Writer of Hebrews said.

> 2 Corinthians 3:6, God, who also has made us sufficient as ministers of a new covenant, not of letter [the law] but of spirit. For the letter kills, but spirit gives life.
>
> Hebrews 8:13, In the saying, "New," he has rendered obsolete the first [the Law], that now growing old and aging, is near vanishing.
>
> Hebrews 9:15, And because of this, he [Jesus Christ] is mediator of a new covenant, so that death having come, for redemption of the transgressions under the first covenant [the Law], those having been called might receive the promise of the eternal inheritance.
>
> Hebrews 10:8–9, Previously saying, "Sacrifice, and offering, and whole burnt offerings, and for sin you did not desire, nor have pleased you, which are offered according to the Law," 9 then he said, "Look, I have come to do your will," he removes the first [the Law] that the second he may establish.

Paul was asked by Christian brethren to compromise for the sake of peace. The believer should never compromise truth for peace. Jesus Christ did not allow Paul to follow through with the vow. Paul's agreement to seek peace by following the Law was the means by which the word from the Holy Spirit came to pass, that "bonds and tribulations" awaited Paul in Jerusalem. The Holy Spirit did not make it happen, Paul's choices caused the prophecy to come true, even as the Holy Spirit knew would come to pass.

The Lord is able to bring good things out of bad choices, and those "bonds and tribulations" were the means by which Paul received an all-expenses paid trip to Rome from the Roman government. There was more than one way to get Paul to Rome, but the Holy Spirit works with and through the believer's freely made choices to accomplish his means and ends. Be wise in your choices.

Translation Acts 21:23–25

23 "This therefore you do what we say to you. There are with us four men having on themselves a vow. 24 Take these men, be purified with them, and bear expense for them, so that they will shave their head, and all will know that of which they have been told about you is nothing: you follow the rule keeping the Law. 25 Now about those of the gentiles having believed, we wrote, giving our judgment, for them to 'avoid the things both sacrificed to idols, and blood, and what is strangled, and sexual immorality.'"

EXPOSITION

The vow is unspecified, but as I discussed in comments at 18:18–23, shaving the head was the conclusion of a Nazirite vow.

> The end of the Nazirite vow required the following offering to the Lord, on the altar in the temple in Jerusalem: one male lamb in its first year without blemish as a burnt offering, one ewe lamb in its first year without blemish as a sin offering, one ram without blemish as a peace offering, a basket of unleavened bread, cakes of fine flour mixed with oil, unleavened wafers anointed with oil, and their grain offering with their drink offerings (Numbers 6:14–15). In addition, the hair must be shaved off at the door of the temple, and put on the fire in the altar when the peace offering was being offered.

They were asking Paul to bear the expenses for the offerings at the conclusion of the vow. They were not asking Paul to participate directly, but indirectly, to create the impression he supported the Mosaic Law.

The point of doing all this was to show to all, "that of which they have been told about you is nothing: you follow the rule keeping the Law." What was it all had been told? "That you [Paul] teach all those Jews among the gentiles to depart from Moses, telling them not to circumcise the children, nor to live according to the customs."

The facts were, Paul did not tell the "Jews among the gentiles" to stop circumcising their children. Paul's message was "in Christ Jesus neither circumcision has any value, nor uncircumcision," Galatians 5:16. Keeping any part of the rituals and ceremonies of the Law had no value for the believer. Those things did not save, they did not give righteousness, they did not give the believer a completed salvation. The salvation of every believer is complete; there is no such thing as a partial salvation. Paul did tell the believing Jews among the believing gentiles, that those believing in Christ as Savior were free from the Law and its customs.

Jacob and the elders were asking Paul to set aside his convictions for the sake of peace.

To be fair to the Jerusalem elders, perhaps Paul had told them he had "shaved his head in Cenchrea," after leaving Corinth on his way to Ephesus, "for he had taken a vow." As I said in earlier comments, I do not believe that vow was a Nazirite vow. Nevertheless, Paul was willing to, "take these men, be purified with them, and bear expense for them, so that they will shave their head, and all will know that of which they have been told about you is nothing: you follow the rule keeping the Law."

Then they justify their proposal by reminding Paul Christianity treats believing gentiles one way, believing Jews another way. No, Christianity does not do that. The Jerusalem Council did address the relationship of believing gentiles with the Law. They had failed to address the relationship of believing Jews to the Law. For that we turn to Paul's letters and discover, Galatians 3:27–28, "For as many as were immersed into Christ have put on Christ. 28 There is not Jew nor Greek," compare Colossians 3:11.

Translation Acts 21:26

26 Then Paul took the men on the following day, having been purified with them, entering into the temple, announced fulfillment of

the days of the purification, until that offering was offered for each one of them.

EXPOSITION

The expression, "Paul ... having been purified with them" may mean the usual immersion into the *mikvah* (bath) prior to entering the temple proper. The meaning cannot be they or Paul shaved their heads, because that was done at the very end, and 21:27 says there were seven more days until that was to be done.

The meaning is not that Paul had taken the Nazarite vow, because Jewish Law seems to have said the minimum for that vow was thirty days, *m. Nazir*, 1.3, "A Nazirite vow that is vowed without a fixed duration is binding for thirty days." The intent seems to be sufficient time for hair to grow. Other passages in *m. Nazir* assume a minimum thirty days.

There is no particular rule I can find for seven days purification. Nor did I see a rule referenced in any of the commentaries I am using. Apparently, according to some custom of the times, those who had taken the vow went to the temple seven days in advance of the termination of the vow and announced their intent to end the vow in seven days. In all these things, Paul did not participate in the vow. His part was to pay for the materials for the offering.

Translation Acts 21:27–29

27 Now when the seven days were about to be completed, Jews from Asia, seeing Paul in the temple, excited all the crowd and laid hands upon him, 28 crying out, "Men, Israelites, help! This is the man who teaches all those everywhere against the people and the Law and this place. And he has brought Greeks into the temple and defiled this holy place." 29 For they had before seen Trophimus the Ephesian in the city with him, and whom they assumed Paul had brought into the temple.

EXPOSITION

The Holy Spirit did not allow Paul to participate in the vow. Why Paul was in the temple is unknown. Luke's phrase, "about to be completed," may mean it was day six of the seven. Or it may mean they ones with the vow were about to shave their heads at the door of the *naós*, the temple proper. Or they had shaved their heads and were on their way to the altar. I do not believe the Holy Spirit allowed Paul to reach day seven, but none of those possibilities may be dismissed.

Longnecker does not express an opinion. Neither does Peterson or Bruce. Alexander says [742] Paul's time was almost ended, which would mean before the seventh day. Conybeare and Howson [576], believe it was the seventh day, but Paul remained at the doors leading into the temple while those with the vow went to offer their sacrifices and burn their hair.

The word used for temple is *hierón*, which incorporated the courts as well as the temple proper (versus *naós*, the temple proper). Paul might have been anywhere within the temple "campus" where gentiles, even proselytes, were not allowed. (The fact the "doors were shut" was a panic response to ensure the *naós* could not be defiled.)

Jews from Asia (Ephesus?) who knew Paul on sight, saw him somewhere in the *hierón*. They attacked Paul and accused him of bringing gentiles into the *hierón*. They had not seen any gentiles with Paul in the *hierón*, but they knew he was in Jerusalem with gentiles, specifically Trophimus the Ephesian. They had previously seen Paul with Trophimus in Ephesus, then in Jerusalem.

The response was typical of the Jewish bigotry of the times. As I mentioned, not even gentile proselytes were accepted as full members of Israel. They were kept out of the temple *hierón* and *naós* except that part of the *hierón* that was the Court of the Gentiles. There was a short wall (4.5 feet high, Edersheim, *Temple*, 22) separating the Court of the Gentiles from the rest of the temple. Signs on the wall at regular intervals advised any gentile, whether proselyte, God-fearer, or a pagan, from entering any other part of the *hierón* or *naós* on pain of death.

The accusation was also typical, a distortion of Paul's message and teachings. Paul did not preach or teach against the people (Israel) or the Law. He taught the Law did not give righteousness and therefore could not save the people.

> Acts 13:38–29, Therefore be it known to you, men, brethren, that through this one, to you forgiveness of sins is proclaimed. 39 And from all things from which you were not able in the Law of Moses to be justified, in him everyone believing is justified.

As I discussed in volume 1, those persecuting Stephen understood that Christianity would replace the Law, even though many Christians had not yet come to that realization. So also here. If, as is the case, there is forgiveness of sins through faith in Christ, then there is no room for the sacrifices for sin required by the Law. The Law never could bring the righteousness necessary for heaven, because no one but Christ could keep the Law perfectly.

The result is this: even though Paul never spoke directly against the Jews or the Law, he did teach the Law had no salvific meaning for those having faith in Christ. The only Jews Paul spoke against were those Jewish Christians who insisted, "If you are not circumcised according to the custom of Moses you are not able to be saved," Acts 15:1. They were still active after the Jerusalem Council. Paul called them dogs, evil workers, and mutilators, Philippians 3:2. The good news is always distorted by those to whom it is absurd, 1 Corinthians 2:14, "But a natural person does not accept things of the Spirit of God, for they are absurd to him, and he is not able to know them, because they are discerned spiritually."

Translation Acts 21:30–32

30 Then the whole city was agitated, and the people ran together. And seizing Paul they dragged him outside the temple, and immediately the doors were shut. 31 Now as they were seeking to kill him, information came to the commander of the cohort, that all Jerusalem was in an uproar, 32 who immediately ran down upon them with soldiers and centurions. And seeing the commander and the soldiers, they stopped beating Paul.

EXPOSITION

The Holy Spirit had plans for Paul that did not include his immediate death. Jerusalem was more of Moses than of Christ, despite the "many thousands there are among the Jews who have believed." News that someone had violated the temple spread quickly throughout the city. Those who had physical contact with Paul were trying to beat him to death. News of a riot in progress was told the Romans. Now the Romans had ratified the rule that gentiles entering the temple were to be put to death. However, Roman law required a trial and confirmation of the violation, not a riot. The soldiers' job was to keep the peace, regardless of the cause by which the peace was disturbed.

The Temple was next door to the Fortress of Antonio where the Roman soldiers had their barracks and offices. They came in force, and were seen running down the stairs to the plaza. At once everyone stepped away from Paul. Riot control then was not like riot control today. Roman soldiers kept the peace by injuring or killing enough of those persons disturbing the peace until peace was restored. A few Jews beating another Jew was ignored. An agitated city participating in a beating, whether actively or as observers, could not be ignored.

Translation Acts 21:33-36

33 Then coming near, the commander took him, and commanded him to be bound with two chains, and began to ask who he might be and what it is he has been doing. 34 But others in the crowd were crying out one thing or another. Now, not being able to discern the facts through the uproar, he ordered him to be brought into the barracks. 35 Now when he came to the stairs, it happened he was carried by the soldiers, because of the violence of the crowd. 36 For the crowd of people were following, crying out, "Away with him!"

EXPOSITION

The Roman commander took physical charge of Paul, and had him bound with two chains; excessive, but it made the point. Then he tried to discover who Paul was and why he was being beaten. Verbal chaos ensued. The commander most reasonably ordered Paul be taken into the barracks, thereby removing the source of the disturbance and keeping Paul safe. Roman law required Paul be kept safe from those who wanted to harm them, without regard to his crime. A trial must be held to verify Paul was guilty.

But the crowd was not pleased Paul was being removed. He had, in their view, defiled the temple, and they wanted revenge, not justice. Some of the soldiers had to lift Paul up and carry him, while other soldiers bodily formed a barrier between the rioters and Paul. The Jews' hatred, their need for vengeance, had become so intense, that some cast away concerns for their safety, that they might kill Paul, even if they were also killed; religious zealotry knows no boundaries. Others continuously raised their voices against Paul. "The crowd of people were following, crying out, 'Away with him!'" Not "take him away," but "kill him."

What we are seeing is false religion at its worst. Genuine Christianity never calls for the death of those opposing Christ. Take a moment and consider the Epistle of Jude. He speaks of heretics and apostates, but his solution is not "kill them" to protect the church, but to preach the gospel and the truth. The truth saves and makes enemies friends, and the truth drives away those not saved. But religion! False religion kills its opponents.

Translation Acts 21:37–40

37 Then about to be brought into the barracks, Paul said to the commander, "Is it allowed to me to say something to you?" Then he was saying, "You know Greek? 38 Then you are not the Egyptian who stirred up sedition before these times and led four thousand men of the assassins out into the wilderness?" 39 Then Paul said, "I am truly a Jew, a man of Tarsus of Cilicia, a citizen of a not insignificant city. Now I implore you, allow me to speak to the people." 40 Then permitting him, Paul stood on the stairs and made a sign with the hand to the people. Then there was great silence, and he spoke to them in the Hebrew language, saying:

EXPOSITION

Paul finds an opportunity to take charge, and perhaps he can stop the violence before anyone gets hurt. He speaks to the commander in the common language spoken by all, the Koine dialect of the Greek language. The commander had assumed Paul was an Egyptian who had tried to arouse sedition. "No," says Paul, "I am a Jew, a citizen of Tarsus in Cilicia, a well-known and respected city. Please let me speak to these people." The commander agreed—Paul might be able to stop his fellow Jews from further disturbance of the peace. Paul stood on the stairs, the soldiers back away a little, he raised his hand, the universal sign to give attention and listen. There was a "great silence," i.e., everyone in the mob was silent. Paul spoke to them as a Jew to Jews, in their native language, Hebrew.

Acts Twenty-two

Translation Acts 22:1–5

1 "Men, brethren, and fathers, now hear my defense to you." 2 Then hearing that he was addressing them in the Hebrew language, they became more quiet. And he says, 3 "I am a man, a Jew, born in Tarsus of Cilicia, but educated in this city at the feet of Gamaliel, being instructed exactly according to the Law of our fathers, being zealous for God, even as all you are this day. 4 Who this Way persecuted as far as death, binding and betraying to prisons both men and women, 5 as also the high priest bears witness to me, and all the elders, from whom I received letters to the brethren. I was on my way to Damascus to bring also those there, being bound, to Jerusalem, in order they might be punished.

EXPOSITION

Paul's introduction was straightforward and requires little comment. He gains their attention by speaking Hebrew, which immediately identifies him as a Jew, like themselves. Most of those in the mob would not have known Paul, only that he had had been reported to have defiled the temple. His recent reputation as a member of the Way was known to some; older men in the audience may have remembered him as a persecutor of the Way.

His beginning was polite, respectful, and a usual way of starting a public speech. If there were women in the audience they would have been swept up by the mob, not deliberately joining with the mob.

Paul gives the particulars: he was a Jew, born in a gentile city, educated in Jerusalem by a well-respected and remembered teacher of the Law. Saying he was "instructed exactly according to the Law of our fathers" may have identified him as a former Pharisee, which he was, Philippians 3:5. That information also implies he was falsely accused of defiling the temple. He was, in fact, remembered for persecuting the Way in his zeal for the Law. Far from being one who would defile the temple, he was the one persecuting those who defiled the Law.

Paul introduces the event that changed his life. Some in the crowd, those who were of the Way (but zealous for the Law, Acts 21:20) knew the story.

Translation Acts 22:6–10

6 "But it happened to me as I traveled and drew near to Damascus, about noon, suddenly out of heaven flashed a great light around me. 7 Then I fell to the ground and heard a voice saying to me, 'Saul, Saul, why do you persecute me?' 8 They I answered, 'Who are you Lord?' Then he said to me, 'I am Jesus of Nazareth, whom you are persecuting.' 9 Now those with me saw the light. But they did not hear the voice of the one speaking to me. 10 Then I said, 'What shall I do, Lord?' Now the Lord said to me, 'Get up, go to Damascus, and there you will be told about all things that it has been appointed you to do.'

EXPOSITION

Paul varies the details of his meeting with Jesus the Christ in every re-telling. For example, in this retelling Paul's question in 22:10 is not in the original account at 9:3–5. These things should not concern us. If the book of Acts was a forgery, i.e., not the product of Luke and the Holy Spirit, the story would be exactly the same every time. Stories repeated by the person who experienced them tend to vary as details are remembered, or not. Divine inspiration means accuracy and authenticity and credibility in reporting events. Luke reports what Paul said.

At Acts 9:5 I translated *kúrios* as "sir," Then he said, "Who are you, Sir?" Translating *kúrios* as sir, master, or Lord, is context sensitive. The context here is not what Paul meant but what the audience understood. Paul is speaking Hebrew, Luke is translating the Hebrew to Greek. Paul might have said YHWH, God's personal name in the Old Testament. Paul might have said *'ādôn*, a Hebrew word equivalent to *kúrios*. The great light that flashed around Paul out of the heaven makes plain God appeared to Paul. Moreover, in 9:5 Paul did not know who was speaking to him. Here in 22:6 he knew who had spoken to him.

In the Acts 9 event, Paul asked "Who are you, Sir?" The answer was "I am Jesus." Paul knew which Jesus. But "Jesus" was the sixth most popular name among the Jews of the times [Bauckham, 85]. In the Acts 22 account Paul specifies which Jesus spoke to him: Jesus of Nazareth.

In the Acts 22 account, Paul adds the detail he asked Jesus, "What shall I do, Lord?" The answer is nearly the same

Acts 9. Get up and enter into the city, and it will be told to you what you must do.

Acts 22. Get up, go to Damascus, and there you will be told about all things that it has been appointed you to do.'

Paul adds a detail that must have come from his three days and nights sitting in the darkness of his blindness, and which Acts 9:16 hints at, "For I [Jesus] will show to him how much he must suffer for my name." Paul includes what he was shown by using the word "appointed." From the perspective of twenty plus years from his conversion, Paul can say the Lord told him "all things that it has been appointed you to do." Jesus did not give Paul a road map during those three days of blindness, but he did give him a mission. It is this mission that is the subject of Paul's defense in Acts 22.

Translation Acts 22:11-16

11 "Now while I could not see for the glory of that light, I being led by the hand by those who were with me, came to Damascus. 12 Then a certain Ananias, a devout man according to the Law, borne witness to by all Jews living there, 13 came to me and stood by me and said to me, 'Brother Saul, receive your sight.' And the same hour I saw him. 14 And he said, 'The God of our fathers has appointed you to know his will, and to see the righteous one, and to hear the voice out of his mouth. 15 Because you will be a witness for him to all men of what you have seen and heard. 16 And now why delay? Get up, be immersed and wash away your sins, calling on his name.'

EXPOSITION

Paul abbreviates what Ananias said to him to the essential message. Ananias actually said, "Brother Saul, the Lord has sent me, Jesus, the one having appeared to you on the road by which you were coming, that you may see again and be filled with the Holy Spirit." Then Paul adds something said by Ananias not reported in Acts 9, but is credible in view of what happened after Paul received his sight.

> Acts 9:18b–20, And getting up he was immersed; 19 and taking food, he was strengthened. Now he was with the disciples in Damascus certain days. 20 And immediately he began proclaiming Jesus in the synagogues, that he is the son of God.

Acts 22:14–16, The God of our fathers has appointed you to know his will, and to see the Righteous One, and to hear the voice out of his mouth, 15 because you will be a witness for him to all men of what you have seen and heard. 16 And now why delay? Get up, be immersed and wash away your sins, calling on his name.

What Ananias said is an important part of Paul's defense in Acts 22.

A comment. Being immersed did not wash away Paul's sins. "calling on his [Jesus'] name" is what washed away Paul's sins.

Translation Acts 22:17–21

17 "Then it happened to me, having returned to Jerusalem, and my praying in the temple, I fell into an ecstasy 18 and saw him saying to me, 'Make haste and go away quickly out of Jerusalem, because they will not receive your testimony about me.' 19 And I said, 'Lord, they know that I was imprisoning and beating in each of those synagogues those believing on you. 20 And when the blood of Stephen was poured out, your witness, I myself also was nearby and approving, and keeping the clothing of those killing him.' 21 And he said to me, 'Go, for I will send you far away to the gentiles.'"

EXPOSITION

Paul leaves out the events of the three years from his conversion in Damascus, his journey into Arabia, his return to and escape from Damascus, and visit to Jerusalem, Acts 9:21–25; Galatians 1:15–19. The event Paul now reports may have occurred at Acts 9:29–30.

Acts 9:29–30, And he was speaking and reasoning with the Hellenist Jews, but they were attempting to kill him. 30 But knowing this, the brethren brought him to Caesarea, and sent him away to Tarsus.

However, what Paul is describing at 22:17–21 most likely coordinates with the time between Acts 11:30; 12:25.

Acts 11:30; 12:25, Which also they [the elders of the local church at Antioch of Syria] did, sending [financial aid] to the elders [of the Jerusalem church] by the hand of Barnabas and Saul .... Then Barnabas and Saul returned, the mission to

Jerusalem completed, bringing with them John, the one called Mark.

Of the two choices, the vision in the temple seems to fit best when Paul and Silas took financial aid to Jerusalem. After returning to the local church in Antioch of Syria, Acts 13:1, Paul and Silas began their first missionary journey, 13:2 ff.

Looking now at 22:17–21. Apparently, the financial aid having been delivered, Paul had considered remaining in Jerusalem for a time to proclaim the good news. At some point he goes into the temple to pray, and Jesus tells him to leave Jerusalem because, "they will not receive your testimony about me." The "they" are the unconverted Jews in Jerusalem. Was Paul's response a defense to remain in Jerusalem, because they knew he had persecuted the Way, so would be more willing to accept his testimony of Jesus as Messiah-Redeemer? That is how I understand Paul's response. But Jesus tells him, "Go." Jesus tells him to go to the gentiles.

Did Paul know before this moment Jesus saved him to go to the gentiles? If we look closely at the account in Acts 9, Jesus told Ananias to go to Paul because "this man is my chosen vessel to carry my name before the gentiles and kings and the sons of Israel. For I will show to him how much he must suffer for my name" 9:15–16. But neither in the Acts 9 account, nor here the Acts 22 retelling, did Ananias tell Paul what Jesus had told Ananias.

> Acts 9:17, Then Ananias went, and he entered into the house, and laying hands upon him, he said, "Brother Saul, the Lord has sent me, Jesus, the one having appeared to you on the road by which you were coming, that you may see again and be filled with the Holy Spirit.
>
> Acts 22:13–16, Then a certain Ananias, a devout man according to the Law, borne witness to by all Jews living there, 13 came to me and stood by me and said to me, 'Brother Saul, receive your sight.' And the same hour I saw him. 14 And he said, 'The God of our fathers has appointed you to know his will, and to see the Righteous One, and to hear the voice out of his mouth, 15 because you will be a witness for him to all men of what you have seen and heard.

Nor do we see between Acts 9 and 13 any time when the Lord told

Paul he would be taking the good news to the gentiles. Paul's visit to Jerusalem during the events of Acts 12, and his vision in the temple during that time, may be the first time Jesus told Paul he would be taking the good news to the gentiles. Certainly we do not see Paul proclaiming the good news to gentiles prior to Acts 13:46 ff.

The word of the Lord in the temple vision, occurring ca. AD 44–45, is shown to still be true in AD 58. The Jews in Jerusalem, including the "many thousands there are among the Jews who have believed," 21:20, did not receive Paul's testimony concerning Jesus the Christ, because Jesus had sent Paul to the gentiles. As I commented earlier, the Lord did not allow this prejudice to stand, but removed his lampstand in Jerusalem, (cf. Revelation 1:20; 2:5).

Translation Acts 22:22–24

22 Now they were listening to him until this word. And they cried out with a loud voice, saying, "Away from the earth with such! For he is not fit to live!" 23 Then they were crying out, and throwing off their clothes, and throwing dust into the air. 24 The commander ordered him to be brought into the barracks, instructing him to be examined by flogging, so he might know why they were crying out against him.

EXPOSITION

The response of this Jewish crowd is irrational. For centuries the Jews had been making proselytes of gentiles. They had not been diligent about it, mostly waiting for a gentile to come to them in the synagogues, not actively pursuing evangelism of the gentile nations. The crowd had accepted Paul's message that the person who met him on the road to Damascus was Jesus of Nazareth, the Lord. But Paul had probably used the Hebrew word 'ādôn, not YHWH.

When Paul had said Ananias told him (22:14) he would be "a witness for him [the God of our fathers; the Righteous One] to all men," they had thought all Jewish men, not gentiles. Gentiles were dogs, unless converted to Judaism. Let us bear in mind that even the saved Jews in the crowd were "zealous for the Law," 21:20, not zealous for Jesus the Christ.

To the Jew of the times, saved or unsaved, the "Law" was not specifically the Law of Moses (although they named it that), but the Judaism their ancestors had made out of the Law. Judaism set legal, social, and moral barriers between Jews and gentiles, forbidding any kind of contact; the Law of Moses did not (the Law forbid participation in pagan religion).

Therefore, these Jews listening to Paul could not accept that the Lord, the God of our fathers, the Righteous One, had sent Paul far away from Jerusalem to the gentiles. They had been (falsely) told the consequence of Paul's misguided belief: Paul had been reported as having defiled the temple by bringing one of the hated gentiles into the temple. The very temple where even proselytes were forbidden.

Their response was sadly predictable: "And they cried out with a loud voice, saying, 'Away from the earth with such! For he is not fit to live!'" Imagine that, not fit to live for telling people the good news of salvation by faith in Jesus the Christ. Yet, that had been the Jewish response in every gentile city where there was a synagogue. That was the response in this Jewish city where it was reliably reported, "a great number of the priests were becoming obedient to the faith," Acts 6:7, and "you see, brother, how many thousands there are among the Jews who have believed," Acts 21:20.

"Throwing off their clothes, and throwing dust into the air" was a cultural means of expressing great anger or frustration. The actions were a means to add emphasis to their desire for Paul to be executed.

The Roman commander's response was conditioned by his obedience to his law, Roman law. First, he protected the accused by taking him to a place safe from the crowds: "the commander ordered Paul to be brought into the barracks." Then the commander set about investigating the accused: "instructing him to be examined by flogging." Keep in mind Paul had been speaking in Hebrew, which the Roman commander did not understand. He wanted to know "why they were crying out against Paul," so an examination was appropriate.

Use of torture during an investigation was a lawful and acceptable means of interrogation. Remember, someone arrested had been arrested because presumed guilty. Guilty persons had no rights—civil rights as we know them today (in some countries not others) did not exist before, during, and for centuries after first century Roman times. Only Roman citizens had legal rights bearing some similarity what we have today.

Translation Acts 22:25–29

25 But as he stretched him out with the thongs, Paul said to the centurion nearby, "Is it lawful for you to flog a man, a Roman, uncondemned?" 26 Then hearing this, the centurion went to the commander, reported it, saying, "What are you going to do? For this man is a Roman."

27 Then coming near, the commander said to him, "Tell me, are you a Roman?" And he said, "Yes." 28 Then the commander said, "With a great sum I bought this citizenship." But Paul said, "But I was so born." 29 Immediately those about to examine him left, and the commander also was afraid, knowing he is a Roman, and because he had bound him.

EXPOSITION

In comments at Acts 16:22–24, I discussed flogging and prison. From that discussion.

> Flogging was used in four circumstances: (1) as torture during questioning of a prisoner; (2) as punishment (the fustigatio and the flagellatio); (3) for execution (the verberatio); (4) as preparation for crucifixion (the verberatio).
>
> In ancient times, imprisonment was not used for punishment. A person was imprisoned to hold them until a trial was held. A person might be imprisoned during an investigation and released if there was insufficient evidence for a trial.

Paul was properly imprisoned, because he was at the least guilty of creating a public disturbance. Whether or not a Roman citizen could be flogged as part of an interrogation is debated among historians and Bible commentators. However, 22:29 answers that question, at least in AD 58. As a Roman citizen Paul might be imprisoned, even permitted house arrest (28:16), but not bound and not flogged.

How a person proved his Roman citizenship is also debated, with some saying a Roman citizen carried a *titulus*, or as we might say today "papers," proving his citizenship. However, the Roman Commander accepts Paul's testimony of Roman citizenship.

The commander was afraid, but Paul does not make an issue of his Roman citizenship, content to remain safe in the prison, unbound and not flogged. Paul needed the protection the commander could give him.

Translation Acts 22:30

30 Now the next day, wanting to know with certainty why he is accused by the Jews, he unbound him and commanded the chief priest and all the council to meet with him. And bringing Paul, he set him among them.

EXPOSITION

The commander proceeds with a bit of extra caution. He is not sure of Paul is guilty of anything, but under Roman law he must be certain before he can release him. Because his normal interrogation procedures are hindered by Paul's Roman citizenship, he holds what we might name a pre-trial hearing. He summons the Sanhedrin.

"All the council" may have been left to the discretion of the high priest, with a minimum number of council members, three to seven [*m. Sanhedrin*, 1.1–1.5]. However, the division Paul creates between council members suggests at the least the lesser Sanhedrim of twenty-three members [*m. Sanhedrin*, 1.6], possibly the full seventy-one.

The commander's intent was to question the Jews, but that is not what happened.

Acts Twenty-three

Translation Acts 23:1–5

1 Then Paul, looking intently at the council, said, "Men, brethren, I in all good conscience have lived as a good citizen of God up to this day." 2 Then the high priest, Ananias, told those nearby to hit him on his mouth. 3 Then Paul said to him, "God is about to hit you, whitewashed wall! And do you sit judging me according to the Law, and violate the Law, commanding me to be struck?" 4 Now those nearby said, "Do you reproach the high priest of God?" 5 The Paul said, I did not know, brethren, that he is high priest. For it is written, 'You shall not speak evil of the ruler of the people.'"

EXPOSITION

Paul focuses his attention on the council, his eyes scanning across the assembled faces. He has their attention. He makes his defense. He has not violated the Law but acted in ways pleasing to God.

That does not sit well with the high priest. The problem with this or any high priest is his authority over Jewish matters was usually unchallenged. However, Josephus [*Antiquities*, 20.9.2] describes Ananias as greedy and prone to violence. Commanding another to strike Paul violated the Law because Paul was neither accused nor convicted under the Law.

Paul's comment in 23:5 is not irony. Paul had not been in Jerusalem for years, so he may not have known who was high priest, and certainly did not know him by sight. In addition, this hearing was chaired by the Roman commander in his building, so the high priest was not in his usual place, and may not have worn his usual robes, as when head of the council in their own meeting place.

The scripture Paul quotes is Exodus 22:28 (ESV), "You shall not revile God, nor curse a ruler of your people."

Translation Acts 23:6–8

6 Then Paul, knowing that the one part is Sadducees but the other Pharisees, exclaimed to the council, "Men, brethren, I am the son of a Pharisee. I am judged concerning the hope and resurrection of the dead." 7 Then him saying this, a dispute began between the Pharisees and Sadducees, and the crowd was divided. 8 For truly Sadducees say

there is no resurrection, no messenger (no spirit). But Pharisees confess both.

EXPOSITION

Paul knows from the poor beginning he will not get a fair hearing. He appeals to the natural divisions among the council. The Sanhedrin was usually chaired by a Sadducee, and many of the council members were Sadducees. The two political and religious factions, Sadducees and Pharisees, had little respect for one another. Paul framed the issue as between an innocent Pharisee who kept the Law, and the secular Sadducees who had little respect for the Law, except when it suited their purposes.

Luke makes sure the reader understands the essential nature of the conflict: "truly Sadducees say there is no resurrection, no messenger (no spirit). But Pharisees confess both." The issue was no longer what Paul might have done, but the veracity of the Scripture on which Paul based his life and message. Fellow Pharisees, "brethren," felt compelled to defend a brother Pharisee.

Paul does not mention the resurrection of the dead as a trick to divide the council, although he is aware it will cause dissension in the ranks. We must look back to the first good news during the apostolic age: the Messiah must die and resurrect; Jesus of Nazareth crucified and resurrected is the Messiah; through faith in his name there is forgiveness of sins. The Sadducees denied the basics of the message.

The Jews from Asia who accused Paul of bringing a gentile into the temple, hated Paul because of that message. They hated Paul for proclaiming that message not only to Jews, but to gentiles. They hated Paul because of the success of that message among the gentiles. Their hatred took advantage of the circumstances, they imagined the worst of Paul, and started a riot with the intent to see Paul murdered.

Therefore, for Paul, "the hope and resurrection of the dead" in both the Old Testament revelation and the New Testament revelation was the essence of his good news message. He was and would continue to be judged (in the sense of condemned) by the Jews for proclaiming Jesus of Nazareth fulfilled "the hope and resurrection of the dead."

Translation Acts 23:9–10

9 Then began a great clamor, and some of the scribes rose up, of the party of the Pharisees, disputing earnestly, saying, "Nothing evil we find in this man. Now what if a spirit has spoken to him, or a messenger?" 10 Then a great dissension began. The commander, fearing lest Paul be torn to pieces by them, commanded the soldiers to go down and take him by force from their midst, then bring him into the barracks.

EXPOSITION

The Pharisees came from all walks of life. However, most tended to be successful businessmen, priests, Levites, or scribes. Scribes who were Pharisees stood up and defended not only Paul a brother Pharisee—they would have been appalled to think they were defending a Christian—but the Old Testament Scripture that spoke of resurrection and the spirit beings known as messengers (Hebrew: *mă'lāk*; Greek: *ággelos*). "What if a spirit has spoken to him, or a *ággelos*?" The Sadducees rejected anything supra-natural, but the Pharisees were now willing to accept Paul's testimony, Acts 22:6–10.

The place where the commander, Paul, and the Sanhedrin met was a very large conference room for public discussions (Luke and other friends of Paul would have been in the audience). Not, however, a conference room with a table and chairs in the middle. More like a tiny stadium with Paul on the field, the commander at one of the goal posts, and audience and Sanhedrin facing one another in seating on both sides of the field. A very small amphitheater with seating on both sides of the stage is also an appropriate image.

When dissension broke out among the members of the Sanhedrin, Paul was not out of reach. A few steps down from the seating onto the stage and they had him. Whether held by Pharisees defending or Sadducees attacking made little difference to Paul's safety. Once again, Roman law compelled the commander to see to Paul's safety. He "commanded the soldiers to go down and take him by force from their midst" and return him to the barracks' prison.

Translation Acts 23:11

11 Now the following night, the Lord stood near him, saying, "Have courage. For as you have repeatedly testified about me in Jerusalem, so it is necessary you also testify in Rome."

EXPOSITION

Paul was a normal person such as you or me. To be discouraged would be natural. To be apprehensive as to the outcome, death or freedom, would also be normal. Innocent men are sometimes executed, under any legal system; mob violence takes a life almost daily, somewhere in the world. If Paul came to be considered a troublemaker under Roman Law, he could be banished to some remote island prison (e.g. Patmos) or executed.

The "following night" might be the night immediately following the pre-trial hearing, or the night of the following day. In the night the Lord Jesus Christ made a personal appearance to Paul to encourage him. Paul must have been wondering if he would get to Rome, as he had planned. Jesus told him he would get to Rome.

If we pay attention we will see Jesus also told Paul how he would get to Rome. Jesus said, "as you have repeatedly testified about me in Jerusalem, so it is necessary you also testify in Rome." In what way had Paul repeatedly testified in Jerusalem? In conflict, against opposition, during a legal hearing, Acts 9:29; 15:12; 22:1–21.; 23:1–10. Paul's request, after a two year wait, to be heard by Caesar, 25:10–12, seems appropriate.

Translation Acts 23:12–15

12 Now when it was day, the Jews, having made a conspiracy, placed themselves under an oath, saying neither to eat nor to drink until that they might kill Paul. 13 Now there were more than forty having made this oath. 14 They came to the chief priests and elders, saying, "We have bound ourselves with an oath, to eat nothing, until that we should kill Paul. 15 Now therefore, you make known to the commander, along with the council, that he might bring him to you, to examine the things about him more accurately. We then, before he comes near, are ready to kill him."

EXPOSITION

Nothing good may be said about this. This is man-made religion, pure and undefiled: kill those who oppose your beliefs.

There were several death penalty crimes in the Law of Moses. Paul is not guilty of any. Bringing a gentile into the temple was not a death penalty crime under the Law of Moses—in Judaism, yes, but not under the law. At the most a Christian might be accused of slander against God—but at this time in the history of Christianity, believers were not proclaiming Jesus of Nazareth was God in the flesh, but that he was the Messiah-Redeemer.

Acts 2:22, Jesus of Nazareth, a man approved by God.

Acts 2:32, This Jesus [Acts 31] God has raised up.

Acts 4:10, Jesus Christ of Nazareth, whom you crucified, whom God raised out from the dead.

Acts 5:30, the God of our fathers raised up Jesus, whom you killed.

Acts 10:38, Jesus of Nazareth, how God appointed him with the Holy Spirit and with power.

Some Christians understood Jesus was God incarnate, but they were not making that fact a condition of salvation. They proclaimed he was Lord of all, e.g., Acts 10:36, but Lord in the sense of Messiah king and redeemer.

Contrary to the Law, "more than forty" men "made a conspiracy, placed themselves under an oath, saying neither to eat nor to drink until that they might kill Paul." The high priest and elders were co-conspirators, 23:14–15.

Why more than forty men? To overcome the Roman soldiers who protected Paul wherever he left the barracks. Their oath shows not only the urgency of the task, but their commitment to the task. They were prepared to give their lives to take Paul's life.

Translation Acts 23:16–19

16 But hearing of this ambush, Paul's nephew, his sister's son, came near and entered the barracks, telling Paul. 17 Then Paul called to himself one of the centurions, saying, "Take this young man to the commander, for he has something to report to him." 18 Therefore indeed, the one taking him brought him to the commander, and he said, "The prisoner Paul called to me, asking me to lead this young man to you." 19 Then holding his hand, the commander, withdrawing to a private place, asked, "What is it you have to report to me?"

EXPOSITION

Paul had a sister, and a nephew! The sister would have grown up in Tarsus with Paul, and probably married in Tarsus. Her husband must have moved to Jerusalem. The age of the nephew is of some interest. Paul died ca. AD 68, and in AD 62 told Philemon he was "Paul the aged," meaning he was over 60 years of age. Paul was saved ca. AD 36–38, so between 25–30 years of age when saved. The year in Acts 23 is ca. AD 58, meaning Paul is about 50 years of age. Paul's sister would be a younger sister, married when about 13–14 years of age. Paul's nephew, the "young man," is *neanískos* [Zodhiates, s. v. 3495], a man "in the prime of manhood up to the age of forty." This was no adolescent as portrayed in children's Sunday School lessons, but an adult. The word *neanískos* is used to describe Paul in Acts 7:58, when he was in his mid to late twenties.

The nephew told Paul about the ambush. Paul followed the chain of command and told one of the centurions. The centurion was cooperative because of Paul's Roman citizenship and took the nephew to his commander. The commander took Paul's nephew by the hand and led him to a private place. In that private place the commander questioned the young man. Everyone in the chain of events gave the young man respect and credibility because he was an adult not a boy.

Translation Acts 23:20–22

20 Then he said, "The Jews have agreed to ask you that tomorrow you might bring Paul into the council, as though something more accurately to ask about him. 21 You therefore should not be persuaded by them. For they lie in wait for him, more than forty men, who took an oath neither to eat nor to drink until that they have killed him. And now they are ready, waiting for your order." 22 Therefore then, the commander released the young man, instructing him, "Tell no one of this you made known to me."

EXPOSITION

In what manner did Paul's nephew come to know about the conspiracy? Certainly it would not have been advantageous for any to know he was Paul's nephew. In that time and place that information would not have been safe for others to know. Perhaps he himself did not know until told by his mother.

We see here something implied but never stated by Luke. Paul's sister knew he was in town. Paul visited her shortly after his arrival in the city (during the days he was purified with those of the vow), or he sent someone to let her know he was there, or after his arrest one of his friends had notified his sister at his request.

How did the nephew know of the conspiracy? He was among that group of young men, or had a friend who was part of that group. He had direct knowledge of the conspiracy to kill Paul. Though Luke does not say, the commander would have carefully questioned the man to validate the information. Having determined the information was genuine and accurate, the commander let the man go, cautioning him to "tell no one." To have told anyone would put the nephew in danger, and allowed the conspirators to change their plans.

Translation Acts 23:23-24

23 And calling a certain two of the centurions, he said, "Prepare two hundred soldiers, in order they might go as far as Caesarea, and seventy horsemen, and two hundred spearmen for the third hour of the night. 24 Provide horses for Paul to ride, that they may bring him safely to Felix the procurator."

EXPOSITION

A centurion normally was in charge of about 100 soldiers; two centurions commanded about 200 men. The commander had these two centurions gather 470 men. The Fortress of Antionio in Jerusalem is estimated to have been large enough to house a Roman legion, which in the first century AD was 5,200 infantry and 200 calvary.

The word used to describe the Roman commander (e.g., Acts 21:31) is *chiliarchos* [Zodhiates, s. v. 5506], technically a military commander who commands a thousand men. Silva [4:672] says *chiliarchos* "was used in Roman times of the *tribunus militum*, the commander of a cohort that consisted of about 600 men. The commander of the Jerusalem cohort greatly depleted his unit to protect Paul.

The infantry need not go all the way to Caesarea. The verb "they might go" is in the subjunctive mood, the mood of possibility-probability. The centurions had permission to take the 200 infantry and 200 spearmen (specialized infantry) as far as Caesarea if the centurions thought their presence was needed. The horsemen would go all the way with Paul, and probably only one of the centurions, the other taking the 400 infantry back to Jerusalem. The flexibility in Paul's protection means the commander had briefed his centurions on the reason for the mission.

Horses, plural, were to be provided for Paul, more than one in case a horse became lame on the journey. The third hour of the night was about 9:00 p.m. Roman infantry were conditioned to march 20 miles in a day. This does not seem far (thirty miles in a 12 hour day was possible), but Roman soldiers, like soldiers in any century, carried armor and supplies, and had to break camp at the beginning of the day, and set up camp at the end of the day. However, they could march further in a day as the need might require.

This may have been the first time in his life Paul rode a horse. Horses were the property of the military, kings, emperors, important Roman officials, and the very rich,

Translation Acts 23:25–30

25 He wrote a letter, having this form: 26 "Claudius Lysias, to the most excellent procurator Felix, greetings. 27 This man, having been seized by the Jews, and about to be killed by them, I came with soldiers and rescued him, having learned he is a Roman. 28 Determining then to know the crime of which they were accusing him, I took him to their council; 29 I discovered he was accused about questions of their Law, but no accusation worthy of death or of chains. 30 Then I was told of a conspiracy that would be against the man. I at once sent him to you, instructing also the accusers to speak these things against him before you."

EXPOSITION

We learn the name of the Roman commander. He is known only from the Book of Acts. He was a military tribune commanding about 600 men. His last name suggests he was of Greek origin. He was not born in a Roman city, as was Paul, because he bought his Roman citizenship.

Felix was a procurator, not a governor. Most versions translate Luke's *hēgemṓn* [Zodhiates, s. v. 2232], as "governor" versus the correct translation "procurator." Luke, being Greek, and writing in Greek, often used equivalent Greek words for specific Latin terms indicating Roman government positions. We know Luke does not mean "governor" because he names Quirinius *hēgemōn* of Syria, Luke 2:2, and Pilate *hēgemōn* of Judea. Quirinius was *legatos Aogusti*, "Lieutenant of Augustus" at the time Varus was governor of Syria. Pilate could not be the governor of Judea because Judea was under the authority of Flaccus, the governor of the Syrian province.

To settle the matter, The New Schaff-Herzog Encyclopedia of Religious knowledge, s. v. "Quirinius."

> Quirinius was a special *legatos Aogusti* to Syria, invested with the command of the army and entrusted with its foreign affairs, such as the relations between its several states and Rome, particularly where tension existed and military intervention might be necessary. Quirinius stood in exactly the same relation to Varus, the governor of Syria, as at a later time Vespasian did to Mucianus. Vespasian conducted the war in Palestine while Mucianus was governor of Syria; and Vespasian was *Legatus Augusti*, holding precisely the same title and technical rank as Mucianus.
>
> http://www.ccel.org/s/schaff/encyc/encyc09/htm/iv.vi.xii.htm

Antonius Felix was procurator of the Judean province AD 52–60. Josephus [*Antiquities*, 20.7] writes about him. The Roman title procurator meant "manager." The title was variously used of persons who managed public finances or Imperial provinces (an Imperial province was under military control, versus a Senatorial province which was not under military control).

The Roman commander gives an abbreviated account that makes him the hero of the incident, and what he says is true, although it seems he places learning Paul was a Roman citizen out of chronological order. The most important part of his letter is this bit, "I took him to their council; I discovered he was accused about questions of their Law, but no accusation worthy of death or of chains." This will prove true every time Paul is examined. Paul did not start the disturbance, he was its victim.

Claudius Lysias makes a report that ensures the procurator knows why he sent Paul, a Roman citizen, under guard: he did his duty as a soldier. If you have served in a military force (I have) you will understand the importance. Now, having referred Paul's case to his boss, procurator Felix, he has told Paul's accusers they will have to pursue their case in Caesarea.

The continued legal pursuit of Paul over the next two years gives the reader an understanding of Paul's importance to the early church. No apostle, no pastor, no elder in Jerusalem was in danger of the mob or the courts. Those days had passed when Saul the persecutor was saved by Jesus Christ. Since that time the Jerusalem church had made peace with the Jews, being also zealous for the Law. Only where Paul served Christ, in gentile lands, was there trouble from the Jews, and only from the gentiles when the Jews roused them to mob violence. That trouble followed him to Jerusalem, and beyond. By the time of Paul's death in AD 68, the Jews had begun to make trouble for gentile converts with Rome, and eventually Rome picked up the gauntlet and persecuted the Christians as traitors to the Roman state, for over 200 years, until Constantine's Edict of Tolerance in AD 313.

Translation Acts 23:31–35

31 Therefore the soldiers indeed did as ordered, taking Paul and bringing him by night to Antipatris. 32 Then on the next day, after committing the horsemen go with him, they returned to the barracks. 33 Those entered into Caesarea, and delivering the letter to the procurator, also presented Paul to him. 34 Then having read it, and asking from what province he is, and learning that he is from Cilicia, 35 said, "I will fully hear you, when also your accusers may arrive." He commanded him to be guarded in the praetorium of Herod.

EXPOSITION

The road from Jerusalem to Caesarea went north, then northwest, passing through Lydda, then to Antipatris, then another thirty miles north and west to Caesarea. Antipatris was the half-way point from Jerusalem to Caesarea. The military group accompanying Paul left about 9:00 p.m. Luke says they brought "him by night to Antipatris," a distance of about thirty miles, so arriving sometime before sunrise. The "on the next day" may mean the next day after arriving at Antipatris, but having marched all night, thirty miles, they would have made camp and rested for a day. If the unit of 470 soldiers left Jerusalem Monday at 9:00 p.m., and arrived at Antipatris before sunrise Tuesday, then they left Antipatris Wednesday morning. One centurion and the 200 infantry returned the thirty miles to Jerusalem on Wednesday. The other centurion, the seventy calvary, and Paul continued the thirty miles to Caesarea on Wednesday, arriving late Wednesday afternoon or early evening, calvary being able to make better time on the road than infantry.

The centurion delivered Paul and the letter to procurator Felix. Felix asked Paul "from what province he is" and learning Paul was from Cilicia, he accepted custody. Now Felix was procurator over the Judean province. So why did he accept custody of a prisoner from the far away province of Cilicia? Longnecker [537] has a reasonable answer.

> Had Paul been from one of the client kingdoms in Syria or Asia [western Turkey], Felix would probably have wanted to consult the ruler of the kingdom. But on learning Paul was from the Roman province of Cilicia, he felt competent as a provincial governor to hear the case himself.

Felix took custody of Paul and "commanded him to be guarded in the praetorium of Herod." Paul was not put in a prison cell, but under what we might name house arrest within what had been Herod's palace in Caesarea, but now housed the Roman provincial procurator. Here Paul waited until his accusers might come to Caesarea for another pre-trial hearing.

Acts Twenty-four

Translation Acts 24:1–2a

1 Then, after five days, the high priest Ananias came down, with some elders and a certain advocate Tertullus, who made to the governor their accusations against Paul. 2 Then being called, Tertullus began to accuse him, saying,

EXPOSITION

In v. 1 Luke summarizes. In v. 2 Luke begins with the details. The word translated "advocate" is *rhḗtōr* [Zodhiates. s. v. 4489], a speaker, orator, advocate. The context calls for a legal advocate, a lawyer. Luke says after five days the accusers came to Caesarea, the high priest and some elders, with the advocate. The sixty miles from Jerusalem to Caesarea was probably a two and a half-day walk, meeting with the procurator the following day. For the high priest, pursuing Paul to death was worth a five day walk: there and back again.

Translation Acts 24:2b–6a

"Much peace we have on account of you, and reforms are happening to this nation through your prudence. 3 In every way and everywhere we embrace these things, most noble Felix, with all gratitude. 4 However, in order not to delay you any longer, I beg your courtesy to hear us in a few words. 5 For we have discovered this man to be a pestilence, and exciting sedition among all the Jews in the world, and a leader of the sect of the Nazarenes, 6a who also tried to profane the temple, and whom we seized. [Verses 24:6b-8a see Translation Note.]

TRANSLATION NOTE

The passage identified as 24:6b–8a is in doubt, being found only in the Western family of manuscripts, and from there into the Textus Receptus [Metzger, *Textual*, 434]. Of the modern versions only the HCSB includes it, but in brackets to indicate it is in doubt. The passage makes sense with or without 24:6b–8a. The passage in doubt is, "6b and according to our Law wished to judge. 7 but Lysias the commander coming up with great violence took him away out of our hands, 8a commanding his accusers to come to you."

What seems likely is some scribe thought some background information was needed for the reader. However, one doubts Tertullus would have accused a soldier under Felix of interfering with a unlawful assembly. Bringing it up was a distraction from the focus of their case against Paul. Tertullus would have assumed the Roman commander had written a letter to Felix presenting the event differently than what is in 24:6b–8a. Considering all these things, I chose not to include the passage in the translation.

EXPOSITION

Tertullus begins with the usual and expected flattery. The Jews were in fact not happy with Roman reforms. The first Jewish revolt began eight years later, in AD 66. Tertullus makes the issue with Paul seem minor and quickly resolved. Paul's crimes are stated in four accusations.

> We have discovered this man to be a pestilence
>
> We have discovered this man to be exciting sedition among all the Jews in the world
>
> We have discovered this man to be a leader of the sect of the Nazarenes
>
> We discovered this man trying to profane the temple

As we will see, Paul confesses to the third accusation, disputes the fourth, and denies the first two for lack of evidence.

Of the four accusations, Felix would have interest in the sedition charge. Everything else was of no value under Roman law. However, Felix knew the sedition charge was untrue. This was the same charge the Jews of Thessalonica tried against Paul, "all these things are opposed to the decrees of Caesar, saying Jesus to be another king," Acts 17:7. The accusation had not worked there either. Felix knew if Paul had been "exciting sedition" he would have already been arrested, tried, and executed. Felix also had "an accurate knowledge of the things concerning the Way," 24:22.

Tertullus the lawyer was not unlike lawyers of any and every time: make as many accusations as circumstances allowed, hoping to convict on at least one.

Translation Acts 24:8b–9

8b "From him you will be able yourself, having examined him about all these things, to know what we accuse him." 9 Then the Jews agreed together, affirming these things were so.

EXPOSITION

Tertullus sums up: examine Paul yourself. There wasn't much more he could say, having no proof to substantiate any of the accusations. Felix would have noticed they did not bring any witnesses. Their true goal was for Felix to release Paul into their custody. To that end, the high priest and elders agreed Paul was guilty as charged.

Once they had Paul in their custody, the Jews had the right under a long-standing agreement with the provincial procurators they could put to death any person profaning the temple (hence the warning on the low wall between the temple and the Court of the Gentiles). But under that agreement, they should also have accused Trophimus the gentile, whom those Jews from Asia had assumed Paul had brought into the temple, Acts 21:29.

Any investigation into the incident in the temple would reveal the charge was false, and the Jews knew this. They gambled that Felix would "take their word for it," being too busy and uninterested to trouble with Jewish matters.

Translation Acts 24:10–16

10 Then Paul answered when the governor made a sign to him to speak. "Knowing that for many years you have been a judge to this nation, I cheerfully make a defense to the things concerning myself. 11 You are able to know that not more than twelve days have passed from when I went up to worship in Jerusalem. 12 And neither in the temple did they find me discussing anything with anyone, or making a disturbance of a crowd, nor in the synagogues, nor in the city.

13 "Nor are they able to prove to you any of the things of which they now accuse me. 14 But I confess this to you, that according to the way they call a sect, so I serve the God of our fathers, believing all things throughout the Law and that have been written in the prophets, 15 having in God a hope which they themselves also await, there is about to be a resurrection of both just and unjust. 16 In this also I myself strive to have a conscience without offence toward God and men, through all things.

EXPOSITION

Felix did not bother to question Paul. Felix, like the Roman commander before him, had already decided "Paul was accused about questions of their Law, but no accusation worthy of death or of chains." He allowed Paul to defend himself, already knowing the outcome.

Paul also begins with a polite address to Felix, as social custom required. Paul denies any charges of causing trouble. He says, I was worshiping, I was not "discussing anything with anyone, or making a disturbance of a crowd, nor in the synagogues, nor in the city."

Paul denies charge of sedition: "Nor are they able to prove to you any of the things of which they now accuse me." He was not worried Felix might give the charge any credence. He denies the charge of being a leader of the sect Nazarenes, although he confesses he is a member. But he denies "the way they call a sect" is against Jewish or Roman Law. Paul "serves the God of our fathers" by "believing all things throughout the Law and that have been written in the prophets."

Then Paul claims the sect of the Nazarenes has the exact same hope in the Law and the prophets as do all Jews, "there is about to be a resurrection of both just and unjust." Paul is not addressing Christian eschatology. All Jews expected the Messiah to appear at any moment, and the resurrection of the just and unjust (Daniel 12:2) to take place.

There is some irony, and a not-so-friendly poke, at the high priest, who was a Sadducee; and probably the elders with him; Sadducees denied the resurrection, Acts 23:6–10. The high priest wasn't going to repeat the mistake at the trial with the Roman commander.

Paul brings his defense to a close: I am just a Jew worshiping YHWH, not unlike my accusers. "I myself strive to have a conscience without offence toward God and men, through all things."

Translation Acts 24:17–21

17 "Now after many years, I came to bring alms and offerings to my country, 18 in which they found me purified in the temple, not with a crowd, nor in tumult. But some Jews from Asia, 19 who ought to appear before you and make accusation, if they may have anything against me. 20 Otherwise, let these themselves say they found any unrighteousness when I stood before the council, 21 than about this one statement which I cried out standing among them, 'concerning the

resurrection of the dead I am judged this day by you.'"

EXPOSITION

Paul comes to the crux of the accusation of profaning the temple. Where are my accusers? Roman law required the accusers to appear in court. Paul was aware that under these circumstances, Felix could dismiss all charges and set Paul free.

He confronts the accusers present: when I stood before the council, Acts 21, did you find any unrighteousness in me? Of course, they did not, but they do not respond to Paul's question. The high priest and those with him would disagree 'concerning the resurrection of the dead I am judged this day by you," was the key issue at that first pre-trial hearing. But they make no protest; at least, Luke does not record a further word from the Jews at this meeting.

The case the Jews have against Paul is lost. But Felix does not dismiss the charges. In 24:26 we discover why: Felix desires to gain favor with the Jews.

Translation Acts 24:22–23

22 But Felix, having an accurate knowledge of the things concerning the Way, put them off, saying, "When Lysias the commander may come, I will examine the things respecting you." 23 Then he commanded the centurion to keep him, to have liberty, and not to forbid his own to minister to him.

EXPOSITION

Felix has heard of the Way, aka Christianity, and had investigated the activities of the followers of the Way. He already knew none of the accusations was true. But he keeps Paul in custody, and politely dismisses the Jews. Of course, Lysias the commander is not going to come and speak to Felix about Paul. He had said all he needed to say in his letter; the Jews would expect Lysias had written a letter, but they did not know the contents. The Jews did understand the case would be idle unless or until Felix decided to reopen it. So they and Paul are left to wait.

A centurion is assigned to "keep" Paul, allowing him to roam about freely in Herod's Praetorium, if not also in Caesarea. Of course, the centurion assigned soldiers from his unit, on a rotating basis, to be with

Paul, ostensibly to keep him from escaping. Paul's friends were to be allowed to "minister to him," a way of saying bring him food and whatever else he might need. Paul was not in prison, but he was also a prisoner, not a guest, of the Roman government. In those times, relatives and friends took care for the needs of those imprisoned. Let Paul and his friends bear the expenses.

Translation Acts 24:24–27

24 Then after some days, he came with Drusilla, his wife, who was Jewish. And he sent for Paul and heard him concerning the faith in Jesus Christ. 25 Then he conversed about righteousness and self-control and the coming judgment. Becoming frightened, Felix responded, "For the present moment go away. Then when I have a suitable time I will call for you." 26 Also at the same time he was hoping that Paul would give him something useful. Therefore, also, often, sending for Paul, he conversed with him. 27 But after two years were completed Felix received his successor Porcius Festus. Then desiring to gain favor with the Jews, Felix left Paul bound.

EXPOSITION

After a while, "some days," Felix "came with Drusilla, his wife" who was a Jew. Provincial procurators split their time between Caesarea and other important cities, notably Jerusalem. For example, like Pilate, Felix was probably in Jerusalem during the major feasts. At one of those times when he was in residence in Caesarea, he sent for Paul. Paul told him the good news message: the messiah must die and resurrect; Jesus who died and resurrected is the messiah; by faith in him all sins are forgiven.

Then Felix and Paul spoke about "righteousness and self-control and the coming judgment." In more modern words, they spoke of sin and the penalty for sin. But Felix, although frightened concerning judgment against sin, was too attached to the things of this world. The third soil of Christ's parable is in view.

The truth was more than Felix could bear, but he kept on speaking with Paul from time to time. Never again did Paul speak so much about the gospel, although I feel certain Paul continued to repeat the good news in one way or another. Felix also thought "that Paul would give him something useful," i.e., that Paul would buy his freedom with money. But Paul was safe, the Christian church seldom has that kind of money, and if I and others are right, Paul was working with Luke on the Gospel According to Luke during those two years.

When after two years, a new provincial procurator was appointed, one Porcius Festus, Felix left Paul bound, desiring to gain favor with the Jews. The Jews must have decided if Paul was being kept in Caesarea, then he was not causing trouble with the Jews. And, if he was a prisoner of the Romans, they might still have opportunity to kill him.

Acts Twenty-five

Translation Acts 25:1–5

1 Therefore Festus arrived in the province. After three days he went up to Jerusalem from Caesarea. 2 Then the chief priests and the leaders of the Jews made their accusations against Paul. And they were urging him, 3 begging a favor against him, that he may send for him to Jerusalem, forming an ambush to kill him on the way. 4 Then indeed Festus responded, "Paul is to be kept in Caesarea." But he himself is ready to quickly leave. 5 "Therefore those among you," he said, "in authority, go down also. If there is anything wrong in the man, let them accuse him."

EXPOSITION

Felix has left, Festus has arrived. After taking up residence in Caesarea, and sorting out things there, he travels to Jerusalem, a place of frequent residence for the procurator of Judea. We must assume that Felix, or one of the ever-present bureaucrats in every government, had briefed Festus concerning Paul, including the Roman commander's letter, and the minutes of the pre-trial hearing. We should not think records were not kept and meetings not stenographically recorded. The Romans did not rule an Empire, so large that in modern times consists of forty nations, by being administratively sloppy or lazy.

About two years have passed since the high priest and the elders pressed their case against Paul before Felix. Nothing has changed. The plot to ambush and kill Paul is still active—probably with the same actors. We may assume Festus knows the letter from the Roman commander: "Paul is to be kept in Caesarea." He has a legal obligation to protect a Roman citizen.

Festus also knows he could set Paul free. But Acts 25:9, "desiring to lay a favor on the Jews," Festus does not free Paul. Political favors are the language of politics. So Festus continues to play the game begun by Felix. The Jews can come to Caesarea and make their accusations.

Translation Acts 25:6–7

6 Now having spent with them not more than eight or ten days, he returned to Caesarea. On the next day, sitting on the judgment seat,

he commanded Paul to be brought. 7 Then when he was present, the Jews who came down from Jerusalem stood around him, bringing many and weighty charges, which they were not able to prove.

EXPOSITION

Luke estimates the time Festus was in Jerusalem. Bear in mind a round trip, Caesarea to Jerusalem and back, took about five days. That plus the "eight or ten days" in Jerusalem, made about two weeks he was absent from his administrative headquarters in Caesarea. He would have naturally checked in with the military commander in Jerusalem, probably a new commander, but Claudius Lysis would have left written records. Porcius Festus had full knowledge of the circumstances concerning Paul.

Looking to v. 7, the Jews who would accuse Paul had traveled with Festus to Caesarea, or at the most had left Jerusalem for Caesarea the day after Festus left. The day after his arrival, Festus told the centurion to bring Paul to the audience room. The accusing Jews made their accusations, which were as fruitless, unprovable, unchanged, and absent eyewitnesses as the first time, two years earlier.

Translation Acts 25:8–9

8 Paul made his defense. "Neither against the Law of the Jews, nor against the temple, nor against Caesar, have I sinned in anything." 9 But Festus, desiring to lay a favor on the Jews, responding to Paul, saying, "Are you willing to go up to Jerusalem and there be judged before me concerning these things?"

EXPOSITION

Paul's defense is a statement of innocence. Nor does he need to say more. The Jews brought accusations, not witnesses of wrong doing. But Festus wanted to have the Jews "owe him one," for some unknown future contingency. So he attempted to change the venue from Caesarea to Jerusalem. Paul would still be judged by Festus, but the trial would be held in Jerusalem.

On the surface this is a reasonable request. The alleged crimes were committed in Jerusalem; the eyewitnesses lived in Jerusalem. But Paul knows the Jews have not wavered in their desire to kill him, and undoubtedly suspects another ambush had been planned. Festus trusts in his military to keep Paul safe. Even if he does not suspect the Jews will try to kill Paul on the way, he knows the outcome of a trial will set Paul free, as he has not broken any Roman Law. Regardless, desiring to lay a favor on the Jews, Festus asks Paul if he is willing to go to Jerusalem. The choice is Paul's not Festus', because a Roman citizen was to be tried in a Roman court, and then if appropriate turned over to local authorities.

Translation Acts 25:10–12

10 Then Paul said, "I am standing before the judgment seat of Caesar, where I ought to be judged. Toward the Jews I have done nothing wrong, as also you know very well. 11 Truly if I have done anything wrong and deserving of death I do not refuse to die. But if there is nothing of which they accuse me, no one can hand me over to them. I appeal to Caesar." 12 Then Festus, having spoken with the council, responded, "You have appealed to Caesar, to Caesar you will go."

EXPOSITION

Paul's answer is sensible, he knows his legal rights as a citizen. "I am standing before the judgment seat of Caesar, where I ought to be judged." Paul understands the political game, and refuses to play. He has done nothing wrong, nor are the Jews able to prove any wrongdoing, Festus knows these things. If guilty, Paul would willingly suffer the consequences. But he cannot be turned over to the Jews for punishment under baseless, unsubstantiated, and unproveable accusations.

Fearing he might be handed over to the Jews, Paul exercises an inalienable right. Any Roman citizen could ask to be tried in person by the Emperor. This was a fact that often prevented a miscarriage of justice, as was happening with Paul. Many hesitated to invoke the right, because there was no appeal from a decision by the Emperor.

Festus probably thought if Paul was going to demand a trial before the Emperor, he would have done so in the past two years. Paul's appeal to Caesar probably caught him off guard. Festus spoke with his legal counselors. Festus could have right then and there set Paul free. But the Holy Spirit more often than not chooses to work through others, and he is working through Festus to send Paul to Rome. Paul was within his legal rights, and it was a way to get rid of the case once for all. If the Jews were willing to pursue Paul for the past two years, and come twice to Caesarea to accuse Paul, then they also could go to Rome with their accusations. There were no consequences for Festus, Roman law allowed Paul to make that appeal. Festus would write a legal brief, Paul would go under guard to Rome. That would be the end of the matter for the provincial procurator. "You have appealed to Caesar, to Caesar you will go."

Translation Acts 25:13–16

13 Now some days having passed, Agrippa the king and Bernice came down to Caesarea, greeting Festus. 14 Now as they stayed there many days, Festus set before the king the things about Paul, saying, "There is a certain man left by Felix a prisoner, 15 concerning whom, my being in Jerusalem, the chief priests and the elders of the Jews made accusations, begging judgment against him, 16 to whom I responded is it not customary with Romans to hand over any person before that one accused may face his accusers, and may have the opportunity of defense concerning the accusation.

EXPOSITION

King Agrippa and Festus were not in the same chain of command, This was a social visit to greet the new procurator. Marcus Julius, Agrippa II, great grandson of Herod the Great, had grown up in Rome during the time Claudius was emperor. He was at the time of Acts 25:13 (AD 61) king of Trachonitis, formerly ruled by Herod Philip, son of Herod the Great, and then by Herod Agrippa I.

In the course of the visit, Festus mentioned Paul the prisoner. Naturally he defends keeping Paul a prisoner, conveniently not mentioning Paul had been a prisoner for two years, and had a previous hearing before his accusers.

Translation Acts 25:17–22

17 "Therefore, making no delay coming here, the next day sitting on the judgment seat, I commanded the man to be brought, 18 concerning whom the accusers, having stood, brought no charge of wrong doing, which I was expecting. 19 But they had against him certain questions concerning their own religion, and concerning a

certain Jesus, who having been dead, Paul was affirming to be alive. 20 Now being perplexed concerning this inquiry, I asked if he was willing to go to Jerusalem and there be judged concerning these things. 21 But Paul, calling himself to be kept for the Emperor's decision, I commanded him to be kept until that I might send him to Caesar." 22 Then Agrippa said to Festus, "I have also been desirous myself to hear the man." He says, "Tomorrow you will hear him."

EXPOSITION

What Festus doesn't mention, is he could have set Paul free on the lack of evidence. Because Festus rehearses to Agrippa things you and I have previously read as they happened, I will not make further comments.

Agrippa, who has no interest in the outcome of a trial, also wants to hear what Paul might have to say about "certain questions concerning their [the Jews] own religion, and concerning a certain Jesus, who having been dead, Paul was affirming to be alive." Festus responds, "Tomorrow you will hear him."

Translation Acts 25:23–27

23 Therefore on the next day, Agrippa and Bernice having arrived with much splendor, and entering into the audience room, with both military officers and men of prominence in the city, and Festus having given command, Paul was brought. 24 And Festus said, "King Agrippa, and all the people present with us, you see this one, concerning whom all the multitude of the Jews applied to me, in both Jerusalem and here, crying out that he ought not to live no more. 25 But I understood him to have done nothing worthy of his death. But he having appealed to the Emperor, I determined to send him. 26 Now concerning him, I have nothing definite to write to my Lord. Therefore I brought him before you all, and especially before you, King Agrippa, so that an examination having taken place, I might have something to write. 27 For it seems irrational to me sending a prisoner without also accusations to declare against him."

EXPOSITION

Festus takes advantage of the circumstances to let those in authority know he will be a fair and just administer of Jewish affairs—

he invited all the important people.

> The charge against Paul is summarized: the Jews want Paul executed.
>
> The reason Paul is alive is stated: he has done nothing worthy of death.
>
> A half-truth is told: I would have released him, but he appealed to Caesar.
>
> A reason is given for the gathering: I need to send a legal brief to Caesar, but have nothing to say, so maybe you all can help me examine him.

There is also a bit of honesty. "For it seems irrational to me sending a prisoner without also accusations to declare against him." Indeed, it had been irrational to keep Paul prisoner.

Acts Twenty-six

Translation Acts 26:1–3

1 The Agrippa said to Paul, "It is permitted you to speak for yourself." Then Paul, having stretched out the hand, began his defense. 2 "Concerning all which I am accused by Jews, King Agrippa, I count myself blessed before you, on this day about to defend myself, 3 you being especially knowing of all the customs of the Jews, and also disputes. Therefore I request you patiently hear me.

EXPOSITION

Festus said he brought out Paul to speak to all, but primarily to King Agrippa, Acts 25:26. Therefore it is the king, not Festus, who gives Paul permission to speak. Paul may not have known prior to being brought into the audience hall he was going to give yet another defense. But the wise believer is always preparing himself for opportunities to speak the good news. The principle of Matthew 10:19–20 is at work in Paul, "But when they deliver you, do not be anxious how or what you might say. For it will be given you in that hour what you should say; for you are not the ones speaking, but the Spirit of your Father is speaking through you."

Paul "stretches out the hand," his usual sign to gain the attention of his audience. He begins by acknowledging he is a prisoner accused by the Jews of certain crimes. Paul knows nothing can prevent him going to trial before Caesar. His defense will also be a testimony.

King Agrippa had been raised and educated in Rome—having the child of a client ruler as hostage was standard political policy in the Roman Empire. His father and grandfather had also been raised in Rome. However, he had been out of Rome and ruling for many years, and as a Herod knew his family history and the history of the Jews whom he ruled in the name of Rome. Like all Roman government administrators he was aware of the customs, religion, and conflicts of the people under his authority. Paul is confident King Agrippa was aware of the Hebrew scriptures.

Translation Acts 26:4–8

4 "Truly then the manner of my life from youth, from the first, was among my nation, also in Jerusalem, know all Jews, 5 knowing me from

the first, if they wish to testify, that according to the strictest sect of our religion, I lived as a Pharisee. 6 And now for the hope of the promise made by God to our fathers I stand, being judged, 7 for which our twelve tribes in earnestness, night and day serving, hope to attain. Concerning which hope I am accused by the Jews, O king. 8 Why is it considered unbelievable to you if God raises the dead?

EXPOSITION

Paul was born and raised in Tarsus of Cilicia among the Jewish community in that city. At an early age he was sent to Jerusalem, which became his permanent residence. He was discipled by one of the top educators of the day, Rabbi Gamaliel, Acts 22:3, in the Old Testament Scripture, as a Pharisee.

Paul knew the Old Testament scripture, and like others in that sect had memorized much of the Old Testament. He had been given an Old Testament understanding by Gamaliel. Then he had been given a New Testament understanding of the Old Testament Scripture by the Holy Spirit when he believed on Christ as Savior. Let us remember he spent time in Arabia, Galatians 1:17, working out a New Testament understanding of the Old Testament scriptures, being discipled by Christ, Galatians 1:11–12.

Although one might point to many promises YHWH made to national ethnic Israel, the context tells the reader the promise Paul had in mind was redemption from sin. "How can that be," you might ask, because Paul speaks of resurrection not sin. In Paul's understanding, resurrection summarized personal redemption from the penalty of sin. To enter Messiah's kingdom one must be resurrected, e.g., Daniel 12:2. To be resurrected one must be righteous. Resurrection out from the dead summarized the righteous life necessary to enter Messiah's kingdom. The good news Paul proclaimed was the Messiah had to die, and be resurrected, so that sinners could be forgiven the penalty due sin, and thereby attain the righteousness necessary to be resurrected and enter Messiah's kingdom.

Jesus had died, and he had not brought Messiah's Davidic kingdom with him. Therefore, in the Jewish view, Jesus could not have resurrected, nor could he be their Messiah. The Old Testament spoke of a Messiah-Redeemer from sin, e.g., Daniel 9:26. However, without the New Testament revelation that particular line of messianic prophecy was not easily accessible to the Old Testament sinner—the prophets focused more on national deliverance than individual redemption. For example, Isaiah 53 was not about a coming redeemer, but the future deliverance of the nation, 52:15; and the Hebrew word *māshîah* is not in Isaiah 53. But with the New Testament revelation? See Acts 8:32–38.

Without the New Testament revelation that Jesus died and resurrected to be the Redeemer, scriptures such as Daniel 9:26; Isaiah 53, Psalm 22, and others were not understandable of a coming Redeemer. Indeed, why would the Holy Spirit teach sinners to place faith in a not present, yet-to-come Redeemer, when the ever-present Redeemer, YHWH, was on the scene redeeming sinners from their sins, through the Old Testament revelation they had received of YHWH the Redeemer?

The Jews rejected Jesus Christ as their Messiah-Redeemer and Messiah-King. They rejected the reports of Jesus' resurrection out from the dead. For the Jews, the issue was a Messiah-King who would rescue the nation from gentile oppression, Genesis 49:10; 2 Samuel 7:13–16; Psalm 2, not a Messiah-Redeemer to rescue individuals from the penalty due sin. The Messiah-King could not die and be king, therefore a dead Jesus could not be the Messiah.

From the Jewish point of view, they must continue to obey the Law of Moses until the King appeared. If the King was also a redeemer from sin, then he would redeem as high priest through the Law of Moses, because that was where YHWH had placed redemption from sin. Therefore they rejected a dead Jesus and his resurrection.

Paul says this hope of resurrection into Messiah's kingdom, for which "our twelve tribes in earnestness, night and day serving, hope to attain," is the "hope I am accused by the Jews, O king." Paul had said that hope was fulfilled in Jesus of Nazareth. The Jews said no, and accused Paul of heresy and blasphemy. The "defiling the temple" accusation was simple a means to an end: to get Paul into their hands so they might execute him for heresy and blasphemy.

Because Messiah's kingdom had not been realized in Jesus of Nazareth, the Jews refused to believe Jesus of Nazareth had resurrected. When Paul asks Agrippa, "Why is it considered unbelievable to you if God raises the dead?" Paul is not speaking of resurrection in general, which every Jew believed was part of Messiah's kingdom, but that one specific resurrection Paul proclaimed, the resurrection of Jesus of Nazareth, that proved him to be the Messiah-Redeemer, and therefore the Messiah-King.

Translation Acts 26:9–11

9 "Therefore, truly, I thought in myself I ought to do much opposed the name of Jesus, 10 which also I did in Jerusalem; then also I confined in prisons many of the saints, receiving authority from the chief priests. When they were put to death I voiced my assent against them. 11 And in all the synagogues often punishing them, I was compelling them to revile God. Then being vehemently furious against them I continued to persecute them, even as far as to foreign cities.

EXPOSITION

Paul returns to the narrative of his salvation, that he had interrupted to present a defense of his message. The interruption was important, because it had set the accusation of defiling the temple in its proper light, which was a false accusation maintained because he had preached the good news. Why had Paul preached that good news of Jesus the Christ resurrected? Paul again tells the story that many had heard, perhaps even Agrippa had heard.

As we read again the story of Paul's salvation, we should keep in mind new details, or missing details, give credibility to the story. This was not the kind of memorized and empty profession taught by some over-zealous "evangelist" seeking conversions like trophies justifying contributions to his ministry. This was real life. Paul adds or subtracts as his memory provides—now over twenty years after the event—and as the needs of the moment may require. I remember the moment of my salvation on May 19, 1974: Wednesday night; a hymn (not remembered) was being sung; the incredible moment of conviction and faith. But I know that over the years I have not told the story with the same details the same way every time, but as memory serves and audience requires. Paul's "defense" is a testimony, and the purpose of that testimony is to proclaim the good news.

The key point of this introduction was his vehement zealousness for YHWH. The Jesus-believers were blaspheming YHWH, heretics to the orthodox faith. What, then, might have changed such a man from violent persecutor to zealous servant?

Paul speaks of punishing people for their faith, and confining people in prison for their faith, and assenting to their death for their faith. Such things happen today, but why were they happening then? One reason was the Romans let conquered nations rule themselves as long as they did not violate certain Roman laws. The Romans wanted peace and taxes. If peace was maintained, and taxes paid, and laws obeyed, the people lived their lives without Roman interference.

Religions were left alone, as long as the Roman religion was respected—or in the case of Judaism, by treaty to worship YHWH only. By that rule the Jews were left alone to manage their religion as they saw fit. By an unwritten rule, no one cared what one Jew might do to another Jew.

If Paul had not been a Roman citizen, the Roman commander would have turned him over to the Sanhedrin after the riot had been dispersed. By Roman law and custom, and by Jewish authority, Paul the zealous Pharisee could punish people for their faith, and confine people in prison for their faith, and assent to their death for their faith, "even as far as to foreign cities," such as Damascus.

Translation Acts 26:12–14

12 "Then when travelling to Damascus with authority and commission of the chief priests, 13 at mid-day on the road I saw, O king, from heaven above, the brightness of the sun, a light shining around me and those travelling with me. 14 All of us fell down to the ground. I heard a voice saying to me in the Hebrew language, 'Saul, Saul, why do you persecute me? It is hard for you to kick against the goads.'

EXPOSITION

Why did Jesus wait to save Paul until after Paul had persecuted Christians in Jerusalem? The first answer is to bow before God's sovereignty to determine times and seasons. However, God does graciously provide one answer, Acts 8:1, "Now Saul was there approving the murder. Then on that day began a great persecution against the church which was in Jerusalem. Then all were dispersed throughout the lands of Judea and Samaria, except the apostles." As I explained in vol. 1, the believers had not obeyed the command to take the gospel out of Jerusalem, Acts 1:8. The Lord gave them a push to do their duty.

Another reason is the strength persecution gives to the faith and the faithful. Believers are refined by trials, the scum of worldliness is removed by the Refiner's fire. A third reason is Christ's plans for Paul. If Paul had been saved in Jerusalem, he would have suffered the persecution he had given to others, and might have been executed for his faith. Paul's salvation was not delayed, it happened exactly where and when and how God had planned for it to happen, to meet not only Paul's spiritual needs, but the spiritual needs of many others.

On his way to Damascus to persecute Christians, about noon as they approached the city, Jesus appeared to Saul-Paul. Not in his natural appearance as a resurrected person, but in the brightness of his essential deity glory, and as a disembodied voice. The brightness of that glory surrounded Paul and his travelling companions. All fell to the ground—they were walking, not riding horses as is often depicted in paintings.

Paul heard a voice speaking in Hebrew. "Saul, Saul, why do you persecute me? It is hard for you to kick against the goads." The second sentence is new to Paul's telling of the event. Paul has told this story before, without that particular sentence from Jesus. In fact, the sentence is not in the original narrative in Acts 9:5.

Some translations do include the second sentence at Acts 9:5. The textual issue at 9:5 is the best manuscripts end with "Jesus, whom you are persecuting." The second sentence is sometimes attached to the end of 9:5 or the beginning of 9:6, depending on the manuscript [Metzger, *Textual*, 317–318]. The fact the sentences appear in different locations in different manuscripts is itself suspicious. The fact that the sentence parallels 26:14–15 decides the issue. A scribe assimilated the 26:14–15 passage to 9:5 or 9:6, and other scribes repeated the error. The sentence came into the Textus Receptus through the Latin Vulgate used by Erasmus.

The sentence is not in the original narrative in Acts 9:5, which means when Paul told Luke about his salvation, he did not include the second sentence in the telling. So why include the second sentence here and not elsewhere? Perhaps because at least one person in the audience, King Agrippa, was "kicking against the goads," 26:27.

A "goad" [*kéntron*, Zodhiates, s. v. 2759] is literally a sharp stick used to poke animals, such as oxen pulling a cart, to protest unruly behavior. From that pointed use, the word developed the metaphorical meaning of a sharp point in a discussion that prods the listener to evaluate his argument. To "kick against the goads" became a proverbial expression meaning, "to offer vain and rash resistance." More pointedly, the saying was applied to those "who by unruly rage hurt themselves." That is Jesus' point within the context of Paul's salvation.

The "goads" were everything Saul-Paul had heard the faithful say about their faith in Jesus as the Christ. The testimony he had heard from those he persecuted illuminated the Old Testament revelation he had learned in his youth. Those facts pressed against his unruly behavior and rash resistance. But every one of us knows from Scripture testimony and personal experience that when sinners are confronted by the Word, they reject it as absurd, until and unless the Holy Spirit takes action to enliven spiritual perception, and give conviction leading to saving faith. That moment comes to everyone who is brought to faith. That moment had come to Saul the persecutor.

Translation Acts 26:15–18

15 "Then I said, 'Who are you Lord?' And the Lord said, 'I am Jesus, whom you are persecuting. 16 But get up and stand on your feet. For this purpose I have appeared to you: to appoint you a servant and a witness of that which you have both seen of me, then of that I will show to you, 17 delivering you out from the people and out from the gentiles to whom I am sending you 18 to open their eyes, that they might turn from darkness to light, and from the authority of Satan to God, that they may receive forgiveness of sins and an inheritance among those who have been sanctified by faith that is in me.'

EXPOSITION

Paul summarizes the consequences of meeting the risen Jesus Christ. His appointment to proclaim the good news was not told him immediately, but was a testimony of facts and events accumulated over time. Jesus had told Ananias, Acts 9:16, "For I will show to him how much he must suffer for my name," the future tense of the verb indicating the full revelation to Paul of his life's mission was yet to come. In Acts 22:13, Paul reports when Ananias came to him he said, "The

God of our fathers has appointed you to know his will, and to see the Righteous One, and to hear the voice out of his mouth, because you will be a witness for him to all men of what you have seen and heard." Paul himself speaks of receiving the good news from Christ, Galatians 1:11–12.

In this particular setting, before King Agrippa, a gentile (the Herodians were out of Esau not Isaac), Paul summarizes his mission.

> Sent by Christ to the gentiles to open their eyes,
>
> that they might turn from darkness to light,
>
> that they might turn from ... the authority of Satan to God,
>
> in order that that they may receive forgiveness of sins,
>
> in order that that they may receive an inheritance among those who have been sanctified by faith that is in Christ.

Is that not the good news? Each of those statements appears in Paul's letters. For example, Colossians 1:13, "who has delivered us out of the authority of darkness and has transferred us into the kingdom of the Son of his love." Compare 1 Peter 2:9, Christ has called the believer "out of darkness into his wondrous light."

Paul's mission was not only to proclaim the good news of salvation, but also the discipling that is to follow salvation. But before discipling there must be salvation, and that was Paul's intent for his audience before King Agrippa.

More might be said here. Satan's authority is exercised through his power of temptation. Satan has been given authority to tempt human beings, in many ways, to commit acts of sinning, witness Job's temptations. But that is his only authority and his only power. He is said to have "the power of death," Hebrews 2:14, but that power is exercised through temptation. Satan's power of death is the consequence of God's laws, "the wages of sin is death," not any authority or power intrinsic to Satan himself.

Even the believer suffers death when he responds to temptation by committing an act of sinning—the separation from fellowship with God. Death is separation: physical death is the separation of the soul from the body; spiritual death is the separation of the soul from communion with God. In the unsaved the consequence of spiritual separation due to sin is the spiritual state of permanently unsaved;

should there not be salvation during this mortal life. In the saved the consequence of spiritual separation due to sin is the spiritual state of temporary loss of fellowship, restored upon confession and repentance. The unsaved person does not have a relationship with God. The saved person has a permanent relationship with God, and fellowship as a result.

The inheritance of those "sanctified by faith" is in some ways Christ himself. The New Testament church is a "joint-heir" with Christ. He is their representative in all things concerning their relationship with God. Therefore, in whatever he receives, the New Testament church participates. John 17:24, "Father, those you have given me, I desire that where I am they also might be with me, that they might behold my glory that you gave me because you loved me before the foundation of the world."

Paul testifies of salvation, because for this he was saved and called, and who knows whom among crowd God may save?

Translation Acts 26:19–20

19 "Whereupon, O King Agrippa, I was not disobedient to the heavenly vision, 20 but first to those in Damascus, and all in Jerusalem, and the region of Judea, and to the gentiles, I kept on declaring to convert and to turn to God, habitually doing works suitable to repentance.

EXPOSITION

Paul was obedient to Christ. He summarizes his life's mission by listing the people to whom he proclaimed the good news. He summarizes the message: "convert" from sin to faith; "turn to God" for salvation from sin and its penalty; "do works" that reveal one has converted and turned to God. Works "justify" in the sense they demonstrate a genuine profession of saving faith. See Jacob's argument, the Book of James 2:20–26.

Translation Acts 26:21–23

21 "On account of these things the Jews seized me as I was in the temple; they were trying to kill me. 22 Therefore, having received help from God unto this day, I have stood bearing witness to both small and great, saying nothing other than what both the prophets said was about

to happen, and Moses: 23 that the Christ would suffer. As first out of resurrection from the dead ones, he is about to preach light to both our people and to the gentiles."

EXPOSITION

Paul's profession of the good news throughout the Greco-Roman world is why the Jews were trying to kill him. In the Book of Acts, to this point in time, we have seen time and time again the jealousy of the Jews as God saved both Jews and gentiles through Paul's proclamation. The Jews were not as successful in gaining coverts, from a man-ward point of view.

A story is told of the American evangelist D.L. Moody (1837–1899). The morning after an evangelistic campaign in a particular American city, Mr. Moody was walking downtown with a friend. They both saw a poor man passed out in gutter, the victim of alcohol abuse.

> "Look," said Mr. Moody's friend, "one of your converts, who came forward the other night to profess salvation."
>
> "He must be one of my converts," replied Moody, "for if he was Christ's convert he would not be in the gutter."

During his lifetime, D.L. Moody saw thousands of people in the USA and England come forward and profess Christ. But he understood there was a difference between his converts and Christ's converts. Many today have forgotten that needful principle, as they seek to convert this or that person, this or that religious group, to win the world for Christ. The world is littered with our converts, who have returned to the gutters of their sinfulness, never having been Christ's converts.

The Jews were trying to convert people to Judaism. Paul was preaching the good news as the means whereby Christ converted people to himself, "from darkness to light ... from the authority of Satan to God ... [to] receive forgiveness of sins and an inheritance."

Some among the Jews understood the consequence of Pau's good news, even as Paul had taught the Jews at Antioch of Pisidia, Acts 13:38–39.

> Therefore be it known to you, men, brethren, that through this one, to you forgiveness of sins is proclaimed. And from all things from which you were not able in the Law of Moses to be justified, in him everyone believing is justified.

Judaism and the Law were becoming obsolete, growing old, near vanishing, Hebrews 8:13, being replaced by a new covenant made in the death and resurrection of Jesus the Christ, Hebrews 8:7–13.

Paul says the Jews should have understood the good news he proclaimed, because "I have [said] … nothing other than what both the prophets said was about to happen, and Moses: that the Christ would suffer." Paul does not mean the Jews understood the Old Testament message that "the Christ would suffer" prior to their hearing the good news. He means that having heard the good news he was proclaiming, they should have understood. Think on this. If the Old Testament peoples had understood from the revelation they had received, that there was a coming redeemer who would suffer, die, and resurrect, would those living when that coming redeemer arrived, have rejected the one who came and suffered, and died, and resurrected? Would not the ones educated in the Scripture—the scribes and Pharisees—have believed Jesus was the Christ sent by God to redeem sinners, and led others to do the same?

The Old Testament revelation of a coming Messiah-Redeemer is understood through the New Testament revelation of that Messiah-Redeemer having come. Paul's message to the Jews, that the Messiah must come and die and resurrect, was straight out of the Old Testament revelation, but—and it is an important objection—only in the light of the New Testament revelation was that Old Testament revelation understood.

> Acts 8:34–35, Now responding, the eunuch said to Philip, "I beseech you, concerning whom the prophet [Isaish 53] says this? Concerning himself, or concerning some other?" 35 Then Philip, having opened his mouth, and beginning from that Scripture, proclaimed the good news to him—Jesus.

Paul proved from the Old Testament revelation Messiah must die and resurrect to provide redemption from sin, by using the New Testament revelation that Jesus of Nazareth proved, by his words and works, that he was that Messiah, who did die, and did resurrect, and in whom is forgiveness of sins.

> As first out of resurrection from the dead ones, he [Jesus the Christ] is about to preach light to both our people and to the gentiles."

That is the message. The word translated "about" [Zodhiates, a. v. 3195], in used in the sense of intent. The intent of the crucifixion, death, and resurrection of Jesus the Christ, is to "preach light to both our people and to the gentiles." That was why Paul had been sent; that was Paul's good news; that was why the Jews wanted to kill Paul.

Paul is innocent of the accusations made against him, because he is doing nothing more nor less than proclaiming the truth that God proclaimed to the Jews.

Translation Acts 26:24–27

24 Now of the things he said in his defense, Festus in a loud voice said, "Paul, you are out of your mind! Your much learning turns you to madness." 25 But Paul said, "No, I am not out of my mind, most excellent Festus, but of truth and of sound mind I speak every word. 26 For concerning these things the king understands, to whom also being bold I speak. For not any of these things are hidden from him. For I am persuaded no not one of these things is done in a corner. 27 King Agrippa, believe you the prophets? I know that you believe."

EXPOSITION

Festus loudly reveals the truth of the unsaved soul: "Christ having been crucified—truly to the Jewish a scandal, but to gentiles absurd" and "a natural person does not accept things of the Spirit of God, for they are absurd to him, and he is not able to know them, because they are discerned spiritually" (1 Corinthians 1:23; 2:14). Though Luke does not tell us specifically what prompted Festus, the context, 26:23, does tell us: Festus considered resurrection out of the dead to be an insane belief. Festus does not know the Hebrew prophets.

Agrippa does understand these things—but not quite the spiritual understanding that leads to salvation. Agrippa understands Paul is innocent because he speaks nothing not already said by YHWH to the Jews. In terms of Roman law and their treaty with the Jews, Paul is proselytizing, a lawful practice. Agrippa understands Paul's message is about redemption from sin through the Messiah sent by God. Agrippa, says Paul, believes the prophets: that a Messiah is coming. Agrippa understands Paul's message that this Jesus of Nazareth is that Messiah.

Translation Acts 26:28–29

28 Now Agrippa said to Paul, "With so little do you persuade me to be made a Christian?" 29 And Paul said, "I would wish to God, both in little and in much, not only you but also all those hearing me this day to become such as I also am, except these bonds."

EXPOSITION

Agrippa tells the problem, but not in the way he thinks. No amount of knowledge or facts persuades the sinner. The sinner does not possess the spiritual perception to be persuaded, unless and until God enlivens the soul's faculty of spiritual perception through his gift of grace-faith-salvation. Agrippa has a natural understanding of the prophets, and Paul's message, but is unable to make an application to his own spiritual state, because he lacks the necessary spiritual perception—he does not even understand he is spiritually dead in trespasses and sins.

Paul prays for Agrippa, and all those present. God will respond to that prayer, by saving some, and by allowing the Word spoken but rejected to judge others. Perhaps some in the audience were saved. We cannot know because it is not our place to know what the Lord does not reveal.

Translation Acts 26:30–32

30 Then the king got up, and the procurator, and Bernice, and those sitting with them. 31 Withdrawing, they began speaking to one another, saying, "This man is doing nothing worthy of bonds or of death." 32 Then Agrippa said to Festus, "This man could have been set at liberty if he had not appealed to Caesar."

EXPOSITION

Perhaps Festus was too dull to understand, and perhaps the King did not mean it this way, but Agrippa has rebuked both Felix and Festus for not setting Paul free long ago.

But God—those precious words–but God, knowing the end from the beginning, had already chosen to use Paul's circumstances to accomplish his will: that Paul be brought to Rome by the Romans in order to "also testify in Rome," as he had "repeatedly testified about me in Jerusalem," Acts 23:11.

There is a God-designed agreement between man's free will and

God's foreordination of events, that causes our freely made choices to work out to accomplish God's will through our circumstances. Knowing the end—his purpose in creating—from before the beginning, God so designed the universe, and all that is in it, including humankind, to freely choose, and in those freely made choices, to accomplish God's purpose in creating. Thus, human beings freely act together to create the web and pattern and complex interconnection of actions and consequences, that all together work together toward the foreordained end.

(Foreordination, briefly, in the timeless eternity before God created, from within himself knowing all things and all possible choices, [omniscience] God sovereignly effectuated from possible to actual only those particular freely made choices that would accomplish his purpose, plans, and processes in the universe he created. Freely made choices are certain because foreordained, but not necessary because freely made.)

Paul's choice to go leave Corinth and go to Jerusalem (he speaks of this in 1 Corinthians 16:3–4), instead of going to Rome from Corinth, a choice made more than two years before he stood before King Agrippa, set his feet on a path leading to this moment when, "This man could have been set at liberty if he had not appealed to Caesar." Small things often lead us unaware to larger events. Let us be careful to order our behavior and choices according to God's values, and principles, and precepts. Let us also remember Paul did nothing wrong. He simply made choices, step by step, to meet his goals, which the Lord had foreordained to accomplish his will.

Acts Twenty-seven

Translation Acts 27:1–4

1 Now when our sailing to Italy was chosen, they delivered both Paul and certain other prisoners to a centurion named Julius, of the Augustus' cohort. 2 Then boarding a ship of Adramyttium, about to sail to the along-the-way places in Asia, we set sail. Aristarchus, a Macedonian of Thessalonica, was with us. 3 Then the next day we made port at Sidon. Then Julius, having treated Paul kindly, allowed him to go to his friends to receive care. 4 From there, putting out to sea, we sailed under the shelter of Cyprus, though the winds being contrary.

EXPOSITION

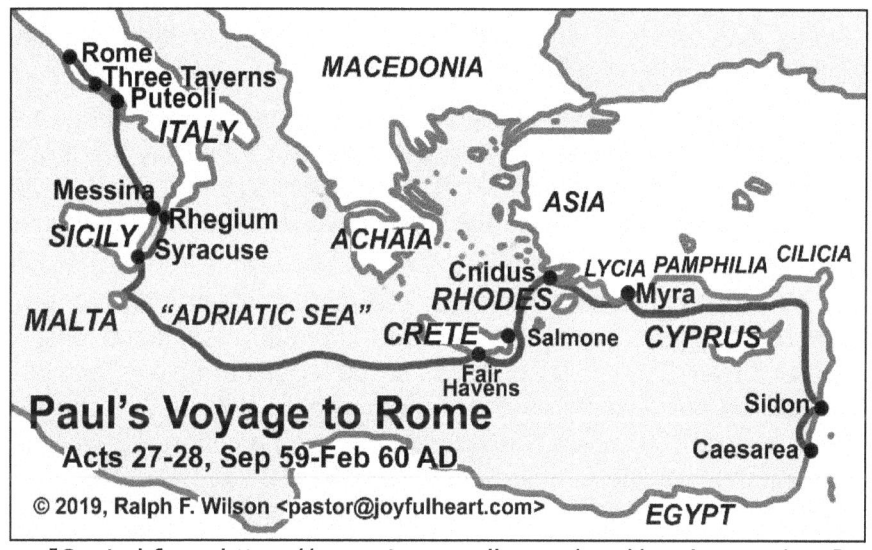

[Copied from https://www.jesuswalk.com/paul/paul-maps.htm]

Perhaps the most unusual aspect of Paul's trip by ship to Rome, is the course from Crete to Malta. Most ships—all ships were cargo ships that also carried passengers—sailed along the coast, not only to sell their cargo and pick up more, but to avoid the kind of storms on the open sea that sank ships.

One wonders why the Holy Spirit thought it necessary to give Luke's travelogues. A little history reveals a good reason. For a few centuries, especially in the 17th and 18th centuries following the birth of a hostile historical-critical method in biblical studies, Luke's gospel and the Acts were viewed by certain scholars as historically inaccurate, because many of the villages he mentions were unknown. That criticism sparked a surge in biblical archaeology in the 19th century. All the places mentioned by Luke were located. The Acts is a credible history of the 1st century New Testament church. Small and unlikely facts, such as a voyage across open sea, are the mark of an eyewitness.

The people Luke mentions add to the eyewitness quality of the Acts. We first meet Aristarchus during the "Great is Artemis" riot in Ephesus, Acts 19:29. He becomes a traveling companion of Paul, 20:4, one among many. Here he is two-plus years later, having stayed with Paul, and now going with him to Rome. We find him in Rome, two-plus years later on, in the letters Colossians 4:10, "Aristarchus, my fellow prisoner greets you," and Philemon 24, "my fellow laborers Mark, Aristarchus, Demas, Luke."

Did Aristarchus ever make it back home to Thessalonica in Macedonia? We do not know; nor is it important. The Holy Spirit gives him to us as an example of the kind of faithfulness required in a servant of Christ. He walked the path the Spirit gave him. He fought the good fight. He kept the faith. Thereby we know he finished with joy.

"A centurion named Julius, of the Augustus' cohort," has given some trouble, as a Roman cohort was 500–600 men, depending on whether it was of the auxiliary troops or the regular army (respectively). The issue is resolved by paying attention to what Luke and the Holy Spirit have written. Julius was not commanding a cohort, he was "of," i.e., a member of the Augustus' cohort.

Ramsay says [315], "the cohorts [of the regular army] never bore surnames, and it would therefore seem that this 'Augustus cohort' was one of the auxiliary cohorts." However, auxiliary officers never performed the duty described of Julius, but only regular army officers. How then to resolve the conflict? Ramsay notes Luke, who is a Greek, does not use Latin forms or names in their technical sense. There were apparently regular army centurions [Ramsay] "on detached service for communication between the Emperor and his armies in the provinces" who were known as "the troop of the Emperor."

Every military organization has groups of officers and enlisted assigned to special duties. For example, in the USA, the "White House

Military Office," supplies military aides for special duties, such as food service, presidential transportation, medical support, emergency medical services and hospitality services; the officer who carries the "nuclear football" (a briefcase with nuclear launch codes that always accompanies the President); the marines that guard certain government offices in the USA and foreign countries. They might be described as "the troop of the President." Julius the centurion of the "Augustus cohort" is not a technical term for this special group, but used by Luke to identify a corps of officer-couriers directly serving the Emperor in a special capacity.

How were Luke and Aristarchus, and possibly others, able to accompany Paul? Prisoners were not allowed friends and guests. Even family members were prevented from accompanying a prisoner [Ramsay, 315–316]. They may have paid their way as coincidentally traveling in the same direction as Julius and his prisoners. But the respect and freedom Julius gives Paul suggests they convinced Julius they were Paul's slaves [Ramsay, 316], giving Paul an importance, in the centurion's estimation, Paul did not actually possess. Paul did not appear as a penniless traveler, but an important man with servants. In the Roman Empire, social status affected the way those charged with a crime were treated.

Translation Acts 27:5–8

5 And then sailing along Cilicia and Pamphylia, we landed at Myra of Lycia. 6 And there the centurion found a ship of Alexandria sailing to Italy. He entered us into it. 7 Now for many days, sailing slowly and with difficulty, we came near Cnidus. The wind not permitting us, we sailed under the shelter of Crete, near Salmone. 8 With difficulty and sailing near it, we came to a certain place called "Fair Havens," to which nearby was Lasea city.

EXPOSITION

A "ship of Alexandria" would be a cargo ship from Alexandria, Egypt, most likely carrying grain going to Rome. Egypt was the granary of Rome during the 1st century. Looking at the map, above, Myra to Cnidus is along the coast, as the ship slowly made its way to Italy. The ship wisely sailed along the coast rather than the open sea. The next leg of the journey should have been across the Adriatic Sea to Corinth.

As I noted in comments at Acts 18:1–3, 8–11, Corinth was located on a narrow isthmus between the shipping ports on the Ionian and Aegean seas. What I did not mention in those comments is there was a paved trackway (with rails similar to a train track) across the isthmus, known as the Diolkos, that allowed ships to be moved overland across the isthmus.

> [https://greekreporter.com/2023/05/07/diolkos-stone-road-ships-ionian-aegean/].

The most natural path of a ship to take sailing to Italy was to Corinth to use the Diolkos. Such a course would keep the ship away from the open sea. Why then did the ship turn south from Cnidus to Crete? Luke says "sailing slowly and with difficulty, we came near Cnidus. The wind not permitting us, we sailed under the shelter of Crete." Sailing ships make way against contrary winds slowly and with great difficulty. From Myra to Cnidus the prevailing winds were from the north.

The ship might have sailed across the Aegean Sea from Cnidus to the Peloponnese peninsula then around the peninsula into the Ionian Sea, and across the Adriatic Sea to Italy. But apparently the winds were too strong to allow even that course. The ship was driven by the winds south to Crete, and from there they sailed into the larger open expanse of the Adriatic Sea between Crete and Malta. Perhaps their initial thought had been to sail "under the shelter of Crete" and then turn north to the Peloponnese peninsula, hoping the winds would change. Because of the prevailing wind, the ship sailed from Cnidus to the south side of Crete, stopping at the seaport known as "Fair Havens."

Translation Acts 27:9–12

9 Now enough time passed, and the voyage already dangerous (the Day of Atonement already past), Paul was exhorting them, 10 saying to them, "Men. I understand that the voyage is about to be with damage and much loss, not only of the cargo and of the ship, but also our lives." 11 But the centurion was persuaded by the pilot and ship owner, rather than the things spoken by Paul. 12 Now as the harbor was unsuitable to spend the winter, the majority, looking toward the southwest and toward the northwest, reached a decision to set sail from there, if somehow that they may be able to attain to Phoenix, a harbor of Crete, to winter there.

EXPOSITION

Here Luke gives his readers information missing from 27:1, the time of year when "our sailing to Italy was chosen." Several days—a week or more—had passed since setting sail from Caesarea. When they harbored at Fair Havens the Day of Atonement was "already past." The Day of Atonement falls between September 14 and October 14 on the modern calendar. Even today weather on the Adriatic Sea tends to strong winds and storms in the fall and winter.

The ship left Crete under good conditions. Paul had given a word of warning, apparently having been informed by the Holy Spirit. "But the centurion was persuaded by the pilot and ship owner, rather than the things spoken by Paul." Paul was not a sailor, and so his warning was ignored.

Those in charge decided to attempt to sail to "Phoenix, a harbor of Crete, to winter there." Phoenix was about thirty-five miles west of Fair Havens, so they could again sail within sight of the coastline. There they would wait until spring to continue the voyage under safer conditions. Regardless of whether they went west or northwest from Crete, fall and winter were dangerous times for a sailing vessel.

Translation Acts 27:13–17

13 Now a south wind blowing gently, they thought they had achieved their purpose. Then taking up, they began sailing near Crete. 14 But not long after there came down from there a violent wind called Euroclydon. 15 Then the ship being caught, and not able to bear up against the wind, we put the ship into the wind to be driven along. 16 Then having sheltered under a certain island called Cauda, we were able, with difficulty, to gain control of the ship's boat, 17 which raising up, they made use of helps, girding the ship across the keel and deck. Then fearing lest they should fall into the sandbank, they lowered the mast, in this manner being driven along.

EXPOSITION

A gentle warm wind was blowing from the south, which fit their plans to sail to Pheonix. The wind changed. A "Euroclydon," literally "north wind," is "a stormy wind from the north or northeast that occurs" in that area [Dictionary.com]. The stormy north wind sent the ship south. Rather than allowing the ship to be blown further south, the crew turned the ship "into the wind." This is a maneuver known as "tacking."

[Image: https://en.wikipedia.org/wiki/Tacking_%28sailing%29].

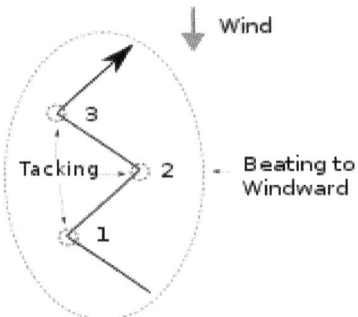

When a sailing vessel wants to go in the direction the wind is coming from, the ship is oriented so the wind blows at an angle across the front of the ship, setting up a conflict between the sail and the keel, so the ship is moved forward as seen in the image. Paul's ship wanted to go north, against the wind, so they performed a tacking maneuver to go north. By using a tacking maneuver, the ship sailed north to Cauda, a small island south of Crete, about twenty miles directly south of Pheonix. [Image is Cauda.]

The phrase "raising up," usually means to set sail or raise the anchor, but here it is connected with *skáphē* [Zodhiates, s. v. 4627], a small boat used for rowing to shore, floating alongside the main ship. They lifted that boat onto the ship's deck. Then they used ropes or chains in order strengthen the hull of the ship by compressing the hull: "girding the ship across the keel [bottom] and deck [top]." (The "keel" of a ship is a structural beam inside the ship's hull running from bow to stern. The keel is the lowest point in the hull, and therefore at the intersection of the hull and the water. By a metonymy the keel refers to the bottom of the hull.)

From Luke's description, it is impossible to know where the ship was located with respect to the shape of Cauda, the modern Gavdos (see image, below). On the east side, there is a wide bay where they might have sheltered from the wind.

Luke reports, "fearing lest they should fall into the sandbank, they lowered the mast." My guess is the ship had been driven by the wind to the northwest corner of the island. Fearing being driven aground, they lowered the mast, and let the wind control the ship. The north wind and the waves must have carried the ship to the south and west, away from the island. [https://en.wikipedia.org/wiki/Gavdos].

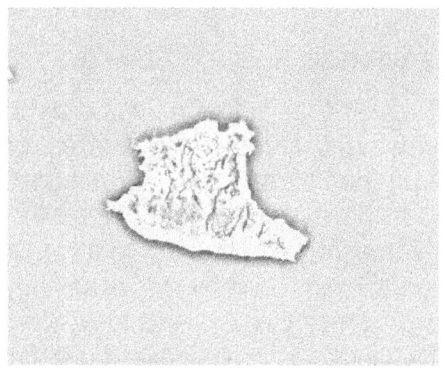

Translation Acts 27:18–21a

18 Now we being violently storm-tossed, on the next day they prepare to cast out the ship's load, 19 and on the third day, by their own hands, they cast away the ship's equipment. 20 Then neither sun nor stars showing for many days, and no small tempest pressing upon us, from then on all hope of our deliverance was abandoned. 21a There was also much time without food.

EXPOSITION

The ship is no longer under the sailors' control. The Eyroclydon developed into a storm at sea, probably because of the interaction between north and south blowing winds, one being wetter than the other. Tropical-like cyclones do occur in the Mediterranean between September and January, with strong winds and lots of rain. Cyclones (aka: hurricane, aka: typhoon, depending on where in the world it occurs) have sustained winds of seventy-four miles per hour or greater. They move slowly across the body of water where they formed. This particular cyclone in Acts 27 moved in a west to northwest direction, taking the ship to Malta, 28:1.

Luke gives an almost day-by-day experience. The ship's equipment was cast into the ocean, to lighten the ship so it sat higher in the water, thereby less likely to be submerged by the waves. The crew and passengers gave up hope of deliverance. There was food, 27:33, but the violent tossing of the ship in the sea prevented food preparation, and most likely many suffered nausea.

Translation Acts 27:21b–26

21b At that time Paul stood up in the midst of them, saying, "Truly it was right, O men, giving attention to me, not to have set sail from Crete, than to have gained this damage and loss. 22 And now I exhort you to be of good cheer. For loss of life there will be none from you, only the ship. 23 For this night, of God whose I am and whom I serve, a messenger stood by me, 24 saying, 'fear not, Paul, it is necessary you stand before Caesar. And look, God has given to you all those sailing with you.' 25 Therefore be of good cheer, men. For I believe God, that thus it will be according to the way it was said to me. 26 But it is necessary us to fall upon a certain island."

EXPOSITION

On a day between the third day and the fourteenth day, Paul revels he had received a message from God. He gains their attention by reminding them—at the least the centurion, the pilot, and ship owner—that he had advised them to remain at Fair Havens, 27:10, warning them "that the voyage is about to be with damage and much loss, not only of the cargo and of the ship, but also our lives." Having been proven right brings credibility to his next words.

This time Paul's message is of hope. The ship will be lost, as he had said before, but no lives will be lost. Paul selects his words carefully. Paul belongs to God and serves God. The gentiles would have interpreted that to mean Paul had a special relationship with one of the gods. Yes, they knew he was Hebrew and worshiped one God, but people tend to understand what is said to them within their own particular personal and cultural circumstances.

Paul's God sent a messenger to Paul (it seems Paul was praying for the lives of those with him). Paul repeats the message; not an interpretation as sometimes happened with false prophets; not some arcane or mysterious riddle for them to solve, as also happens with false prophets. God's messenger said things plainly and Paul repeats the plain things God's messenger said.

> Fear not, Paul, it is necessary you stand before Caesar. And look, God has given to you all those sailing with you.

Paul will complete his journey to Rome, and all those with Paul at this very moment will survive the loss of the ship. For two hundred seventy-five people, Acts 27:37 (Paul being the 276th), that was good news.

Paul believes God; they should also believe. Paul then adds one more detail, "it is necessary we be cast upon a certain island." Again, the people will survive the loss of the ship.

Translation Acts 27:27–29

27 Then when the fourteenth night had come, we being driven about the Adriatic, toward the middle of the night, the sailors suspected that they were drawing near to some land. 28 And testing the depth of the water, they found twenty fathoms. Then a little farther and again testing the depth of the water, they found fifteen fathoms. 29 Then fearing lest we might fall somewhere on rocky places, four anchors were cast out of the stern; and they were praying for day to come.

EXPOSITION

On the fourteenth might, experience in the ways of the sea suggested to some of the ship's crew the ship was approaching land. Experienced crews of sailing ships understand the behavior of ocean waves. An ocean wave approaching land looks different from a wave in the deep ocean. Waves become steeper in shallower water. There are also small changes in the movement of the ship in the water as the depth of water decreases.

The sailors tested the depth: twenty fathoms, which is about 120 feet. A "fathom" is nominally six feet. A depth of 120 feet meant they were close. What is known as the "surface ocean" extends from zero depth to 300 feet in depth; several miles away from land the depth is about 650 feet. The deeper water is far from land.

The sailors waited a bit and again checked the depth. This time the depth was ninety feet. They were not close enough to hear waves hitting the shore, but they were close enough to stop the boat and wait for day.

Translation Acts 27:30–34

30 Then some sailors sought to escape out of the ship, and let down the ship's boat into the sea, under pretense, as being about to cast out

bow anchors. 31 Paul said to the centurion and to the soldiers, if these do not remain in the ship, you are not able to be saved. 32 Then the soldiers cut the ropes of the ship's boat and allowed her to fall away. 33 Then until day was dawning Paul kept on urging all to partake of food, saying, "Today is the fourteenth day which you continue waiting without eating, having taken nothing. 34 Therefore, I exhort you to take food. For this is for your deliverance. For not one of you, a hair of the head will be lost."

EXPOSITION

Some sailors tried to leave the ship, not willing to chance crashing upon the shore. They might row the smaller boat safely to land, but the much larger ship might be damaged by the waves as it attempted to make land on an unknown shore. Paul makes sure they are stopped from leaving. Paul's credibility is high, and respected. Then Paul went around the ship urging everyone to eat. They would need the strength food provided to go safely to the shore that day. He reassures them not one of them would come to harm.

Translation Acts 27:35–39

35 Then having said those things, and taking bread, he gave thanks to God before all. And breaking it he began to eat. 36 Then having been cheered, all also took food. 37 Then we were all the souls in the ship, two hundred seventy-six. 38 Then, having been filled with food, they began to lighten the ship, casting the wheat into the sea. 39 Now when it was day, they did not recognize the land, but they noticed a certain bay, having a coast on which they decided, if they were able, to drive the ship.

EXPOSITION

Paul sets the example. He believes what he is saying, and proves it by eating, giving thanks to the God who had told him everyone with him on the ship would live. So encouraged, they all eat. Having been strengthened, they all work together to "lighten the ship, casting the wheat into the sea." This ship is not coming into a seaport, but to a shoreline, where there is no depth of water. The ship needs to set as high in the water as possible, to be able to get as close to the shore as possible, before breaking up in the waves.

Day breaks, land is seen. No one has seen this land before. But there is a bay, which indicates deeper water close to the shore. They begin to drive the ship into the bay. How did they do that? They lifted the mast into place and set the sails.

Translation Acts 27:40–41

40 And cutting the anchors, leaving them in the sea, at the same time they loosened the ropes of the rudders. And hoisting the foresail to the blowing wind, they began bringing the ship toward the coast. 41 But falling into a place between two currents, they ran the ship aground. And truly the bow sticking firm it remained unmovable. And the stern was being broken by the violence of the waves.

EXPOSITION

Luke is not a sailor, but he reports in detail what the sailors did to bring the ship into the bay. The "foresail" is the principle sail on the foremast, which is the main mast on large sailing vessels. Despite their best efforts, the ship was taken aground by the currents in the bay. The ship ran aground hard, lodging firmly into the shore, making the ship rigid against the waves. The waves battered the stern and the ship began to break apart.

Translation Acts 27:42–44

42 Now of the soldiers, the decision was that they should kill the prisoners, lest any swimming away should escape. 43 But the centurion, desiring to save Paul, prevented them from their purpose. Then he commanded those being able to swim to let themselves down from the ship to go out on the land, 44 and the rest, indeed some on boards, then some on things from the ship. And thereby it happened that all were brought safely to the land.

EXPOSITION

The solders knew that if any prisoner escaped, even under the current circumstances, they might suffer the penalty due the escapees. But the centurion, desiring to save the man who had saved them all, stopped their murderous intent. The centurion gave permission for all to leave the ship and swim to shore. Luke does not say, but the soldiers must have made sure they arrived before or with the prisoners, and gathered them into one group in one place where they could keep them from escaping. As Paul had promised, i.e., as he had reported the Word of the Lord, all 276 persons made it safely to shore.

Acts Twenty-eight

Translation Acts 28:1–4

1 And having been delivered, then we learned that the island is called Malta. 2 And the barbarians were showing us no ordinary kindness. For having kindled a fire, they received all of us because of the coming rain and because of the cold. 3 Now Paul gathered together many sticks and laid them on the fire. A viper came out from the heat, fastening on Paul's hand. 4 Now when the barbarians saw the beast suspended from his hand, they said to one another, "Assuredly this man is a murderer, who having been saved from the sea, justice has not permitted to live."

EXPOSITION

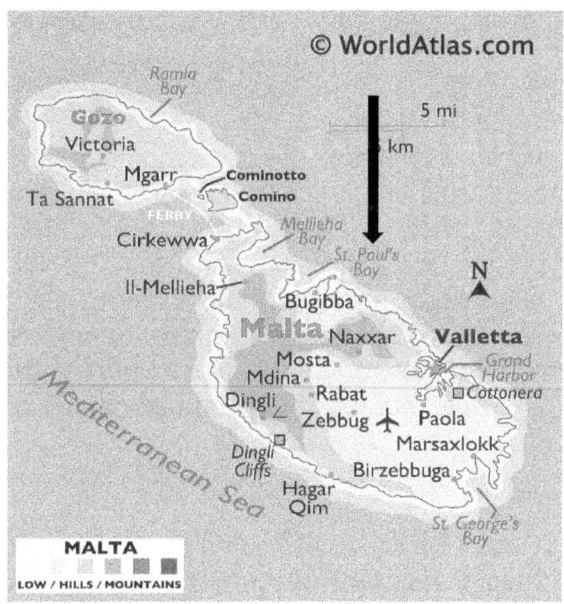

Malta is an island located 103 miles south of Sicily (there is a nearby smaller island named Gozo), by car a one hour, forty-five minute ferry ride from Sicily; by plane 113 miles. The Romans had conquered Malta in 218 BC during one of the three Punic Wars (264–146 BC). When the ship crashed into Malta, the island had a Roman ruler and legislature. However, ancestors of the original settlers, Phoenicians from Carthage (a coastal city in what is now Tunisia), retained their own distinct culture and language. They are the ones Luke refers to as "the barbarians." On the map, "St. Paul's Bay" is the traditional place (see arrow) where Paul's ship made land. [https://www.worldatlas.com/maps/malta.]

The "barbarians" assisted the shipwrecked crew and passengers, building a fire, from which others could be built, and also probably giving other assistance. Most likely the presence of Roman soldiers helped the situation.

Paul helped by gathering sticks for the fire(s). As he lay his gathered sticks on the fire, a venomous snake (for so is the meaning of "viper") drew away from the heat, and being frightened attacked the moving first object it saw, Paul's nearby hand. Superstitions ruled the age, and so the barbarians believed they were seeing one of their gods enacting justice against one of the Roman prisoners, who had seemingly escaped justice by not drowning.

Translation Acts 28:5–6

5 Then, indeed, he shook off the creature into the fire, suffering no injury. 6 But they were expecting he was about to become swollen, or to suddenly fall down dead. Now they expected a long time. And seeing nothing hurtful happening to him, they changed their mind and declared him to be a god.

EXPOSITION

In their experience no one survived the bite of a venomous snake. Paul's survival persuaded the barbarians Paul was "a god." Their belief, not encouraged by Paul or the others, led them to treat the visitors as honored guests. We might relate Paul's survival as an instance of Mark 16:18, Christ's servants "will take up snakes" without harm. (For an extended discussion of Mark 16 see my book, *A Private Commentary on the Bible: Mark's Gospel.*) Paul, of course, did not encourage their belief, cf. Acts 14:8–18. Luke does not say if Paul had an opportunity to protest his "godhood" and present the good news to them.

Translation Acts 28:7–10

7 Now around that place were fields of the chief of the island, named Publius, who courteously received us three days as guests. 8 Then it happened Publius' father was lying oppressed with fevers and dysentery, to whom Paul, entering and praying, laying his hands on him, healed him. 9 Then this having happened, also the rest in the island who had illness came and were healed. 10 These also honored us with many honors, and on setting sail they gave us the things for our needs.

EXPOSITION

The "chief of the island" would be the Roman administrator, a "procurator" for a place so small, though Luke does not give him that title. If one did not know the history of the island, one might assume from the Scripture account the entire island was peopled by "barbarians." Why Luke and the Holy Spirit do not identify the Roman ownership and administration of the island cannot be known.

The chief of the island, one Publius, had accumulated property on the island. This probably indicates Publius was a permanent resident, of some note among the inhabitants, who had been appointed by the Romans as their representative.

The locals took Paul and his "slaves" (Luke's "received us") to Publius, who received them "three days as guests" in his home. We have before seen the centurion "treated Paul kindly" (27:3) allowing him to receive care from others. Most likely because of Paul's reception by the barbarians, the crew, soldiers, prisoners, and other passengers were made welcome, and long-term accommodations (28:11, "three months) provided. There was most likely a small Roman garrison on the island, where the prisoners could be kept, and serve as a barracks for the soldiers.

When Paul arrived at Publius' home, the man's father was gravely ill. A fever indicates an infection, and dysentery is an infection of the intestines that causes diarrhea containing blood or mucus. Death is possible from the dehydration caused by diarrhea. Paul heals the man, which leads to "the rest in the island who had illness came" to Paul and those ill were healed. The long term effect of this action was the people "honored us with many honors, and on setting sail [three months later] they gave us the things for our needs."

Again, Luke does not tell us if Paul and those with him—who together formed an experienced missionary team—proclaimed the good news. Perhaps Luke and the Holy Spirit knew the reader, such as you and me, would assume the missionary team did what was natural and did proclaim the good news of salvation.

If there was not opposition to the good news, Luke may not have felt the need to tell the story we have heard so many times in the Acts. Luke the Writer is also aware his is about to close his historical account, and may have decided on brevity, knowing those reading would understand. We also do not see any report of Paul proclaiming the good news during the voyage from Caesarea to Rome, and perhaps he did not, but that is difficult to imagine. Regardless, the shipwrecked crew and passengers by necessity spent the winter months in Malta.

Translation Acts 28:11–14

11 Then after three months we sailed in a ship having wintered in the island, Alexandrian, with an ensign of Castor and Pollux. 12 And putting in at Syracuse, we remained three days. 13 From there, taking up the anchors round about, we arrived at Rhegium. And after one day a southwest wind sprang up, the second day we came to Puteoli, 14 where finding some brethren, we were invited to stay with them seven days. And so we came to Rome.

EXPOSITION

The ship that had brought Paul to Malta originated in Alexandria, Acts 27:6, but had traveled a different way to Malta than the ship with an ensign of Castor and Pollux. That ship was also a cargo ship carrying grain from Alexandria, Egypt, to Rome, Italy. That ship would have sailed west from Alexandria, along the African coast, until about (modern day) Tripoli, then north across the sea to Malta. The ensign reveals this was a Roman ship, not Egyptian. Castor and Pollux were twin half-brothers in Greek and Roman mythology. Two stars in the constellation Gemini were named Castor and Pollux.

The ship had room for the soldiers and the prisoners, including Paul's "slaves." Perhaps the rest of the 276 went with them perhaps not. Luke does not say as it is not of interest to Paul's story. The ship set sail and arrived in Puteoli, Italy in seven days.

Puteoli was about 170 miles south of Rome. Paul would not have been allowed to deliver himself to Rome as a prisoner. Did the all soldiers and all prisoners get off the ship at Puteoli and together walk the eight days (or so) to Rome? Unlikely. The ship stopped at Puteoli, and Paul found some believers there. Julius the centurion allowed Paul to remain with those Christian brethren (there is a precedent at 27:3), accompanied by at least one soldier; they stayed in Puteoli for seven days. The ship would have had cargo to unload at Puteoli (else why stop there?), and most likely new cargo to load. Did Paul then reboard the ship, or did he walk to Rome? Luke's account says, "and so we came to Rome," and Luke answers the question in 28:15.

Translation Acts 28:15–16

15 From there the brethren, having heard things concerning us, came out to meet us as far as the market of Appius and Three Taverns. Whom Paul, seeing, took courage, giving thanks to God. 16 Now when we came to Rome, Paul was allowed to stay by himself, with the soldier guarding him. [map: https://bibleatlas.org/three_taverns.htm]

TRANSLATION NOTE

At 28:16, I have not included the words occurring after the word "Rome" which are, "the centurion delivered the prisoners to the captain of the guard; but." These words appear only in the Western family of manuscripts, from there into the Byzantine manuscripts, and from there into the Textus Receptus [Metzger, *Textual*, 443]. Variations in the text in different manuscripts make it likely this was an explanatory addition.

EXPOSITION

In comments above I asked a question, did Paul return to the ship or walk to Rome? If Paul went on the ship from Puteoli to Rome, then where did the ship stop? Rome sat on the Tiber river, and the Port of Ostia was located at the mouth of the Tiber (where it emptied into the sea). But if the ship made port in Ostia, then why did Roman believers meet Paul at Appii Forum and Three Taverns. The Three Taverns was about 30 miles south of Rome, the Appii Forum about six miles further south. The most reasonable answer is Paul the Roman prisoner walked the 140 miles from Puteoli to the Appii Forum, where friends from Rome met him. Julius the centurion would have continued on with the ship.

He would have left one or more soldiers to walk with Paul. How did the brethren in Rome know Paul was coming from Puteoli? Paul spent seven days in Puteoli, plenty of time for a messenger from the Puteoli brethren to travel to the Rome brethren.

It is not too much to think some of the soldiers had heard the good news on the voyage, or during their time at Malta, and believed. Paul tells us that during his time in Rome, some in "Caesar's household," Philippians 4:22, believed, and the palace guard knew Paul's chains were for Christ, Philippians 1:13. The centurion, knowing Paul's character and trusting his soldiers, allowed Paul to walk to Rome from Puteoli.

"When we came to Rome, Paul was allowed to stay by himself, with the soldier guarding him." There was a process of which Luke tells only the result. Of course Paul was delivered to someone in the soldiers' chain of command. Paul's age (if not 60 years old, then almost), his social status (as noted before Luke and Aristarchus were most likely considered Paul's slaves), and probably a recommendation from Julius the centurion, led to allowing Paul house arrest under guard.

Luke never speaks of financial means, but we see Paul had friends in Rome, Acts 28:15, cf. Romans 16:3–16, who may have helped fund a rented house; or a wealthy believer lent him a house. All these things were within the Lord's sovereign command. But the Lord usually chooses to use earthly means to accomplish godly ends: Jesus Christ works through his saved people.

Translation Acts 28:17–20

17 Then it happened after three days he called together those who were leaders of the Jews. Then them coming together, he said to them, "Men, brethren, I have done nothing against the people or the customs of our fathers. I was delivered from Jerusalem a prisoner into the hands of the Romans, 18 who having examined me, were wanting to let me go, because not one cause of death existed in me. 19 But because the Jews contradicted, I was compelled to appeal to Caesar—not as having anything to accuse my nation. 20 Therefore, for this cause, I have called for to see you and to speak to you. On account of the hope of Israel I have this chain hung around me."

EXPOSITION

Paul's first purpose was to assure his fellow Jews his coming to Rome as a prisoner of the Romans was not to harm the Jews in Rome, or the Jewish nation. That is why he asked the Jewish leaders to come to his rented house, he not being able to go to them. Paul was in Rome not because of the Romans, but because Paul's testimony of hope that was contradicted by the Jews in Jerusalem. We the reader know Paul appealed to Caesar because the Jews kept on insisting Paul be turned over to them for trial and execution (or murder in ambush). Having explained why he was in Rome by the Romans, Paul introduces his main subject, "On account of the hope of Israel I have this chain hung around me."

Translation Acts 28:21–23

21 And to him they said, "We received neither letters from Judea concerning you, nor have any of the brethren arriving made known or said anything evil concerning you. 22 But we think it appropriate to hear from you what you think, for truly concerning this sect it is known to us that it is spoken against everywhere." 23 Then appointing him a day, many came to him at the house, to whom he expounded, testifying to the kingdom of God, persuading them concerning Jesus from both the Law of Moses and the prophets, from morning to evening.

EXPOSITION

Now Paul's trip to Rome by ship must have taken about four months, perhaps five, including the three months at Malta. That was time for a letter to travel from Jerusalem over land and sea to Philippi, much the same way Paul had traveled to Philippi, and then overland to Rome using the Via Egnatia, a common route for letter carriers. Also, Paul did not leave immediately after the defense before King Agrippa, giving the Jerusalem Jews more time to inform their brethren in Rome. That they did not is puzzling, but Luke does not give a reason for the omission. One cannot be sure any Jerusalem Jews came to Rome to testify against Paul, although Paul's two years in Rome certainly gave them time to respond. Perhaps Paul was set free because there were no witnesses against him? Certainly the letter from Festus would have exonerated him.

Paul has an opportunity to proclaim the good news with no more than the usual resistance he had experienced in this or that synagogue.

The Jewish leaders were eager to hear from a proponent of that "sect" which "is known to us" and "is spoken against everywhere" within the Jewish world. They had not heard from Jerusalem concerning Paul but they had heard from other Jews concerning the Way; and that may have included negative reports about the chief spokesman for the Way in the gentile world, Paul the former Pharisee.

What did Paul tell them? The very same message he had been saying from the beginning, of which we have an example in Acts 13:15–41. Paul told them the first great truths of Christianity.

> The Messiah must suffer, die, and resurrect out from the dead to redeem his people from their sins.
>
> Jesus of Nazareth is the prophesied Messiah-Redeemer.
>
> Jesus of Nazareth died and God raised him from the dead.
>
> Jesus of Nazareth's death is redemptive.
>
> By the indwelling Holy Spirit Jesus of Nazareth is present with his saved people.

From both the Law of Moses and the prophets, from morning to evening, Paul persuaded those listening concerning Jesus of Nazareth.

Translation Acts 28:24–29

24 And truly some were persuaded of the things he spoke; but some refused to believe. 25 Then disagreeing with one another, they began leaving; Paul said one statement: "Rightly the Holy Spirit spoke through Isaiah the prophet to your fathers, 26 saying, 'Go to this people and say, in hearing you will hear and not understand, and in seeing you will see and no not perceive. 27 For the heart of this people has become dull, and with the ears they hear with difficulty, and their eyes they have shut, lest ever they should see with the eyes and they should hear with the ears and should understand with the heart, and should turn, and I will heal them.' 28 Therefore, be it known to you, that to the gentiles has been sent this salvation of God; and they will listen."

TRANSLATION NOTE

I have not included what certain other translations identify as 28:29, "And when he had said these words, the Jews left, and had much reasoning among themselves," These words appear only in certain manuscripts of the Western family, and from there into the

Byzantine texts [Metzger, *Textual*, 444]. The lack of clear textual support indicates it is probably a scribal addition to make a transition from 28:28 to 28:30. The scribal addition is redundant, see 28:24.

EXPOSITION

The proclamation of the good news does what it always does, from then to now. Some were persuaded; some refused to believe. The resultant conflict between those of faith and those of no faith resulted in "disagreeing with one another." And so they began leaving the house.

Before they all left the house, Paul gave a final word of warning, drawn from Isaiah.

> Isaiah 6:8–10 (ESV), And I heard the voice of the Lord saying, "Whom shall I send, and who will go for us?" Then I said, "Here am I! Send me." 9 And he said, "Go, and say to this people: 'Keep on hearing, but do not understand; keep on seeing, but do not perceive.' 10 Make the heart of this people dull, and their ears heavy, and blind their eyes; lest they see with their eyes, and hear with their ears, and understand with their hearts, and turn and be healed.'"

> Acts 28:25–27 (JQT), Then disagreeing with one another, they began leaving; Paul said one statement: "Rightly the Holy Spirit spoke through Isaiah the prophet to your fathers, 26 saying, 'Go to this people and say, in hearing you will hear and not understand, and in seeing you will see and no not perceive. 27 For the heart of this people has become dull, and with the ears they hear with difficulty, and their eyes they have shut, lest ever they should see with the eyes and they should hear with the ears and should understand with the heart, and should turn, and I will heal them.'

YHWH's statement in Isaiah, and Paul in Acts, is more descriptive than prescriptive. God does not prevent any person from believing and being saved. God acts to save people, that is election (see Appendix: Election), but God's choice to save some does not prevent any from coming and believing. Their own desire for sin causes them to rebel against God and his salvation. God gave human kind the moral authority to make choices, and he has respect for what he has created, blessing the right choices, allowing and warning against the wrong choices (see Appendix: Free will).

Choices have consequences. The good news was to the Jew first, then to the gentiles. In 28:28 Paul does not mean he will no longer proclaim the good news to the Jews, We see that is not the case by comparing Acts 13:46 with the rest of the story of Acts. Paul says nothing more or less than the Old Testament prophets said, that God has sent the Messiah-Redeemer to the gentiles, Acts 13:47, and they will believe and be saved. Not all gentiles will believe, but some gentiles will be persuaded. That is the way of the word of salvation.

Translation Acts 28:30–31

30 Then he remained two whole years in his own rented house, and welcomed all coming to him, 31 proclaiming the kingdom of God and teaching the things concerning the Lord Jesus Christ with all boldness, no one hindering.

EXPOSITION

The consequences of those two years is known from Paul's letters written and sent to local churches from his time as a prisoner in Rome. Paul had his trial before Caesar and was released. During that two whole years many were saved. The respect Paul had from his Roman guards was made known in this, "no one hindering" his proclamation of "the kingdom of God" and "the things concerning the Lord Jesus Christ."

How do I know Paul was released from what came to be his first Roman imprisonment? One reason is what Luke, Paul, and the Holy Spirit tell us. Paul says it here, 28:18, the Romans who sent him to Rome, "having examined me, were wanting to let me go, because not one cause of death existed in me." The letter Festus sent to Rome with Paul, 25:25-26, would have stated that fact. Festus many have included a copy of the letter from Claudius Lysias, the Roman Jerusalem commander, 23:25–30, saying the same thing, "no accusation worthy of death or of chains."

We also have a chain of evidence from Paul's letters. See Appendix: Pauls' Roman Imprisonments. Luke's narrative of the Acts of the Holy Spirit through the Apostles and other disciples has come to an end.

Appendix: Election

This article on election first appeared in my book, *Dispensational Soteriology*, developed over many years from Scripture, historic orthodox creeds, and similar Reformed and Dispensational statements of doctrine.

Election: Statement of the doctrine.

> Election. The choice of a sovereign God (Ephesians 1:4), to give the gift of grace-faith-salvation to effect the salvation of some sinners (Ephesians 2:8), and to take no action, positive or negative, to either effect or deny salvation to other sinners (Romans 10:13; Revelation 22:17).
>
> The decree of election includes all means necessary to effectuate salvation in those elected. God's decree of election ensures the salvation of the elect, but does not prevent any non-elect sinner from coming or willing to be saved. God will act savingly toward any who choose to seek him and come to him for salvation (Rom. 10:13; Eph. 1:4; Rev. 22:17).

God would have all persons to be saved (1 Timothy 2:4), but he wills for certain persons to believe (Ephesians 1:4; 2 Thessalonians 2:13), thereby guaranteeing the elect will believe, without any kind of decree preventing any from believing.

What is election? Election is God's foreordaining choice to give to certain persons his gift of grace-faith-salvation (Ephesians 2:8), so that they will infallibly choose to believe.

Because God would have all persons to be saved (1 Timothy 2:4), God does not will any person to reprobation, but permits any person not elected to choose to believe, if they will.

All persons begin life as reprobate (Romans 3:23). All persons believing are saved from reprobation and have eternal life (John 3:15; 17:2). All persons not believing remain reprobate and will endlessly experience God's just wrath against their sins (Revelation 20:15).

God's wrath is his justice in action against the impenitent.

> God's wrath against the sinner who dies unforgiven and thus unsaved is expressed as endless punishment.

God's wrath against the unrepentant believer who has committed an act of sinning is expressed as chastisement.

Jesus Christ on the cross suffered the wrath of God justly due the unsaved sinner, through the imputation of the sinner's judicial guilt to Christ, 2 Corinthians 5:21.

Discussion of Election

I previously discussed the doctrine of sin in the chapter "Soteriology." All persons are conceived as sinners and unless saved, die as sinners. This chapter will focus on the election of sinners to salvation. Because from the instant of conception all are sinners needing salvation, this chapter will also address election from the moment of conception. It is impossible to discuss election without some mention of the lapsarian orders of God's pre-creation decrees. However, an in depth discussion will not be done here but in the chapter on Propitiation.

I defined election above.

> The choice of a sovereign God (Ephesians 1:4), to give the gift of grace-faith-salvation to effect the salvation of some sinners (Ephesians 2:8), and to take no action, positive or negative, to either effect or deny salvation to other sinners (Romans 10:13; Revelation 22:17).

Election is the consequence of foreordination. Therefore a presentation of foreordination is required.

Foreordination is a very difficult subject. All opinions on foreordination, as may be expressed by any person, are theological constructs: logical and rational reasoning based on the Scripture to arrive at a conclusion not explicitly stated in the Scripture. The scriptures used to derive a doctrine of foreordination are those relevant to God's sovereignty, human nature, and the obvious fact some are saved, some are not.

I will not here discuss the merits of this or that particular view of foreordination, but my own conclusions only. I briefly discussed Arminian foresight (or prescient) election in the chapter "Arminian Soteriology." The consequence of foresight election is God took no foreordaining action resulting in election. Molinism is foresight election, simply on a larger scale.

In Arminian soteriology election is individual. In Molinism

soteriology God chose worlds not individuals: God foresaw all possible universes he might create, and who would believe on each Earth in each universe. God then chose to create one universe where those believing suited his purpose in creating. Thus, foresight election.

Foreordination

For a complete discussion of foreordination see my book, *God's Choices, the Doctrines of Foreordination, Election, and Predestination*.

> Foreordination. The decree of God occurring between his decision to create and his act of creation as to which agents, events, and outcomes, out of all possible agents, events, and outcomes potential in the decision to create, would pass from possible to actual, in which the liberty or contingency of secondary causes is established, in which God is not the author of sin, and in which no violence is done to the free will of his creatures.

Prior to the act of creation, God omnisciently knew within himself whatever might or could come to pass upon all supposed conditions. This was not the knowing of foresight, but God omnisciently understanding all possible agents, events, and outcomes (which outcomes included all possible freely made choices that might be made by all beings he would create and all possible consequences resulting from their choices) that could develop from the act of creation. God did not decree anything because he foresaw it as future, but because he determined all that was possible, and then chose which of all possible agents, events, and outcomes he would foreordain as actual. That choice effectuating possible to actual included freely made choices.

In an illustration, we might say God omnisciently "calculated" that from cause A, events 1, 2, 3, a, b, c were possible, and then chose which possible events to make actual. Not because he foresaw the events, but because he omnisciently understood within himself all that might be possible from his decision to create, and then chose which possible things he would effect in the universe he would create. God then created the universe his choices effectuated.

Foreordination is not fate or determinism. Foreordination makes choices certain but not necessary. The choices we make during our lifetime are certain because foreordained, but not necessary because those choices are freely made, God having effectuated certain possible choices from possible to actual, as fit his purpose in creating the universe. Within the historic moment of decision, all sentient creatures freely decide in agreement with God's choices. That is foreordination through sovereignty not foreknowledge.

Several illustrations will be helpful. What your computer does upon turn-on was foreordained by the computer's programmer. When you drive to the grocery store in your vehicle, at every four-way intersection you have four choices: straight, left, right, U-turn. God chose which of those four possible choices to effect from possible to actual. During a chess game a grandmaster can see up to twenty possible moves ahead. Before the game begins God sees all possible moves from beginning to end and chooses which moves to effect from possible to actual.

How does foreordination interact with election? That depends on your lapsarian view of God's pre-creation decrees. The suffix -lapsarian refers to the "lapse" in man's holiness, i.e., Adam's act of sinning.

When God chose to create a universe, what did he do first, second, third, etc.? The lapsarian views of God's pre-creation decrees are opinions of God's decrees relevant to salvation. Of course, God's creation decree was one decree, but it is helpful to think of that act of creation as we might act, having several rational sequenced steps. For example, my first step in putting together my kid's tricycle for her birthday was to grab the directions, then sort the parts, then inventory the parts, then get the tools, etc., etc., until the tricycle was fully assembled. How did God assemble his universe? More to the point of this discussion, how did God decide whom to save and how to save them.

The supralapsarian view, created by Thomas Beza (1519–1605) says God's first decision was to elect to salvation some of the human beings he would create, and elect to reprobation (damnation) all other human beings he would create. Then God decided to decree Adam would commit an act of sinning, then God decided to send Christ to save those whom God had elected to salvation. I will discuss the ramifications of this view in the chapter on Propitiation.

The infralapsarian view adopted by the Synod of Dort (1618–1619) says God decided to permit Adam's fall into sin. That choice determined all of Adam's descendants would be sinners (see discussion of sin in chapter "Soteriology"). Then, seeing all human beings as sinners, God chose to elect some out of this fallen mass to be saved, and to leave the others as they were, and then chose to provide a redeemer for the elect.

In the sublapsarian view, after the Synod of Dort, God chose to permit the fall, to provide a redeemer, to elect some out of this fallen mass to be saved, and to leave the others as they were.

Those are the three views of God's foreordination to elect some to be saved. But those views do not give the process of election. What I am saying is election was a choice made by God, but how was that choice effectuated? How are those sinners who were to be elected identified as those who were elect? The answer is twofold.

First, God never tells us the basis on which one was elected and another was not. All we know is the choice was not based on foreseeable merit: all were sinners, none had merit. As I explained in an earlier chapter, in Arminian soteriology God looked outside himself into the history of the universe he would create, decided to give all prevenient grace, saw who would believe and who would not believe after receiving prevenient grace, and elected to salvation those he foresaw would believe. In Arminian soteriology God acted because of what he learned.

Reformed-Dispensational soteriology says God looked inside himself (omniscience), and thereby knowing all human beings he would create, decided which of those human beings he would give prevenient grace for salvation (Ephesians 2:8). Those individuals God decided to give prevenient grace are identified as elected to salvation, because of the infallible efficacy of the gift.

That brings us to the second answer: the process of electing is God foreordaining to give to certain sinners his prevenient grace; or as it is otherwise known, God's gift of grace-faith-salvation, Ephesians 2:8. God's decree that a particular person will receive God's gift, at some point during the course of that person's lifetime, is the foreordaining act of electing that person to salvation, an act that occurred before God created the universe.

Therefore election is "the choice of a sovereign God (Ephesians 1:4), to give the gift of grace-faith-salvation to effect the salvation of some sinners (Ephesians 2:8)."

What about those not elected? The traditional Reformed solution, to which many Dispensationalists will agree, is to propose God has a secret will and a revealed will. The revealed will calls all to believe, knowing the secret will says only some can believe because only those elected to believe can believe.

I disagree. None can know the secret will of God, Deuteronomy 29:29, but we can know that what has been revealed to us cannot contradict what has not been revealed to us. Therefore the salvific call of God to "whosoever will" cannot contradict an unknown "secret will." If all are called to believe, then all must have the same opportunity to believe. Therefore election cannot prevent belief in any of the all.

(The supralapsarian gets around this logical reasoning by redefining "all" as "only the elect.")

I believe election guarantees the salvation of those elected but says nothing about those not elected. Thus, in his decree to elect some, God took no action, positive or negative, to either effect or deny salvation to other sinners (Romans 10:13; Revelation 22:17). What stands in the way of salvation is sin—all are sinners—overcome in the elect by God's gift.

I believe Scripture teaches salvation is conditioned upon faith in God and God's testimony as to the way of salvation. There are two consequences of that belief. The first is election guarantees some will believe, that is its purpose, and by election the condition of faith will be met by the elect.

The second consequence is election does not prevent any non-elect from believing. If a non-elect person would choose to repent of his or her sin and freely believe on God and God's testimony as to the way of salvation, God would act savingly toward that person, because the purpose of election is to guarantee salvation, election does not prevent salvation. Thus God's requirement that the proclamation is to be made to all for all to believe, because none are prevented by God from believing.

I have an illustration.

> The river of sinful humankind is justly racing toward the waterfall of death emptying into the lake of eternal fire; God reaches into the river and saves many; he prevents no one from swimming to the safety of the heavenly shore; he puts his saved people on the shore encouraging all to believe on God and his

testimony of salvation and be saved; he saves all that come to him by faith in God and his testimony.

What prevents salvation is the freely made choice to rebel against God. All are infected with this spiritual condition, from birth. God chose to give some his gift of grace-faith-salvation to effect their salvation through his gift. God leaves the others as he found them, unsaved sinners, which also means he leaves them to their own choices. God never prevents the choice to believe and be saved, their own sinful nature makes the choice to reject God and his salvation the natural choice.

Yes, God foreordained every choice, but every choice is a freely made choice, freely made by the person during the course of his or her lifetime. The choice of disbelief is the natural choice of the sinner, there are no other possible choices, hence the gift of grace-faith-salvation. But if there were other possible choices, God has foreordained all are sinners, so the promise of salvation might be given to those who believe.

Even the choice of the elect to believe is a freely made choice, foreordained by God, through his gift, because the gift of God efficaciously changes the moral boundaries of human nature (see chapter "What is Free Will"), changing the unable and unwilling sinner to able and willing. But even the elect would not choose to believe if God had not foreordained to give them his gift. Therefore all are free to make the choice to believe, but the elect are guaranteed to make that choice, because God foreordained those he elected to receive his gift.

Election And The Morally Undeveloped

One of the more troubling issues—and highly charged emotionally—is the relationship God's election has toward those who either have not or never will develop the moral capacity to decide for faith or no faith. Usually these are defined as babies or infants. But the reality is as a group those with an undeveloped moral capacity include human beings from conception to birth; babies, infants, small children; adults who never develop the moral capacity to decide for faith or no faith.

From an observational point of view, we cannot know if the persons in that class of people—the morally undeveloped—have believed unto salvation. Let us be honest: we become aware of who we believe is among the elect through a credible profession of saving faith. That criteria is unavailable in the morally undeveloped group of persons. Because we cannot observe the choice for faith or no faith in that group, we are emotionally distressed that the "innocent" (none are innocent, all are sinful) may be unfairly condemned. The usual solution is to manipulate Scripture to say, "babies and infants are automatically saved," disregarding all others in that group.

Some, who understand that all are sinners from conception forward (the legal guilt of Adam's sin is imputed to every sinner), have a slightly different solution: the intrinsically sinful nature is not counted against the morally undeveloped until they commit an act of sinning. This solution manipulates Scripture to create a standard of moral accountability (an "age" of accountability) that begins with the moral choice to commit an act of sinning. This is similar to that aspect of Arminian soteriology that says inability absolves responsibility.

What says the Scripture? The following is drawn in part from my book, *Adam and Eve, A Biography and Theology*.

Culpability For Sin From Conception

If, as Scripture teaches, all persons are culpable for the moral guilt of sin from the moment of conception (see *Adam and Eve*, arguments under Hamartiology)—which we know is true because physical death, the observable consequence of sin's judicial guilt, may occur between conception and birth—then how are those persons who are morally undeveloped to make a faith-based decision—the unborn (a human being from conception to birth), infants, small children, adults who never became mentally or morally competent—how are they able to express saving faith and be saved from their sin?

The answer, as far as can be known by observation, is that they cannot. I am not saying that a person must verbalize his or her faith in order to be saved. The exercise of saving faith is not necessarily verbal. Saving faith is the positive response of the soul to God's gift of grace-faith-salvation. However, the way a person's saving faith can be known to others (other than God) is when it is verbalized or actualized.

The persons under discussion cannot verbalize faith and they cannot demonstrate their faith by their works. Therefore, we cannot know if this class of persons are saved, because they are not capable of making their salvation (or lack of salvation) known. Since they are culpable for their sin, but as much as we can observe are morally undeveloped to make a faith-based decision, can they be saved? Let me firmly answer that the question is not, "can these persons be saved," because they can, but "how can we know if these persons can be saved?"

The answer is in the efficient cause of salvation and the choices made by God. We will discuss the latter later. As to the former, the one and only basis of salvation is the propitiating death of Christ, decreed in eternity past, effective from eternity past through eternity future, and accomplished in historical space-time. The efficient cause of salvation is the remission of sin's guilt and penalty by the application of Christ's limitless merit.

In those who are mentally competent to make a choice between faith and no-faith, Christ's merit is applied by their receiving God's gift of grace-faith-salvation, and through the means of personal faith in God's revealed means (way) of salvation, they exercise saving faith. However, the unborn, infants, small children, and adults who never became mentally or morally competent cannot, as far as may be known, grasp or express saving faith. Nor does Scripture deal with their need for salvation. Scripture focuses on those who are able to make a decision for faith or no-faith. Scripture does not directly address the salvific needs of the unborn, infants, small children, and adults who never became mentally or morally competent.

Two Scriptures are often used to defend the salvation of infants and small children (neither of which addresses the unborn or the morally undeveloped adult.)

The first is 2 Samuel 12:15–23. The story is familiar to most Christians. David the king committed adultery with Bathsheba and she became pregnant. David recalled her husband from the battlefield so he could have sex with his wife and make it appear he was responsible for the pregnancy. He did not have sex with her, so David had him abandoned on the battlefield so he would die in conflict with the enemy; in God's eyes it was an act of murder. Then David married Bathsheba. The child was born. The child became ill and died.

During the illness, David prostrated himself in prayer and fasts. After the child died, David got up, washed and anointed himself, changed his clothes, went to the tabernacle, and worshiped YHWH. His servants were amazed he did not mourn. David replied,

> When the child was alive I fasted and wept. I said to myself, 'Who is able to know whether YHWH will be gracious to me that the child may live?' But now he is dead; should I continue to fast? Can I bring him back again? I shall go to him, but he shall not return to me.

Was David saying he also would die. Was David saying that when he died he would meet this infant in heaven, i.e., that this one infant had been saved prior to its physical death? (Salvation must occur prior to death, Hebrews 9:27.) To answer this question we must ask, who was speaking? Was it David the prophet or David the grieving father? We must ask, is what David said revelation from God? The words are inspired, which means that what David said was accurately recorded, but was what David said revelation from God the Holy Spirit regarding the spiritual state of all infants? Or even this one infant. David says his son cannot come back from death, but he, David, will go to him, the child, when he, David, dies.

If David was speaking as a prophet, and if David knew by divine revelation the eternal fate of this one infant, does that understanding apply to every other person dying in infancy from Adam forward to the end of the world? No. What David said was a singular statement, meaning that nothing like it, or corresponding to it, or parallel with it, or similar to it in thought or idea, appears anywhere else in Scripture. One of the rules of theology is, do not build a doctrine from a single verse. I will respect that rule in regard to this singular verse. In my view, this one verse only answers the question concerning the salvation of either this one infant or all infants if you bring the answer with you. (And what about all the other morally undeveloped persons?)

The second verse, rather, the incident recorded in Matthew 19, Mark 10, and Luke 18, is Jesus with little children. The passage says nothing conclusive about their salvation. Jesus was displeased that the disciples sought to prevent parents bringing their children to Jesus. However, it was culturally unusual, very unusual, that parents would bring their little children near to any "holy man," such as a rabbi, teacher, or prophet.

In the ancient world children were not prized as they are today. In modern times children are evaluated on their assumed adult potential.

In the ancient world children were evaluated on what they might contribute to society or family as children. As a result, they were not valued at all (a high mortality rate for infants and children did not help the situation). Christianity is actually one of the impelling reasons the attitude toward children changed.

So, it was unusual in those times for parents to bring their children to a teacher, a holy man, a prophet. But they did bring their children to Jesus and he did receive them. He used them as an illustration to teach that saving faith is trusting faith, on the order of the naïve kind of trust expressed by little children: faith without suspicion; faith without doubt. The passage does not say if little children will be saved, but it leaves no doubt they can be saved—if they can express saving faith.

Neither the 2 Samuel passage nor the gospel passages answer the question concerning the salvation of the unborn, infants, small children, and morally undeveloped adults. To answer the question we must return to the basis of salvation, Christ's propitiation and its efficient application, and add in the final point, the choices made by God. What is required to save those who cannot express saving faith, who (as far as we can know) cannot make a choice between faith and no-faith, is the application of the merit of Christ to the sinful condition of their soul.

That is, in fact, the need of everyone. No one seeks after God, no one understands, all have gone the way of sin. If no person seeks God, if the inclination of the sinful nature is to rebel against God, then how is anyone saved? The answer is Ephesians 1:4, "he chose us in him before the beginning of the universe." Not every human being is chosen, but no human being is beyond the reach of God's electing choice, from the moment of conception to physical death.

All those whom God has elected will certainly be saved. Those persons *who are morally developed* will be saved by responding to the good news of salvation with faith; Scripture gives no other way to salvation.

As to the unborn, infants, and others similarly so morally undeveloped that they are unable to make the moral choice between faith and no faith, if they are saved, "it cannot be on their own merits, or on the basis of their own righteousness or innocence, but must be entirely on the basis of Christ's redemptive work and regeneration by the work of the Holy Spirit within them" [Grudem, 500].

What I am saying is that if God has chosen any one of these morally undeveloped persons to salvation, then God will by grace give them the gift of grace-faith-salvation, and by grace they will positively respond to the gift by the exercise of saving faith, and by grace God will apply the merit of Christ to their soul. The manner of their positive response—how they might express saving faith—cannot be known, because they cannot tell us by word or deed.

Is the God who created human beings unable to effectively communicate with the human soul that he designed and created *ex nihilo?* At any stage of human development, beginning at conception? The omnipotent God in whom my faith rests is able.

God's electing choice is the primary condition affecting the salvation of every human being from Adam forward to the end of this present universe: God saves whom he has chosen; he prevents no one from coming to him to be saved. Beyond this no one can go with certainty. No one can say with scriptural certainty that all, some, or none of the unborn, infants, small children, or adults who never became morally developed are saved. Perhaps God has elected every single person who dies without having the moral development to decide for faith or no-faith. Perhaps some of these are saved and some not. Perhaps none are saved. Is God righteous, holy, and just only when I understand? Certainly not! For then how will God judge the world?

Whatever God has decided it is holy, it is righteous, it is just. As Abraham said, God does not execute the righteous with the wicked, Genesis 18:25. What are the options?

> If all the unborn, infants, small children, and morally undeveloped adults are saved, God is just, God is holy.
>
> If only some, or none, are saved God is just, God is holy.

Justice and holiness are essential characteristics of God. God has no sin and takes no action that would be unjust. There is an election according to grace—the blessing of God given to those with no merit. God does make a choice, "Jacob I have loved, but Esau have I hated," meaning God drew one into a covenant with himself but not the other, and "the children not yet being born, nor having done any good or evil, that the purpose of God according to election might stand, not of works, but of him who calls." God has chosen not to reveal the why or who of his electing choice. One must either accept that God is holy, righteous, and just in all his ways, or create a soteriology not based on Scripture.

What has been said about the unborn, infants, small children, and morally undeveloped adults cannot be applied to those who have developed the moral competence to make a decision for faith or no-faith. All morally developed people of any physical age, in all the millennia of humankind on this earth, are morally required to believe in God and God's testimony as to the means of salvation. All Christians are required to go and "disciple all the peoples," Matthew 28:19. How God deals with that one class of sinners without moral development is one of the secret things that belong to YHWH our God (Deuteronomy 29:29). This also is part of the doctrine of soteriology.

Appendix: Free Will

This article on free will first appeared in my book, *Dictionary of Doctrinal Words*.

Free Will, Or Freely Made Choices.

The will is the decision-making faculty of human nature. Free will may be defined as the moral authority God designed into his sentient creatures to make choices within the physical, moral, and spiritual boundaries of their nature, as further influenced by internal and external motivations and consequences.

The two important aspects of that definition are the "physical, moral, and spiritual boundaries," and "internal and external motivations and consequences."

Free will is not a license to think or do anything I want. Free will is limited by the attributes and characteristics of human nature. These form the boundaries in which free will may be exercised. If it helps, think of those attributes and characteristics of human nature as a fence beyond which one cannot go, whether physically, morally, or spiritually. Any decision may be made that the fence allows, including decisions to commit acts of sinning, and the decision to reject God and his salvation. The latter, in fact, that decision to reject God and his salvation, is the only decision regarding God and his salvation that the fence formed by the sinful unsaved human nature will allow.

The other important aspect to the exercise of free will is the influence of internal and external motivations and consequences. The internal motivations of the person, the external motivations applied to the person by influences outside the person, and the consequences arising from a person's freely made choices—all influence the exercise of free will, but do not change the fact the will freely makes decisions.

Right now, you are deciding to continue reading or stop. No one is making that decision for you. Your decision will be influenced by various internal motivations, such as your spiritual state (saved or unsaved), curiosity, the desire to learn, or perhaps the desire to respond to this "bloated windbag of a theologian" (as some have said). You are also experiencing various external motivations, including prior teaching you have received on the subject, and your own investigations of relevant scriptures. Whatever you decision, you exercised your free will.

As sinful human beings we try to hide, or even deny, our free will behind motivations and consequences. If the motivations and consequences are good we claim the choices we made. If the motivations and consequences are bad we say we were forced or coerced to make those choices. No, the choice is always yours, you alone are responsible for your choices.

Even the slave—even a slave to sin—makes a decision to obey or not to obey, as influenced by motivations and by the consequences of his choices. Even the slave is not prevented from exercising his free will because of the consequences of those choices.

So free will, like liberty or freedom, isn't a license to think or do anything I want. Just as a physical fence limits choices to "this far, no further," even so the fence formed by the physical, moral, and spiritual aspects of human nature say "this far, no further"; and these are fences one cannot climb over. One cannot freely choose to flap his arms and fly to the store because of the physical boundaries of human nature. Even so, the moral and spiritual boundaries limit the exercise of free will.

Free will is limited by the attributes and characteristics of human nature. Looking at the spiritual boundaries, the will is not neutrally suspended between good and evil, but is inclined toward one or the other by its spiritual attributes as created by God, corrupted by sin, and in the case of the saved, regenerated by salvation. The spiritual boundary does not allow the sinner to initiate salvation, nor believe and be saved unaided by the efficacious influence of God's gift of grace-faith-salvation (Ephesians 2:8).

In the case of unsaved human beings, the will is inclined toward sin because of the principle of rebellion (the sin attribute) that became part of human nature following Adam's sin and propagation. The inclination of sin is to rebel against God and disobey his commandments, thereby effectively persuading human beings to choose their path in life apart from God. The sinner freely chooses to commit acts of sinning, including the sin to reject God and his salvation. The unsaved human being is unable to overcome the spiritual boundary of the sin attribute without God's gift of grace-faith-salvation.

The sinner freely chooses to sin, his choice conditioned by the moral and spiritual boundaries set by the sin attribute in his or her human nature. Without that freely made choice there is no responsibility, accountability, or liability. When we deny that free exercise of the will, we have denied God made humankind with the power to choose, the moral authority to exercise choice, the responsibility to choose rightly, and equally as important to God's justice, the accountability and liability for every freely made choice. When we deny the free exercise of will, we have proclaimed God made human beings programmed automatons who dance on the string of God's sovereignty.

God changes the spiritual boundary of the sinner through his gift, Ephesians 2:8, thereby changing the kind of choices that may be made. Staying with the same illustration, God moves the fence to a different spiritual boundary, so different choices may be made. God by his gift initiates salvation in the sinner by changing the spiritual boundary (1 Corinthians 2:14; Romans 6:14) in which free will operates. The gift enlivens the person's spiritual perception, whereby the sinner is able to understand the spiritual issues of his sin, Christ the only Savior, salvation by faith alone, and thereby the sinner willingly obeys God's command to believe and be saved, whereupon God completes that salvation through the regeneration of the human nature from unsaved to saved.

The saved, born-again believer freely chooses to deny temptation because those choices are within the spiritual boundary of the born-again human nature.

All decisions made by every human being are made within the limits imposed by the boundaries of the human nature of sinner or saint, as further influenced by internal and external motivations and consequences. That is free will.

Appendix: Paul's Roman Imprisonments

This appendix is an extract from my commentary on the Pastoral Epistles.

In 1 Timothy Paul does not speak of his imprisonment but has an expectation of coming to Timothy, "hoping to come to you in a short time," 1 Timothy 3:14. Paul expects to see Titus, "be diligent to come to me into Nicopolis; for there I have chosen to winter," Titus 2:12. These things speak of Paul released from prison.

In 2 Timothy 4:16–17, Paul speaks of a trial.

> At my first defense no one was present with me, but all left me. May it not be reckoned to them. Now the Lord stood by me and strengthened me, so that through me the proclamation would be fully accomplished, and all the gentiles should hear. And I was delivered out of the mouth of the lion,"

Then he tells Timothy to come to him, 2 Timothy 4:9, "Be diligent to come to me quickly" and 4:21, "Be diligent to come before winter." Timothy was with Paul during his imprisonment in Rome, Colossians 1:11. Mark, whom Paul instructs Timothy to bring with him, 2 Timothy 4:11, was with Paul during his first imprisonment, Philemon 24. These verses tell us Paul was not in prison in 1 Timothy and Titus, but he is in prison in the second letter to Timothy.

Considering the above scriptures, I believe Paul was imprisoned twice. The first was that of Acts 28, beginning ca. AD 61–62, from which Paul was tried and released, ca. AD 63. Then he endured a second imprisonment and trial, ca. AD 67–68, which he did not survive. The issue is debated by many, but two imprisonments seems likely. I have based my belief on Paul's words. Others propose two imprisonments to account for Paul's movements (see below) that are not recorded in Acts.

Clement (AD 30–100), in his first letter to the Corinthians (5.7), wrote that Paul, "After preaching in the east and west ... and come to the extreme limit of the west, suffered martyrdom under the prefects." The debate is whether "extreme limit of the west" meant Rome or Spain. [Roberts, 6]. Eusebius (d. AD 339) knows the tradition of two imprisonments [2.22]. Wiersbe [no page numbers], assumed two imprisonments. Towner [11–12], says a visit to Spain is in the Muratorian Canon (late 2nd century).

The apocryphal book, *Acts of Peter* 1.1, the version known as the "Vercelli Acts," preserves the tradition of Paul's visit to Spain.

> At the time when Paul was sojourning in Rome and confirming many in the faith, it came also to pass that one by name Candida, the wife of Quartus that was over the prisons, heard Paul and paid heed to his words and believed. And when she had instructed her husband also and he believed, Quartus suffered Paul to go whither he would away from the city: to whom Paul said: If it be the will of God, he will reveal it unto me. And after Paul had fasted three days and asked of the Lord that which should be profitable for him, he saw a vision, even the Lord saying unto him: Arise, Paul, and become a physician in thy body (i.e. by going thither in person) to them that are in Spain.
>
> [http://www.earlychristianwritings.com/text/actspeter.html]

The book was written not later than AD 200.

Goodwin [173 ff.; Appendix 13], harmonizes the Scriptures detailing the apostle Paul and his travels. He presents likely scriptures indicating Paul's travels after a first imprisonment, and an appendix discussing the likelihood of a second imprisonment. See also Schaff, *History*, 1:331–333; Conybeare and Howson, *Life*, 2:436–440.

Here is what I believe. Between his imprisonments Paul traveled to these places [Hollingsworth, 201].

Macedonia, Philippians 2:24

Crete, Titus 1:5

Asia Minor, Philemon 22

Troas, 2 Timothy 4:13

Perhaps Spain, Romans 15:22–29

The cities listed *are not* given in a particular or suspected order of travel and visitation. His other obligations probably make Spain last on the list. If Paul did travel to Spain, then it was between his two imprisonments.

Appendix: Paul's Roman Imprisonments

Assuming Paul went to Spain, he ended his time in Spain ca. AD 66, and made his way through Macedonia to Ephesus. First Timothy and Titus were written ca. AD 66–67. Paul's second Roman imprisonment was ca. AD 67–68. Second Timothy was written from prison ca. AD 68.

The first letter to Timothy and the letter to Titus were written before Paul's second imprisonment: 1 Timothy written from Macedonia; Titus from written from Ephesus. The order would be.

Released from prison ca. AD 63

Promised visits, as listed above, ca. AD 63–64

Missionary journey into Spain, ca. AD 64–66

Travel back to Asia Minor from Spain, ca. AD 66

1 Timothy and Titus written, ca. AD 66–67

Visit to Nicopolis, Titus 3:12, ca. AD 66–67

Second Roman imprisonment, ca. AD 67–68

Second Timothy written from prison in Rome, ca. AD 68

Paul Executed by Nero, ca. AD 68.

About three years earlier than his letters to Timothy and Titus, or perhaps two years earlier, Paul had left Ephesus for Macedonia, 1 Timothy 1:3, then on to Spain (his expressed desire in the Romans letter, 15:22–29). From Spain he had returned to Asia Minor and Ephesus. While passing through Macedonia on his way to Ephesus (undoubtedly spending time with the Macedonian churches), he had sent a letter, 1 Timothy, to Timothy in Ephesus, reminding him of a conversation before he went into Spain, 1 Timothy 1:3.

Then, arriving at Ephesus, he had written to Titus who was in Crete, referencing a previous visit there with Titus between his imprisonments, Titus 1:5. He was arrested some unknown length of time after writing those letters. The circumstances leading to his second imprisonment are unknown—but most likely similar to the first time. During this imprisonment he wrote again to Timothy, concerning his (Paul's) impending death, giving final instructions and encouragement.

Sources

Aharoni, Yohanan, and Michael Avi-Yohan. *The MacMillan Bible Atlas*. Rev. New York, NY: 1968.

Alexander, Joseph, Addison. *Commentary on the Acts of the Apostles*. NICNT. 1875. Reprinted. Grand Rapids, MI: Zondervan, 1956.

Black, David Alan. *Why Four Gospels?* Gonzales, FL: Energion Publications, 2010.

Bauckham, Richard. *Jesus and the Eyewitnesses*. Grand Rapids, MI: Eerdmans Publishing, 2006.

Bock, Darrell L., and Gregory J. Herrick. *Jesus in Context*. Grand Rapids, MI: Baker Academic, 2005.

Boyer, James L. *Chronology of the Crucifixion and the Last Week*. Winona Lake, IN: Grace Theological Seminary, 1975.

Bromiley, G. W., ed. *The International Standard Bible Encyclopedia*. Revised 1982. Reprinted, Grand Rapids, MI: William B. Eerdmans Publishing Company, 1992.

_____. *Theological Dictionary of the New Testament*. Abridged. Grand Rapids, MI: Eerdmans Publishing, 1971.

Bruce, F. F. *Commentary on the Book of he Acts*. Grand Rapids, MI: Eerdmans, 1954.

Burton, Ernest De Witt. *The Ancient Synagogue Service*. The Biblical World, Aug., 1896, Vol. 8, No. 2 (Aug., 1896), pp. 143–148 Published by: The University of Chicago Press Stable. URL: http://www.jstor.com/stable/3140264

Charnock, Stephen. *The Works of Stephen Charnock*. Vol. 3. 1865. Reprinted, Carlisle, PA: Banner of Truth Trust, 1986.

Conybeare, W. J. and Howsen, J. S. *The Life and Epistles of St. Paul*. 1864. Reprinted. Grand Rapids, MI: Eerdmans, 1976.

Danby, Herbert. *The Mishnah*. Oxford, England: Oxford University Press, 1933.

Edersheim, Alfred. *The Temple, Its Ministry and Services*. Peabody, MA: Hendrickson Publishers, 1994.

Goodwin, Frank J. *A Harmony of the Life of St. Paul, According to the Acts of the Apostles and the Pauline Epistles*. Grand Rapids, MI:

Baker Book House, 1951.

Harris, R. Laird; Gleason L. Archer, Jr.; and Bruce K. Waltke. *Theological Wordbook of the Old Testament*. 2 vols. Chicago, IL: Moody Press, 1980.

Hollingsworth, David R. and James D. Quiggle. *Old and New Testament Chronology*. Amazon/KDP, 2015.

Kaiser, Walter C., and Moisés Silva. *An Introduction to Biblical Hermeneutics: The Search for Meaning*. Grand Rapids, MI: Zondervan, 1994.

Lightfoot, John. *A Commentary on the New Testament from the Talmud and Hebraica, Matthew—1 Corinthians*. Vol 2. 1859. Reprinted Peabody, MA: Hendrickson Publishers, 1995.

Mauck, John W. *Paul on Trial, The Book of Acts as a Defense of Christianity*, Nashville, YN: Thomas Nelson, 2001.

Metzger, Bruce M. *A Textual Commentary on the Greek New Testament*. 2nd ed. USA: United Bible Societies, 1994.

Page, Frank S. *Jonah*. The New American Commentary. Vol. 19B. Nashville, TN: Broadman and Holman, 1995.

Peterson, David G. *The Acts of the Apostles*. Grand Rapids, MI: Eerdmans, 2009.

Quiggle, James D. *A Private Commentary on the Bible: John 13–21*. Amazon/KDP, 2015.

_____. *A Private Commentary on the Bible: Jonah*. Amazon/KDP, 2012, 2018.

_____. *A Private Commentary on the Bible: Matthew's Gospel*. Amazon/KDP, 2016.

_____. *Covenants and Dispensations In the Scripture*. Amazon/KDP, 2021.

_____. *Dictionary of Doctrinal Words*. Amazon/KDP, 2018.

_____.

_____. *Dispensational Eschatol ogy, An Explanation and Defense of the Doctrine*. Amazon/KDP, 2013.

_____. *Four Voices, One Testimony*. Amazon/KDP, 2022.

_____. *James Quiggle Translation New Testament*. Amazon/KDP, 2023.

_____. *Life, Death, Eternity*. Amazon/KDP, 2019.

_____. *Spiritual Gifts*. Amazon/KDP, 2015.

Ramsay, W. M. *St Paul the Traveller and the Roman Citizen*. London: Hodder and Stoughton, 1895.

Robinson, O. F. *Penal Practice and Penal Policy in Ancient Rome*. New York, NY: Routledge, 2007.

Schurer, Emil. *A History of the Jewish People in the Time Of Jesus Christ*. Division 2, vol. 2. 1890. Reprinted Peabody, MA: Hendrickson Publishers, 2020.

Silva, Moisés. Revision Editor. *New International Dictionary of New Testament Theology and Exegesis*. Grand Rapids, MI: Zondervan, 2014.

Stuart, Douglas. *Hosea–Jonah*. Word Biblical Commentary. Vol. 31. Nashville, TN: Thomas Nelson Publishers, 2003.

Virkler, Henry A., *Hermeneutics, Principles and Processes of Biblical Interpretation*. Grand Rapids, MI: Baker Books, 1981.

Wallace, Daniel B. *Greek Grammar Beyond the Basics*. Grand Rapids, MI: Zondervan, 1996.

Westcott, B. F. *The Gospel According to St. John*. 1881. Reprinted, Grand Rapids, MI: William B. Eerdmans Publishing, 1978.

Wuest, Kenneth. *Wuest's Word Studies From the Greek New Testament*. 3 volumes. Grand Rapids, MI: Eerdman's Publishing, 1973.

Zodhiates, Spiros. *The Complete Word Study Dictionary: New Testament*. Revised. Chattanooga, TN: AMG Publishers, 1993.

www.ingramcontent.com/pod-product-compliance
Lightning Source LLC
Chambersburg PA
CBHW071304110426
42743CB00042B/1167